AF539976

Dictionary of
PRONUNCIATION FOR CURRENT ENGLISH

Dictionary of PRONUNCIATION FOR CURRENT ENGLISH

Sonu Marwah

ANMOL PUBLICATIONS PVT. LTD.
NEW DELHI-110 002 (INDIA)

ANMOL PUBLICATIONS PVT. LTD.

Regd. Office: 4360/4, Ansari Road, Daryaganj,
New Delhi-110002 (India)
Tel.: 23278000, 23261597, 23286875, 23255577
Fax: 91-11-23280289
Email: anmolpub@gmail.com
Visit us at: www.anmolpublications.com

Branch Office: No. 1015, Ist Main Road, BSK IIIrd Stage
IIIrd Phase, IIIrd Block, Bangalore-560 085 (India)
Tel.: 080-41723429 • Fax: 080-26723604
Email: anmolpublicationsbangalore@gmail.com

Dictionary of Pronunciation for Current English

First Edition, 2011

ISBN 978-81-261-4576-8

PRINTED IN INDIA

Printed at Mehra Offset Press, Delhi.

Contents

Preface

Dictionary of Pronunciation for Current English is written for under graduate students of Universities who are pursuing English Courses. The book is a comprehensive reference-cum-textbook suitable for self-study or classroom work which comprises of current English Pronunciation words with their meanings used in day-to-day life.

The book contains easy-to-use units which covers all aspects of pronunciation, including individual sounds, word stress, connected speech and intonation. Each chapter is supported by latest material. In additional to this the students find this book a user friendly tool that helps them in pronuncing numbers and geographical names with lots of exercises and phonemic symbols.

Author

Chapter 1

Introduction

DEFINITION

Pronunciation refers to the way a word or a language is spoken, or the manner in which someone utters a word. If one is said to have"correct pronunciation", then it refers to both within a particular dialect.

A word can be spoken in different ways by various individuals or groups, depending on many factors, such as: the area in which they grew up, the area in which they now live, if they have a speech or voice disorder, their ethnic group, their social class, or their education.[

A dictionary is a list of words with their definitions, a list of characters with their glyphs, or a list of words with corresponding words in other languages. In a few languages, words can appear in many different forms, but only the lemma form appears as the main word or headword in most dictionaries. Many dictionaries also provide pronunciation information; grammatical information; word derivations, histories, or etymologies; illustrations; usage guidance; and examples in phrases or sentences. Dictionaries are most commonly found in the form of a book. Some dictionaries are also found in electronic portable handheld devices. Dictionaries are produced by lexicographers.

DICTIONARY

Today, dictionaries of most languages with alphabetic and syllabic writing systems list words in lexicographic order, usually alphabetical or some analogous phonetic system.

In many languages, words are grouped together according to their true or normal origin ("root"), and these roots are arranged alphabetically. If English dictionaries were arranged like this, the words "import", "export", "support", "report", "porter", "port", "important" and "transportation" would all be listed under "port".

This method has the advantage that all words of a common origin are listed together, but the disadvantage is that you have to know how to disassemble all prefixes of a word before you look it up. Some Sanskrit dictionaries and all Arabic dictionaries work like this.

Dictionaries of languages using ide ographic writing systems, may be sorted either according to one of many schemes based on the component parts of the characters (number of strokes, overall shape, or pronunciation of each letter), or according to the pronunciation of the full words when spelled phonetically.

Due to the unfamiliarity of Chinese speakers with phonetic spellings, phonetic sorts are particularly unsuitable for Chinese dictionaries, while the fluency of Japanese speakers with kana makes kana spelling the most common and convenient method to sort Japanese dictionaries.

The first English alphabetical dictionary came out in 1604 and alphabetical ordering was a rarity until the 18th century. Before alphabetical listings, dictionaries were organized by topic, i.e. a list of animals all together in one topic.

VARIATIONS

Since words and their meanings develop over time, dictionary entries are organized to reflect these changes. Dictionaries may either list meanings in the historical order in which they appeared, or may list meanings in order of popularity and most common use.

Dictionaries also differ in the degree to which they are encyclopedic, providing considerable background information, illustrations, and the like, or linguistic, concentrating on etymology, nuances of meaning, and quotations demonstrating usage.

Any dictionary has been designed to fulfil one or more functions. The dictionary functions chosen by the maker(s) of the dictionary provide the basis for all lexicographic decisions, from the selection of entry words, over the choice of information types, to the choice of place for the information (e.g. in an article or in an appendix). There are two main types of function.

The communication-oriented functions comprise text reception (understanding), text production, text revision, and translation. The knowledge-oriented functions deal with situations where the dictionary is used for acquiring specific knowledge about a particular matter, and for acquiring general knowledge about something. The optimal dictionary is one that contains information directly relevant for the needs of the users relating to one or more of these functions. It is important that the information is presented in a way that keeps the lexicographic information costs at a minimum.

The art and craft of writing dictionaries is called lexicography.One of the earliest dictionaries known, and which is still extant today in an abridged form, was written in Latin during the reign of the emperor Augustus. It is known by the title De Significant Verborum ("On the meaning of words") and was originally compiled by Verrius Flaccus. It was twice abridged in succeeding centuries, first by Sextus Pompeius Festus, and then by Paul the Deacon. Verrius Flaccus' dictionary was an abridged list of difficult or antiquated words, whose usage was illustrated by quotations from early Roman authors.

The Erya, from the early 3rd century BC, was the first Chinese language dictionary. The book organized Chinese characters by semantic groups. The intention of this dictionary was to explain the true meaning and interpretation of words in the context of older ancient texts.

The word "dictionary" comes from neoclassical Latin, diccio, meaning simply "word".

The first true English dictionary was Robert Cawdrey's Table Alphabeticall of 1604, although it only included 3,000 words and the definitions it contained were little more than synonyms. The first one to be at all comprehensive was Thomas Blount's dictionary Glossographia of 1656. This was followed by Samuel Johnson's famous and more complete dictionary of 1755.

In 1806, Noah Webster's dictionary was published by the G and C Merriam Company of Springfield, Massachusetts which still publishes Merriam-Webster dictionaries, but the term Webster's is considered generic and can be used by any dictionary. The most complete dictionary of the English language is the English Dictionary. The first edition was properly begun in 1860 and was completed in 1928, by which time a supplement that took an additional five years to complete was already necessary.

ENGLISH USAGE

Every major hazard in English usage was subjected to reanalysis and, where necessary, provided with sage qualifications or 'Keep Off' signs. MEU is a collection of articles arranged under both ordinary headings (*this, thistle, thither, -th nouns, those, though*) and idiosyncratic ones (*battered ornaments, out of the frying pan, sturdy indefensible, swapping horses*).

This work in particular has made the name Fowler as well known among those interested in usage and the language as Johnson and Webster, a point of reference for both those who venerate and those who regret what he has had to say. Presented as the 3rd edition, this is effectively a new book that sets Fowler himself in historical perspective.

A Dictionary of Modern English Usage is a style guide to English usage, pronunciation, and writing. Ranging from plurals and literary technique to the distinctions among like words (homonyms, synonyms, etc.), to foreign-term use, it became the standard for most style guides that followed — thus, first edition remains in print despite the existence of the second edition, and third edition. The third edition has been largely rewritten along the lines of a modern usage dictionary, making some use of corpus data.

English usage was to encourage a direct, vigourous

writing style, and to oppose all artificiality — firmly advising against unnecessary, convoluted sentence construction, foreign words and phrases, and archaisms. He opposed all pedantry, and notably ridiculed artificial grammatical rules without warrant in natural English usage — such as bans on split infinitives and ending a sentence with a preposition, rules on the placement of the word *only*, and distinctions between *which* and *that*.

He also condemned every cliché, and, in classifying them, coined and popularized the terms *battered ornament*, *Ward our Street*, *vogue words*, and *worn-out humour*, whilst simultaneously defending useful distinctions between words whose meanings were coalescing in practice, and guiding the user away from errors of word misuse, and illogical sentence construction. Like most *practical* guides, its linguistics is a mixture of the prescriptive and the descriptive — thus allowing extremists of both camps to place Fowler in the other.

Quotations

The speaker who has discovered that *Juan* and *Quixote* are not pronounced in Spain as he used to pronounce them as a boy is not content to keep so important a piece of information to himself. Display of superior knowledge is as great a vulgarity as display of superior wealth — greater indeed, inasmuch as knowledge should tend more definitely than wealth towards discretion and good manners. Writers who observe the poignancy sometimes given by inversion, but fail to observe that 'sometimes' means 'when exclamation is appropriate', adopt inversion as an infallible enlivener; they aim at freshness and attain frigidity.

The English-speaking world may be divided into those who neither know nor care what a split infinitive is; those who do not know, but care very much; those who know and condemn; those who know and approve; and those who know and distinguish. It is strange that a people with such a fondness for understatement as the British should have felt the need to keep changing the adverbs by which they hope to convince listeners of the intensity of their feelings.

Henry Fowler researched *A Dictionary of Modern English Usage* with the aid of his younger brother Francis, who died in 1918 from tuberculosis contracted during service with the BEF. The dedication begins: "I think of it as it should have been, with its prolixity's docked, its dullness's enlivened, its fads eliminated, its truths multiplied

Description

Now it is bringing back the original long-out-of-print first edition of this beloved work, enhanced with a new introduction by one of today's leading experts on the language, David Crystal. Drawing on a wealth of entertaining examples, Crystal offers an insightful reassessment Fowler's reputation and his place in the history of linguistic thought.

Fowler, Crystal points out, was far more sophisticated in his analysis of language than most people realise and many of his entries display a concern for descriptive accuracy which would do any modern linguist proud.

And although the book is full of his personal likes and dislikes, Fowler's prescriptivism is usually intelligent and reasoned. Crystal concludes warmly that Fowler was like "an endearingly eccentric, schoolmasterly character, driven at times to exasperation by the infelicities of his wayward pupils, but always wanting the best for them and hoping to provide the best guidance for them.... He may shake his stick at us, but we never feel we are actually going to be beaten."

In the concluding section of the book, Crystal examines nearly many entries in detail, offers a modern perspective on them, and shows how English has changed since the 1920s. This exciting and long awaited re-release of one of the classic works of English reference will delight everyone interested in language.

Dictionary makers apply two basic philosophies to the defining of words: prescriptive or descriptive. The Oxford English Dictionary (OED) is descriptive, and attempts to describe the actual use of words. Noah Webster, on the other hand, intent on forging a distinct identity for the American language, altered spellings and accentuated differences in meaning and pronunciation of numerous words. This is why American English now uses the spelling "colour" while the rest of the world uses "colour" While disapproved of in the UK, the US spellings are universally understood; likewise the British spellings are not acceptable in America.

While descriptivists argue that prescriptivism is an unnatural attempt to dictate usage or curtail change, prescriptivists argue that to indiscriminately document "improper" or "inferior" usages sanctions those usages by default and causes language to "deteriorate". Although the debate can become very heated, only a small number of controversial words are usually affected. But the softening of usage notations, from the previous edition, for two words, ain't and regardless, out of over 450,000 Third, was enough to provoke outrage among many with prescriptivist leanings, who branded the dictionary as "permissive."

The prescriptive/descriptive issue has been given so much consideration in modern times that most dictionaries of English apply the descriptive method to definitions, while additionally informing readers of attitudes which may influence their choices on words often considered vulgar, offensive, erroneous, or easily confused. Merriam-Webster is subtle, only adding italicized notations such as, sometimes offensive or nonstand (nonstandard.) American Heritage goes further, discussing issues separately in numerous "usage notes." Encarta provides similar notes, but is more prescriptive, offering warnings and admonitions against the use of certain words considered by many to be offensive or illiterate, such as, "an offensive term for..." or "a taboo term meaning..."

Because of the broad use of dictionaries, and their acceptance by many as language authorities, their treatment of the language does affect usage to some degree, even the most descriptive dictionaries providing conservative continuity. In the long run, however, usage primarily determines the meanings of words in English, and the language is being changed and created every day. As Jorge Luis Borges says in the prologue to "El otro, el mismo": "It is often forgotten that (dictionaries) are artificial repositories, put together well after the languages they define. The roots of language are irrational and of a magical nature."

Features

The dictionary was called "permissive" and details of its perfidy were aired, mocked, and distorted until the publisher was put on notice that it might be bought out to prevent further circulation of this insidious thirteen-and-a-half–pound, four-inch–thick doorstop of a book. *Webster's Third New International* (Unabridged) wasn't just any dictionary, of course, but the most up-to-date and complete offering from America's oldest and most respected name in lexicography.

The dictionary's previous edition, *Webster's New International* Second Edition (Unabridged), was the great American dictionary with 600,000 entries and numerous competitors but no rivals.

With a six-inch-wide binding, it weighed four pounds more than *Webster's Third* and possessed an almost unanswerable air of authority. If you wanted to know how to pronounce *chaise longue,* it told you, shâz long, end of discussion. It did not stoop to correct or even mention the vulgarization that sounds like "Che's lounge." When to use *less* and when to use *fewer*? It indicated what strict usage prescribed. It defined *celebrant* as "one who celebrates a public religious rite; esp. the officiating priest," not just any old party guest.

Gove, in Morton's telling, comes off as an impatient and technocratic editor. He did not shrink from drawing hard lines. A dictionary should give primacy to generic terms, he asserted, not proper names, not geographical appendixes, not biographical information, not famous sayings, nor names from the Bible and the plays of William Shakespeare. This way of cutting encyclopedic material and proper nouns is also the approach of the *English Dictionary,* but it was completely novel to American dictionaries, which tended to be one-stop, all-purpose reference works, as W2 had been. Gove's decision quickly cleared a lot of dead wood, but deprived users of helpful material and resulted in some general peculiarity. Charles Dickens, for example, no longer warranted an entry but*dickensian* (with a lowercase d) did. Words almost always capitalized in print were shown in lower case but followed by the notation *usu. cap* (usually capitalized)—a policy Morton wrote was "universally deplored."

SCOPE OF DICTIONARY

The dictionary invites a playful reading. It challenges anyone to sit down with it in an idle moment only to find an hour gone by without being bored. Recently I noticed an advertisement for a dictionary as a wonder book. "Astonished Actually Means Thunderstruck" was the headline, written obviously in the hope that the prospective buyer would be thunderstruck, or wonderstruck, enough to look further. And the rest of the ad listed such tidbits as a "*disaster* literally means the stars are against you!" or "to tantalize is to torment with the punishment of Tantalus as told in Greek mythology."

While do not think astonishment is the dictionary's main mission in life, It cannot resist reporting some of the things It discovered, that the word "solecism" derives from Soli, the name of a Greek colony in Cilicia, whose inhabitants were thought by the Athenians to speak bad Greek; hence, "solecism" was probably the equivalent in Greek slang for a Bostonian's contemptuous reference to "New Yorkese." I learned that "coal" originally meant charred wood. It was then applied to mineral coal when this was first introduced, under such names as "sea-coal" and "pitcoal." Now that mineral coal is the more common variety, we redundantly refer to charred wood as "charcoal." I was edified by the fact that the drink "Tom and Jerry" derives its name from the two chief characters in Evan's "Life of London", that in England a low beer joint is called a "Tom and Jerry Shop," and, that indulgence in riotous behaviour is called "to tom and jerry." It was always thought that a forlorn hope was really a hope on the verge of turning into despair, but it seems that it isn't a hope at all, "Hope" here is a misspelling of the Dutch word "hoop" meaning heap. A forlorn hope is a storming party, a band of heroes who willing to end up in a heap for their country's cause. And most shocking of all was the discovery that one theory about the origin of the magician's "hocus pocus" accounts for it as a corruption of *"hoc est corous"* — the sacred words accompanying the sacrament of the Eucharist. This, together with the reversal in meaning of "dunce" — from the proper name of Duns Scotus, the subtlest doctor of the Church, to naming a numbskull provides a two-word commentary on the transition from the Middle Ages to modern times.

The staid modern dictionary is full of such wit even when it doesn't try to be funny, as Dr. Johnson did when he defined "oats" as "a grain which in England is generally given to horses, but in Scotland supports the people." Look up "Welsh rabbit," for example, or "scotch capon" or "swiss steak," and you will discover gentle jokes about national shortcomings in diet. What interests me most of all are the shifts in meaning of common words in daily use. From meaning an attendant on horses, "marshall" has come to mean a leader of men; though also originating in the stable, "constable" has gone in the reverse direction from signifying an officer of highest rank to denoting a policeman; "boon" has done an about-face by becoming the gift which answers a petition, having been the prayer which asked for it; "magistrate" and "minister" have changed places with each other in the ups and downs of words, for in current political usage, "magistrate" usually names a minor official, whereas "minister" refers to a major diplomatic or cabinet post.

It is often hard to remember that a minister is a servant of the people, and harder, still to recall the precise point of religious controversy which caused the substitution of "minister" for "priest" as the name for one who served in the performance of sacerdotal functions. And readers of our Constitution should have their attention called to a shift in the word "citizen" from meaning any one who, by birth or choice, owes allegiance to the state, to the narrower designation of those who are granted the right to vote. Similarly, "commerce" has narrowed in meaning; like "trade," it once meant every dealing in merchandise, but now is distinguished from industry according to the difference between distributing commodities and producing them.

The word "commerce" reminds me of one other sort of incidental inquiry the dictionary lures you into. You discover that "commerce" and "mercenary" have the same root in "*mercis,*" wares, and that leads you to the closely related root "*merces,*" pay or reward, which is embodied in the word "mercy." If you start this game of research, you will find such roots as "*spec*" from "*spectare*"meaning to look at or see, which generates a family of English words (species, speculate, specimen, specify, spectacle, inspect, respect, aspect, etc.); or "*press*" from "*primo*"; meaning to squeeze, which has an equally large family (impress, repress, pressing, compress, suppress, oppress, depress, express, etc.).

It is almost as hard to stop writing about the dictionary in this way as to stop reading one when you are in hot pursuit of the mysteries of human speech. But, over and above such fascinations, the dictionary has its sobre uses. To make the most of these one has to know how to read the special sort of book a dictionary is. But, before I state the rules, let me see if I can explain why most people today don't use dictionaries in a manner befitting the purpose for which they were originally created.

In its various sizes and editions, the dictionary is an unlisted bestseller on every season's list. To be able to get along without one would be a sign of supreme literacy — of complete competence as a reader and writer. The dictionary exists, of course, because there is no one in that condition. But, if the dictionary is the necessity we all acknowledge, why is it so infrequently used by the man who owns one? And even when we do consult it, why do most of us misuse the dictionary or use it poorly?

The answer to both questions may be that few of us make efforts at reading or writing anything above the present level of our literary competence. The books — or maybe it is just the newspapers and magazines — we read, and the things we write, don't send us to the dictionary for help. Our vocabularies are quite adequate, because the first rule in most contemporary writing is the taboo against strange words, or familiar words in strange senses.

Of course, there are always people (not-excluding college graduates) who have difficulty with spelling or pronouncing even the common words in daily discourse. That, by the way, is the source of the most frequent impulse to go to the dictionary. There is nothing wrong about this! The dictionary is there to render this simple service – in fact, Noah Webster began his career as the compiler of a spelling book which sold in the millions. But my point remains – the dictionary has other and more important uses, and the reason we do not generally avail ourselves of these services is not our superiority, but rather our lack of need as the life of letters is currently lived.

The history of dictionaries, I think, will bear me out on this point. The Greeks did not have a dictionary, even though "lexicon" is the Greek word for it. They had no need for foreign language dictionaries because there was no literature in a foreign language they cared to read. They had no need for a Greek word-book because the small educated class already knew what such a book would contain. This small group of literate men would have been, like the modern French Academy, the makers of the dictionary, the arbiters of good usage. But at a time when so sharp a line separated the learned from the lewd (which, in an obsolete usage, means*unlettered*), there was no occasion for the few men who could make a dictionary to prefer one for the others.

George Santayana's remark about the Greeks – that they were the uneducated people in European history – has a double significance. The masses were, of course, uneducated, but even the learned few were not educated in the sense that they had to sit at the feet of foreign masters. Education, in that sense, begins with the Romans, who went to school to Greek pedagogues, and became cultivated through contact with Greek culture. It is not surprising, therefore, that the first dictionaries were glossaries of Homeric words. The earliest lexicon which is still extant is such a glossary, prepared by a Greek, Apollonius, in the fifth century of our era, obviously intended to help Romans read the "Iliad" and "Odyssey" of Homer, as well as other Greek literature which employed the Homeric vocabulary. Most of us today need similar glossaries to read Shakespeare well.

There were dictionaries in the Middle Ages — a famous Latin one by the Spaniard, Isidore of Seville, which was really a philosophical work, a sort of encyclopedia of worldly knowledge accomplished by discussions of the most important technical terms occurring in learned discourse. There were foreign-language dictionaries in the Renaissance made necessary by the fact that the *humane letters* which dominated the education of the period were from the ancient languages. Even when the vulgar tongues — English, French, or Italian — gradually displaced Latin as the language of learning, the pursuit of learning was still the privilege of the few. Under such circumstances, dictionaries were intended for a limited audience, mainly as an aid to reading the most worthy literature. In attempting to compile a standard dictionary, that is would furnish a guide to others who tried to read them, or who tied to write as well.

The beginning the educational motive dominated the making of dictionaries, though, as in the case of Dr. Johnson, and the work of the French and Italian Academies, there was also an interest in preserving the purity and order of the language. As against the latter interest, the English Dictionary, was a new departure, in that it did not try to dictate the best usage but rather to present an accurate historical record of every type of usage — the worst as well as the best, taken from popular as well as stylish writing. But this conflict between the mission of the lexicographer as self-appointed arbiter and his function as historian can regarded as a side-issue, for the dictionary, however constructed, is primarily an educational instrument. And the problem is whether that instrument is currently well used.

Noah Webster is in a sense the hero of the story. Alarmed by the state into which learning had fallen after the Revolutionary War, Webster sought to make a one volume dictionary which would serve in the self-education of the semiliterate masses. He was concerned with the masses, not the elite, and with selfeducation, at a time when this country had not yet become democratic enough to regard the public education of all its children as a primary obligation of the state. The Webster dictionary was probably one of the first self-help books to become a popular bestseller. And the paradox is that now, with public education widely established in this country, with literacy as universal as suffrage, the self-help potentialities of a dictionary are seldom realised by the millions who own one.

I am not thinking merely of children from progressive schools who cannot use a dictionary because they do not know the alphabet. This brief history of dictionaries is relevant to the rules for reading and using them well.

One of the first rules as to how to read a book is to know what sort of book it is. That means knowing what the author's intention was and what sort of thing you can expect to find in his work. If you look upon a dictionary merely as a spelling book or a guide to pronunciation, you will use it accordingly. If you realise that it contains a wealth of historical information, crystallized in the growth of language; you will pay attention, not merely to the variety of meanings which are listed under each word, but to their order.

And above all if you are interested in advancing your own education, you will use a dictionary according to its primary intention — as a help in reading hooks that might otherwise be too difficult because their vocabulary includes technical words, archaic words, literary allusions or even familiar words used in now obsolete senses.

The number of words in a man's vocabulary is as definite as the number of dollars he has in the bank; equally definite is the number of senses in which a man is able to use any given word. But there is this difference: a man cannot draw upon the public treasury when his bank-balance is overdrawn, but we can all draw upon the dictionary to get the coin we need to carry on the transaction of reading anything we want to read. Let be sure that it not misunderstood, not saying that a dictionary is all you need in order to move anywhere in the realms of literature. There are many problems to be solved, in reading a book well, other than those arising from the author's vocabulary.

And even with respect to vocabulary, the dictionary's primary service is on those occasions when you are confronted with a technical word or with a word that is wholly new to you — such as "costard" (an apple), or "hontzin" (a South American bird), or "rabato" (a kind of flaring collar). More frequently the problem of interpretation arises because a relatively familiar word seems to be used in a strange sense.

Here the dictionary will help, but it will not solve the problem. The dictionary may suggest the variety of senses in which the troublesome word can be used, but it can never determine how the author you are reading used it. That you must decide by wrestling with the context.

More often, than not; especially with distinguished writers, the word may be given a special, an almost unique, shade of meaning. The growth of your own vocabulary, in the important dimension of multiple meanings, as well as in mere quantity of words will depend, first of all, upon the character of the books you read, and secondly, upon the use you make of the dictionary as a guide. You will misuse it — you will stultify rather than enlighten yourself — if you substitute the dictionary for the exercise of your own interpretative judgment in reading.

This suggests several other rules as to how *not* to read a dictionary. There is no more irritating fellow than the man who tries to settle an argument about communism, or justice, or liberty, by quoting from Webster. Webster and all his fellow lexicographers may be respected as authorities on word-usage, but they are not the ultimate founts of wisdom.

They are no Supreme Court to which we can appeal for a decision of those fundamental controversies which, despite the warnings of semanticists, get us involved with abstract words. It is well to remember that the dictionary's authority can, for obvious reasons, be surer in the field of concrete words, and even in the field of the abstract technical words of science, than it ever can be with respect to philosophical words. Yet these words are indispensable if we are going to talk, read, or write about the things that matter most.

Another negative rule is: Don't swallow the dictionary. Don't try to get word-rich quick, by memorizing a lot of fancy words whose meanings are unconnected with any actual experience.

Merely verbal knowledge is almost worse than no knowledge at all. If learning consisted in nothing but knowing the meanings of words, we could abolish all our courses of study, and substitute the dictionary for every other sort of book. But no one except a pedant or a fool would regard it as profitable or wise to read the dictionary from cover to cover.

In short, don't forget that the dictionary is a book about words, not about things. It can tell you how men have used words, but it does not define the nature of the things the words name.

A Scandinavian university undertook a "linguistic experiment" to prove that human arguments always reduce to verbal differences: Seven lawyers were given seven dictionary definitions of truth and asked to defend them. They soon forgot to stick to the "verbal meanings" they had been assigned, and became vehemently involved in defending or opposing certain fundamental views about the nature of truth. The experiment showed that discussions may start about the meanings of words, but that, when interest in the problem is aroused, they seldom end there. Men pass from words to things, from names to natures. The dictionary can start an argument, but only thought or research can end it.

USING DICTIONARY

When reading this guide, if you are in doubt as to which part of speech is which, consult the Grammar, where each word class is presented separately in tabular form.

The guide assumes your familiarity with a number of terms. If you are not acquainted with them you may find the following, radically simplified, definitions helpful:

Case: The specification of the syntactic function of a noun, pronoun or adjective by means of an inflectional ending. In

Icelandic the cases comprise the nominative (for subject and subjective completions, etc.), the genitive (for possession, with certain prepositions, and certain verbs, etc.), the accusative (with many verbs for the direct object, but also with certain prepositions, etc.), and the dative (for indirect object, with certain verbs and prepositions, etc.)

Compound: A word composed of two or more words or word elements joined together

Inflection: The systematic alteration of word forms (usually by the addition or alteration of an ending) to indicate differences of meaning or syntactic function, as in: I go, she goes; girl, girls; he, him; sing, sang, sung

Morphology: The inflectional system of a given word

The contains the headword, information on word class, and morphological details.

THE HEADWORD

Order of Entries

All headwords are printed in bold and presented in the alphabetical order that is now standard for Modern Icelandic.

a, á, b, d, ð, e, é,s f, g, h, i, í, j, k, l, m,
n, o, ó, p, r, s, t, u, ú, v, x, y, ý, þ, æ, ö

This means, for example, that all words beginning with i- are listed before words beginning with í-. Consequently, when two headwords are distinguished only by the presence or absence of an accent over a vowel, the form without the accent is placed first.

hlið *f*
hlíð *f*

When headwords with the same spelling (homonyms) introduce successive entries, they are distinguished by means of superscript numbers.

á·líka *adj indecl*
á·líka *adv*

Presentation of Headwords

A headword is often divided into parts: by means of a dot or by means of a slash/.

A dot marks a division of a compound word into constituent parts. Only one such division is noted.

tilviljunar·kenndur

A slash in a headword marks the point at which any inflectional endings given later in the lemma should be added.

borð/a *v* (*acc*) (**-aði**)

indicates that the preterite of borða is **borðaði;**

stelp/a *f* (**–u**, **–ur**)

indicates that the genitive singular of **stelpa** is **stelpu** and that the nominative plural is **stelpur**.

In the case of a compound word whose second segment displays the effects of mutation, this segment is separated from the first by the slash rather than by the dot.

hólm/ganga *f* (**–göngu, –göngur**)

Lemmas that Consist of Cross-references

A headword can take the form of a reference from an inflected form with a different spelling.

hættir –> háttur

A headword can be a reference from a second word with an exactly similar meaning.

einskis·virði *adj indecl*

= einskisverður

First elements of Compound Words

A headword can consist purely of the first element of a compound word followed by suggestions as to how the element is to be understood in compound words that are not included in the dictionary.

meðal- *in compounds*

average

PARTS OF SPEECH

The following main distinctions are commonly made: *adj* = adjective, *adv* = adverb, *conj* = conjunction, *interj*= interjection, *num* = numeral, *prep* = preposition, *pron* = pronoun, *v* = verb. Dual function is sometimes indicated as follows:

ótal *adj /adv*

Nouns

Nouns are not identified as such. Instead, their gender is given (*m* for masculine, *f* for feminine, *n* for neuter), and where relevant they are given additional markers to show that they are registered only in the plural form or are indeclinable.

land *n*
sifjar *f pl*
var·kárni *f indecl*

Verbs

Verbs are identified by the marker *v*. Note also *v refl* for a verb used in the reflexive form, and *v impers* for a verb that is always used in impersonal constructions.

éta *v* (*acc*)
fast/a *v*
á·girn/ast *v refl*
lang/a *v impers*

Case markers. In the preceding example the first instance, **éta,** has the additional information (*acc*) after the verb marker.

This indicates that the verb in question *can* be used transitively and that in transitive use the object of the verb is in the accusative case (as opposed to the dative (*dat*) or genitive (*gen*)).

The absence of a case marker indicates that the verb in question is registered only in an intransitive sense or senses. Case markers are never given for reflexive verb forms, but case usage is usually indicated by an example.

á·girn/ast *v refl* (**-tist, -st**)
desire, crave
~~ **e-ð**
crave sth

Some verbs are frequently used with double objects, one in the accusative (the direct object), the other in the dative (the indirect object).

A typical example of this is **bjóða e-m e-ð** 'offer sby sth' where in Icelandic the sby (**e-m**) is in the dative and the sth (**e-ð**) in the accusative. Verbs of this type are marked (*dat+acc*).

Adjectives

Where adjectives are indeclinable this is shown by the marker *adj indecl,* and when an adjective in origin is the past participle of a verb its source is often identified.

búinn *adj*

< búa

Where an adjective governs the dative case in its noun phrase, it is shown as follows:

[2]líkur *adj* (*dat*)

similar, resembling, like

vera ~ e-m

be like sby

INFLECTED FORMS

Inflectional endings or inflected forms of nouns, pronouns, verbs and adjectives are given in bold type in round brackets immediately after the indication of word class

In cases where there is mutation the portion of the word that includes the vowel (or the whole of the word) is presented in its entirety in the round brackets

[1]höll *f* (**hallar, hallir**)

fé/lag *n* (**-lags, -lög**)

Some words occur with alternative endings for a given case; these are separated by *or*. Thus in the following example the genitive singular of **liður** appears both as **liðs** and **liðar**.

lið/ur *m* (**-s** *or* **-ar, -ir**)

Nouns

For nouns, the endings usually given are the genitive singular and the nominative plural. If only one ending is given it is always the genitive singular, and the absence of the plural form indicates that plural usage is unknown or extremely rare.

and·úð *f* (**-ar**)

antipathy

Where the dative singular of a noun has a vowel change, this form is entered as a headword with a cross-reference.

ketti -> köttur

Verbs

For verbs that belong to the strong declension, the third person singular present (followed by a semicolon) is only given if the vowel differs from the vowel of the infinitive (the headword); otherwise only the third person singular preterite, the third person preterite plural, and the past participle are given, separated by commas.

bjóða *v* (*dat+acc*) (**býður** ; **bauð, buðu, boðið**)

bera *v* (*acc*) (**bar, báru, borið**)

For most classes of weak verbs only the third person singular preterite and the past participle are given. For the largest and most regular class of weak verbs (Class 1, those marked like **borg/a** *v* (**-aði**)) the past participle is, however, not given, since it is formed completely regularly by the addition of a final **-ð** to the infinitive (thus**borgað, kallað**, etc.).

Where the preterite subjunctive of a verb has a vowel change, the form is entered as a headword with a cross-reference.

byði *subj*

-> bjóða

Adjectives

For adjectives, mutated forms (feminine singular) are given (this form is the same as the neuter plural). Further details on the inflection of adjectives is to be found in the Grammar.

ban·eitr/aður *adj* (*f* **-uð**)

DEFINITION

The primary spelling and usage of the definitions represent standard North American English. Spelling and usage variants in British English are also given, preceded by the marker (*UK*). These variants are to be regarded purely as the *preferred* British form, and it is not necessarily implied that they cannot be used in American English./(*UK*) introduces a British variant within a phrase.

gefa í botn

step on the gas (*UK*) accelerate

erfið/a *v* **(-aði)**
work hard, toil, labour (*UK*) labour
það er orðið ~
it has gotten light/(*UK*) got light

There is a deliberate bias toward everyday speech in the English renderings; thus contracted forms such as 'couldn't' (rather than 'could not') are frequently found.

Basic form of Definition

The basic form of definition is used for an Icelandic word for which a single meaning is registered and for which one or more English equivalents are provided.

háðung *f* **(-ar)**
shame, disgrace, ignominy

Within a definition, round brackets may be used to enclose part of an explanation that is optional in English (often dependent on the context).

kyn·þroska *adj indecl*
(sexually) mature

Collocations/illustrative Phrases

The English equivalents of the Icelandic headword may be supplemented by collocations or illustrative phrases. They are printed in bold type and followed by a translation. Collocations ('fixed phrases') often demonstrate idiomatic usage;

fanta·brögð *n pl*
dirty tricks
beita ~um
hit below the belt

illustrative phrases, on the other hand, demonstrate how an Icelandic word is used in one or more of its senses, and the translation shows how the phrase in which it appears can be conveniently rendered into English:

fern *adj*
four (of a type)
~ar buxur
four pairs of pants/(*UK*) trousers

Especially in the representation of phrases there is a tendency in this as in any dictionary of Icelandic to use masculine grammatical forms as illustrative material. This is done to avoid introducing variations to the headwords which, where applicable, in accordance with tradition are given in the masculine form. Grammatical gender is arbitrary (its roots are too deeply embedded in the history of language for us to be able to see any logic in it) and it has no sexist connotations.

hugsa um e-n
care for sby, care to sby's needs

Use of the tilde (~). In the Icelandic phrases incorporated in the definitions the sign ~ (single tilde) and ~~(double tilde) are used as abbreviations for all or part of the headword.

~ is used to represent the whole of a headword that is not broken up by slash.

iðinn *adj*
diligent, industrious
~ við kolann (= iðinn við kolann)
persevering
í·grip *n pl*
gera e-ð í ~um (= gera e-ð í ígripum)
do sth on the side

~ is also used to represent the part of the headword that precedes the slash.

ímugust/ur *m*
hafa ~ á e-m (= hafa ímugust á e-m)
dislike sby

~~ is used where the headword is broken up by a vertical slash but both parts (the whole of the divided headword) are to be inserted in the example.

kynn/ast *v refl* **(-tist, -st)**
~~ e-m
get acquainted with sby, get to know sby

Round brackets are used to enclose part of an Icelandic phrase that is optional and may therefore be missing in a specific occurrence.

þol·rif *n pl*
reyna (á) ~in í e-m

put sby to the test

The slash is used to indicate alternatives in collocations and phrases.

fisk/ur *m* (**-s, -ar**)

fish

e-ð/e-r er ekki upp á marga ~a

sth/sby is not up to much

Collocations on Own

When use of a headword outside a particular collocation or phrase is not registered in this dictionary, only the collocation itself (introduced by a colon) and its translation are given.

þrándur *m*

vera e-m ~ í götu

be an obstacle to sby

Complex Entries for Words with Multiple Meanings

Many of the Icelandic headwords in the dictionary have more than one meaning. Where this is the case the different senses are numbered separately, and as a rule the numbered definitions are distinguished from each other for the Icelandic user by means of a semantic indicator written in Icelandic and italicized in parenthesis.

ná·kvæmur *adj*

1. (*áreiðanlegur*) exact, precise
2. (*gaumgæfilegur*) thorough, thoroughgoing
3. (*vandlegur*) careful

A phrase may also be placed in an individually numbered section.

reynd *f* (**-ar, -ir**)

1. (*reynsla*) experience
2. (*veruleiki*) reality
3. **í** ~ in practice

Where the headword is registered in many phrases, they are grouped together in a separate numbered section marked *phrases*. Within this numbered section, the instances are arranged in roughly alphabetical order, usually according to the prepositions or adverbs incorporated in the phrases.

kast/a *v* (*dat*) (**-aði**)

1. (*varpa*) throw, fling, hurl
2. (*ala afkvæmi*) foal
3. *phrases*

~~ **eign sinni á e-ð**

claim sth as one's own

~~ **kveðju á e-n**

greet sby briefly

~~ **rýrð á e-ð**

belittle sth

~~ **af sér vatni**

make water, take a leak

~~ **aftur**

reflect

~~ **e-u fram**

throw out a remark

~~ **fram vísu**

make up a quatrain on the spot

~~ **mæðinni**

take a breather

~~ **upp**

vomit, throw up

Chapter 2

Dictionary

a	ad. one; any; each
able	v. having the power to do something
about	ad. almost ("about half"); of or having a relation to ("We talk about the weather.")
above	ad. at a higher place
accept	v. to agree to receive
accident	n. something that happens by chance or mistake; an unplanned event
accuse	v. to say a person is responsible for an act or crime; to make a statement against someone
across	ad. from side to side; to the other side
act	v. to do something
activist	n. one who seeks change through action
advise	v. to help with information, knowledge or ideas in making a decision
affect	v. to produce an effect on; to influence ("A lack of sleep affected the singer's performance.")
afraid	ad. feeling fear
after	ad. later; behind
again	ad. another time; as before
against	ad. opposed to; not agreeing with something
age	n. how old a person or thing is
agency	n. an organization that is part of a larger group ("an agency of the United Nations")
aggression	n. an attack against a person or country; the violation of a country's borders
ago	ad. of time past; before now

agree : v. to have the same belief as someone; to be willing to do something
agriculture : n. farming
aid : v. to help; to support; n. help, assistance
airplane : n. a vehicle with wings that flies
airport : n. a place where airplanes take off and land
album : n. a collection of recorded music

alone : ad. separated from others
along : ad. near or on ("along the road")
already : ad. before now; even now
also : ad. added to; too
although : conj. even if it is true that
always : ad. at all times; every time
ambassador : n. a nation's highest diplomatic representative (to another government)
amend : v. to add to or to change (a proposal or law)
ammunition : n. the bullets or shells fired from guns
among : ad. in or part of (a group)
amount : n. the number, size or weight of anything
anarchy : n. a lack of order; lawlessness
ancestor : n. a family member from the past
ancient : ad. very old; long ago
and : conj. also; in addition to; with
another : ad. one more; a different one
answer : n. a statement produced by a question; v. to make a statement after being asked a question
any : ad. one or more of no special kind
apologize : v. to express regret for a mistake or accident for which one accepts responsibility
appeal : v. to take to a higher court, person or group for a decision; to call on somebody for help
appear : v. to show oneself; to come into sight; to seem
appoint : v. to name; to choose ("appoint a judge")
approve : v. to agree with; to agree to support
archeology : n. the scientific study of past human life and activities

area : n. any place or part of it
argue : v. to offer reasons for or against something; to dispute; to disagree
arms : n. military equipment; weapons
army : n. military ground forces
around : ad. on every side (of)
arrest : v. to seize a person for legal action; to take as a prisoner
astronaut : n. a person who travels in space
astronomy : n. the scientific study of stars and the universe
asylum : n. political protection given by a government to a person from another country
at : prep. in or near ("at the edge"); where ("look at"); when ("at noon")
atmosphere : n. the gases surrounding any star or planet
attach : v. to tie together; to connect
attack : n. a violent attempt to damage, injure or kill; v. to start a fight
attempt : v. to work toward something; to try; to make an effort
attend : v. to be present at
automobile : n. a vehicle with wheels used to carry people; a car
autumn : n. the time of the year between summer and winter
average : n. something (a number) representing the middle; ad. common; normal
avoid : v. to stay away from
awake : ad. not sleeping
award : n. an honour or prize for an act or service
away : ad. not near
baby : n. a newly born creature
back : n. the part behind the front; ad. the other way from forward
bad : ad. wrong; acting against the law; not good
balance : v. to make two sides or forces equal
ball : n. something round

balloon : n. a device of strong, light material that rises when filled with gas lighter than air
ballot : n. a piece of paper used for voting
ban : v. to not permit; to stop; n. an official restriction
bank : n. an organization that keeps and lends money
bar : v. to prevent or block
barrier : n. anything that blocks or makes an action difficult
base : n. a military centre; v. to establish as a fact ("Her research was based on experiments.")
battle : n. a fight between opposing armed forces
be : v. to live; to happen; to exist
beat : v. to hit again and again
beauty : ad. that which pleases the eye, ear or spirit
because : prep. for the reason that ("He left because he was sick.")
become : v. to come to be
bed : n. a sleeping place
before : prep. earlier
begin : v. to do the first part of an action; to start
behind : ad. at the back of; in back of
believe : v. to think; to feel sure of; to accept as true; to trust
bell : n. an instrument that makes a musical sound ("a church bell")
belong : v. to be owned by; to be a member of
below : ad. lower than
best : ad. the most good
betray : v. to turn against; to be false to
better : ad. more good than
biology : n. the scientific study of life or living things in all their forms
bird : n. a creature that flies
bite : v. to cut with the teeth
black : ad. dark; having the colour like that of the night sky

blame	:	v. to accuse; to hold responsible
blanket	:	n. a cloth cover used to keep warm
bleed	:	v. to lose blood
blind	:	ad. not able to see
block	:	v. to stop something from being done; to prevent movement
blood	:	n. red fluid in the body
blow	:	v. to move with force, as in air ("The wind blows.")
blue	:	ad. having the colour like that of a clear sky
boat	:	n. something built to travel on water that carries people or goods
body	:	n. all of a person or animal; the remains of a person or animal
boil	:	v. to heat a liquid until it becomes very hot
bomb	:	n. a device that explodes with great force; v. to attack or destroy with bombs
bone	:	n. the hard material in the body
book	:	n. a long written work for reading
border	:	n. a dividing line between nations
born	:	v. to come to life; to come into existence
borrow	:	v. to take as a loan
both	:	ad. not just one of two, but the two together
bottle	:	n. a container, usually made of glass, to hold liquid
bottom	:	ad. the lowest part of something
box	:	n. something to put things into; a container, usually made of paper or wood
boy	:	n. a young male person
boycott	:	v. to refuse to take part in or deal with
brain	:	n. the control centre of thought, emotions and body activity of all creatures
brave	:	ad. having no fear
bread	:	n. a food made from grain
break	:	v. to divide into parts by force; to destroy
breathe	:	v. to take air into the body and let it out again
bring	:	v. to come with something

broadcast : v. to send information, stories or music by radio or television; n. a radio or television programme

brother : n. a male with the same father or mother as another person

brown : ad. having the colour like that of coffee

budget : n. a spending plan

build : v. to join materials together to make something

bus : n. a public vehicle to carry people

business : n. one's work; buying and selling to earn money; trade

busy : ad. doing something; very active

but : conj. however; other than; yet

buy : v. to get by paying something, usually money

by : conj. near; at; next to ("by the road"); from ("a play by William Shakespeare"); not later than ("by midnight")

cabinet : n. a group of ministers that helps lead a government

call : v. to give a name to ("I call myself John."); to ask for or request ("They called for an end to the fighting.")

calm : ad. quiet; peaceful; opposite tense

camera : n. a device for taking pictures

camp : n. a place with temporary housing

campaign : n. a competition by opposing political candidates seeking support from voters; a connected series of military actions during a war

can : v. to be able to; to have the right to; n. a container used to hold liquid or food, usually made of metal

cancel : v. to end; to stop

cancer : n. a disease in which dangerous cells grow quickly and destroy parts of the body

candidate : n. a person who seeks or is nominated for an office or an honour

capital : n. the official centre of a government; the city where a country's government is
capitalism : n. an economic system in which the production of most goods and services is owned and operated for profit by private citizens or companies
capture : v. to make a person or animal a prisoner; to seize or take by force; to get control of
car : n. a vehicle with wheels used to carry people; an automobile; a part of a train
care : v. to like; to protect; to feel worry or interest
careful : ad. acting safely; with much thought
carry : v. to take something or someone from one place to another
catch : v. to seize after a chase; to stop and seize with the hands
cause : v. to make happen; n. the thing or person that produces a result
cease-fire : n. a halt in fighting, usually by agreement
celebrate : v. to honour a person or event with special activities
centre : n. the middle of something; the place in the middle; a place that is the main point of an activity
century : n. one hundred years
ceremony : n. an act or series of acts done in a special way established by tradition
chairman : n. a person leading a meeting or an organized group
champion : n. the best; the winner
chance : n. a possibility of winning or losing or that something will happen
change : v. to make different; to become different
charge : v. to accuse someone of something, usually a crime; n. a statement in which someone is accused of something
chase : v. to run or go after someone or something
cheat : v. to get by a trick; to steal from

cheer : v. to shout approval or praise
chemical : n. elements found in nature or made by people; substances used in the science of chemistry
children : n. more than one child
choose : v. to decide between two or more
circle : n. a closed shape that has all its points equally distant from the centre, like an "O"
citizen : n. a person who is a member of a country by birth or by law
city : n. any important large town
civilian : ad. not military
civil rights : n. the political, economic and social rights given equally to all people of a nation
claim : v. to say something as a fact
clash : n. a battle; v. to fight or oppose
clean : v. to make pure; ad. free from dirt or harmful substances ("clean water")
clear : ad. easy to see or see through; easily understood
clergy : n. a body of officials within a religious organization
climate : n. the normal weather conditions of a place
climb : v. to go up or down something by using the feet and sometimes the hands
clock : n. a device that measures and shows time
close : v. to make something not open; ad. near to
cloth : n. a material made from plants, chemicals, animal hair and other substances
clothes : n. what people wear
cloud : n. a mass of fog high in the sky
coal : n. a solid black substance used as fuel
coalition : n. forces, groups or nations joined together
coast : n. land on the edge of the ocean
coffee : n. a drink made from the plant of the same name
cold : ad. not warm; having or feeling great coolness or a low temperature

collect : v. to bring or gather together in one place; to demand and receive ("collect taxes")

college : n. a small university

colony : n. land controlled by another country or government

colour : n. the different effects of light on the eye, making blue, red, brown, black, yellow and others

combine : v. to mix or bring together

come : v. to move toward; to arrive

command : v. to order; to have power over something

comment : v. to say something about; to express an opinion about something

committee : n. a group of people given special work

common : ad. usual; same for all ("a common purpose")

communicate : v. to tell; to give or exchange information

community : n. a group of people living together in one place or area

company : n. a business organized for trade, industrial or other purposes

compare : v. to examine what is different or similar

compete : v. to try to do as well as, or better than, another or others

complete : ad. having all parts; ended or finished

complex : ad. of or having many parts that are difficult to understand; not simple

compromise : n. the settlement of an argument where each side agrees to accept less than first demanded

computer : n. an electronic machine for storing and organizing information, and for communicating with others

concern : n. interest, worry ("express concern about"); v. to fear ("to be concerned")

condemn : v. to say a person or action is wrong or bad

condition : n. something declared necessary to complete an agreement; a person's health

conference : n. a meeting
confirm : v. to approve; to say that something is true
conflict : n. a fight; a battle, especially a long one
congratulate : v. to praise a person or to express pleasure for success or good luck
Congress : n. the organization of people elected to make the laws of the United States (the House of Representatives and the Senate); a similar organization in other countries
connect : v. to join one thing to another; to unite; to link
conservative : n. one who usually supports tradition and opposes great change
consider : v. to give thought to; to think about carefully
constitution : n. the written general laws and ideas that form a nation's system of government
contain : v. to hold; to include
container : n. a box, bottle or can used to hold something
continent : n. any of the seven great land areas of the world
continue : v. to go on doing or being
control : v. to direct; to have power over
convention : n. a large meeting for a special purpose
cook : v. to heat food before eating it
cool : ad. almost cold
cooperate : v. to act or work together
copy : v. to make something exactly like another; n. something made to look exactly like another
corn : n. a food grain
correct : ad. true; free from mistakes; v. to change to what is right
cost : n. the price or value of something ("The cost of the book is five dollars."); v. to be valued at ("The book costs five dollars.")
cotton : n. a material made from a plant of the same name
count : v. to speak or add numbers

country : n. a nation; the territory of a nation; land away from cities

court : n. where trials take place; where judges make decisions about law

cover : v. to put something over a person or thing; n. anything that is put over a person or thing

cow : n. a farm animal used for its milk

crash : v. to fall violently; to hit with great force

create : v. to make; to give life or form to

creature : n. any living being; any animal or human

credit : n. an agreement that payments will be made at a later time

crew : n. a group of people working together

crime : n. an act that violates a law

criminal : n. a person who is responsible for a crime

crisis : n. an extremely important time when something may become much better or worse; a dangerous situation

criticize : v. to say what is wrong with something or someone; to condemn; to judge

crop : n. plants that are grown and gathered for food, such as grains, fruits and vegetables

cross : v. to go from one side to another; to go across

crowd : n. a large number of people gathered in one place

crush : v. to damage or destroy by great weight; to defeat completely

cry : v. to express or show sorrow or pain

culture : n. all the beliefs, traditions and arts of a group or population

cure : v. to improve health; to make well ("The doctor can cure the disease."); n. something that makes a sick person well ("Antibiotics are a cure for infection.")

curfew : n. an order to people to stay off the streets or to close their businesses current : n. movement of air, water or electricity; ad. belonging to the present time ("She found the report in a current publication.")

custom : n. a long-established belief or activity of a people

customs : n. taxes on imports

cut : v. to divide or injure with a sharp tool; to make less; to reduce

dam : n. a wall built across a river to hold back flowing water

damage : v. to cause injury or destruction; n. harm; hurt or injury, usually to things

date : n. an expression of time; a day, month and year

daughter : n. a person's female child

day : n. twenty-four hours; the hours of sunlight

dead : ad. not living

deaf : ad. not able to hear

deal : v. to have to do with ("The talks will deal with the problem of pollution."); to buy or sell ("Her company deals in plastic.")

debate : v. to argue for or against something; n. a public discussion or argument

debt : n. something that is owed; the condition of owing

decide : v. to choose; to settle; to judge

declare : v. to say; to make a statement

decrease : v. to make less in size or amount

deep : ad. going far down; a long way from top to bottom

defeat : v. to cause to lose in a battle or struggle; n. a loss; the condition of having lost

defend : v. to guard or fight against attack; to protect

deficit : n. a shortage that results when spending is greater than earnings, or imports are greater than exports

define : v. to give the meaning of; to explain

degree	:	n. a measure of temperature
delay	:	v. to decide to do something at a later time; to postpone; to cause to be late
delegate	:	n. one sent to act for another; one who represents another
demand	:	v. to ask by ordering; to ask with force
democracy	:	n. the system of government in which citizens vote to choose leaders or to make other important decisions
deny	:	v. to declare that something is not true; to refuse a request
depend	:	v. to need help and support
deplore	:	v. to regret strongly; to express sadness
deploy	:	v. to move forces or weapons into positions for action
depression	:	n. severe unhappiness; a period of reduced business and economic activity during which many people lose their jobs
describe	:	v. to give a word picture of something; to give details of something
desert	:	n. a dry area of land
design	:	v. to plan or create plans for
desire	:	v. to want very much; to wish for
destroy	:	v. to break into pieces; to end the existence of
detail	:	n. a small part of something; a small piece of information
develop	:	v. to grow; to create; to experience progress
device	:	n. a piece of equipment made for a special purpose
dictator	:	n. a ruler with complete power
die	:	v. to become dead; to stop living; to end
diet	:	n. usual daily food and drink
different	:	ad. not the same
difficult	:	ad. not easy; hard to do, make or carry out
dig	:	v. to make a hole in the ground
diplomat	:	n. a person who represents his or her government in dealing with another government

disappear :	v. to become unseen; to no longer exist
discover :	v. to find or learn something
discuss :	v. to talk about; to exchange ideas
disease :	n. a sickness in living things, often caused by viruses, germs or bacteria
dismiss :	v. to send away; to refuse to consider
dispute :	v. to oppose strongly by argument; n. an angry debate
dissident :	n. a person who strongly disagrees with his or her government
distance :	n. the amount of space between two places or objects ("The distance from my house to your house is two kilometres.")
dive :	v. to jump into water head first
divide :	v. to separate into two or more parts
do :	v. to act; to make an effort
doctor :	n. a person trained in medicine to treat sick people
document :	n. an official piece of paper with facts written on it, used as proof or support of something
dog :	n. a small animal that often lives with humans
dollar :	n. United States money, one hundred cents
door :	n. an opening for entering or leaving a building or room
down :	ad. from higher to lower; in a low place
dream :	v. to have a picture or story in the mind during sleep; n. a picture or story in the mind during sleep; a happy idea about the future
drink :	v. to take liquid into the body through the mouth
drive :	v. to control a moving vehicle
drop :	v. to fall or let fall; to go lower
drown :	v. to die under water
drug :	n. anything used as a medicine or in making medicine; a chemical substance used to ease pain or to affect the mind

dry : ad. not wet; without rain

during : ad. through the whole time; while (something is happening)

dust : n. pieces of matter so small that they can float in the air

duty : n. one's job or responsibility; what one must do because it is right and just

each : ad. every one by itself

early : ad. at or near the beginning, especially the beginning of the day; opposite late

earn : v. to be paid in return for work done

earth : n. the planet we all live on; the ground or soil

earthquake : n. a sudden, violent shaking of the earth's surface

ease : v. to reduce; to make less difficult

east : n. the direction from which the sun rises

easy : ad. not difficult; not hard to do

eat : v. to take food into the body through the mouth

ecology : n. the scientific study of the environment and links among living and material things

economy : n. the system by which money, industry and trade are organized

edge : n. the line where something ends or begins

education : n. the act of teaching

effect : n. the result or change caused by something ("The storm had a serious effect on the economy.")

effort : n. an attempt; the work necessary to do something

egg : n. the rounded object containing unborn young produced by female birds, fish or reptiles; a single cell in a female person or animal that can develop into a baby

either : ad. one of two, but not the other

elect : v. to choose by voting

electricity : n. a form of energy that flows through wires

		to provide heat and light, and power to machines
embassy	:	n. the offices of an ambassador and his or her assistants
emergency	:	n. an unexpected and dangerous situation demanding quick action
emotion	:	n. a strong feeling such as love, hate, fear or sadness
employ	:	v. to give work in return for wages
empty	:	ad. having nothing inside; v. to remove everything
end	:	v. to stop; to finish; n. the part which comes last
enemy	:	n. a person opposing or hating another; a person or people of the other side in a war
energy	:	n. power used to do work, usually with machines; the ability and willingness to be active
enforce	:	v. to make something be done
engine	:	n. a machine that uses energy to cause movement or to do work
engineer	:	n. a person who designs engines, machines, roads, bridges or railroads
enjoy	:	v. to be pleased or satisfied by something
enough	:	ad. as much as necessary; pro. the amount needed
enter	:	v. to come or go into
environment	:	n. all surrounding things, conditions and influences that affect life; the natural world of land, sea, air, plants and animals
equal	:	ad. the same in amount, size, weight or value; having the same rights
equipment	:	n. things, tools or machines needed for a purpose or activity
escape	:	v. to get free; to get away from; to get out of
especially	:	ad. more than others ("We liked the food, especially the fish.")
establish	:	v. to bring into existence; to create

estimate : v. to form an opinion about a value, size or amount using less than complete information

ethnic : ad. of or concerning people belonging to a large group because of their race, religion, language, tribe or where their ancestors lived

evaporate : v. to change from a liquid into a gas

even : ad. in a way not thought possible ("They survived, even though the building was destroyed.")

event : n. that which happens, especially something of importance

ever : ad. at any time

every : ad. each one; all

evidence : n. material or facts that prove something; a reason for believing

evil : ad. not good; extremely bad

exact : ad. having no mistakes; correct in every detail

examine : v. to study closely

example : n. a part that shows what the rest of a thing or group is like

excellent : ad. extremely good

except : prep. but for

exchange : v. to trade; to give or receive one thing for another

excuse : v. to take away blame; to pardon; to forgive; n. a reason (sometimes false) for an action

execute : v. to kill

exercise : n. an activity or effort for the purpose of improving the body or to stay in good health

exile : v. to force a person to leave his or her country; to expel; n. a person who is forced to leave his or her country

exist : v. to be; to live

expand : v. to make larger; to grow larger

expect : v. to think or believe that something will happen; to wait for an event

expel : v. to force out; to remove from; to send away

experience : v. to live through an event, situation or condition ("She experienced great pain."); n. something that one has done or lived through ("The experience caused her great pain.")

experiment : v. to test; n. a test or trial carried out to prove if an idea is true or false, or to discover something

expert : n. a person with special knowledge or training

explain : v. to give reasons for; to make clear; to tell about; to tell the meaning

explode : v. to break apart violently with a loud noise, like a bomb

explore : v. to travel in a place that is not well known to learn more about it; to make a careful search; to examine closely

export : v. to send to another country; n. something sent to another country, usually for sale

express : v. to say clearly

extend : v. to stretch out in area or length; to continue for a longer time

extra : ad. more than normal, expected or necessary

extreme : ad. more than the usual or accepted

extremist : n. a person with strong religious or political beliefs who acts in an extreme or violent way

face : n. the front of the head:eyes, nose, mouth; v. to look toward; to turn toward; to have before you, such as a problem or danger

fact : n. something known or proved to be true

factory : n. a building or group of buildings where goods are made

fail : v. to not succeed; to not reach a goal

fair : ad. just; honest; what is right

fall : v. to go down quickly; to come down; to drop to the ground or a lower position

false : ad. not true; not correct

family : n. the group that includes children and their

parents

famous : ad. known very well to many people

far : ad. at, to or from a great distance

farm : n. land used to grow crops and animals for food

fast : ad. moving or working at great speed; quick

fat : n. tissue in the bodies of humans and animals used to store energy and to keep warm; ad. thick; heavy

father : n. the male parent; a man who has a child or children

fear : v. to be afraid; to worry that something bad is near or may happen ("He feared falling down."); n. a strong emotion when there is danger or trouble ("He had a fear that he would fall down.")

federal : ad. of or having to do with a national or central government

feed : v. to give food to

feel : v. to have or experience an emotion; to know by touching

female : n. a woman or girl; the sex that gives birth; ad. of or about women

fence : n. something around an area of land to keep animals or people in or out

fertile : ad. rich in production of plants or animals; producing much

few : ad. not many; a small number of

field : n. an area of open land, usually used to grow crops or to raise animals

fierce : ad. extremely strong; violent; angry

fight : v. to use violence or force; to attempt to defeat or destroy an enemy; n. the use of force; a battle

fill : v. to put or pour something into a container until there is space for no more

film : v. to record something so it can be seen again; to make a motion picture or movie; n.

		a thin piece of material for making pictures with a camera; a movie
final	:	ad. at the end; last
financial	:	ad. of or about the system that includes the use of money, credit, investments and banks
find	:	v. to discover or learn something by searching or by accident; to decide a court case ("The jury finds the man guilty of murder.")
fine	:	n. a payment ordered by a court to punish someone for a crime; ad. very good; very small or thin
finish	:	v. to complete; to end
fire	:	v. to shoot a gun; n. the heat and light produced by something burning
firework	:	n. rockets producing bright fire in the sky, used in holiday celebrations
firm	:	ad. not easily moved or changed ("She is firm in her opinion.")
first	:	ad. coming before all others
fish	:	n. a creature that lives and can breathe in water
fit	:	v. to be of the correct size or shape ("These shoes fit my feet.")
fix	:	v. to make good or right again
flag	:	n. a piece of coloured cloth used to represent a nation, government or organization
flat	:	ad. smooth; having no high places
flee	:	v. to run away from
float	:	v. to be on water without sinking; to move or be moved gently on water or through air
flood	:	v. to cover with water; n. the movement of water out of a river, lake or ocean onto land
floor	:	n. the bottom part of a room for walking on ("The book fell to the floor."); the level of a building ("The fire was on the first floor.")
flow	:	v. to move like a liquid
flower	:	n. the coloured part of plants that carry seeds

fluid	:	n. any substance that can flow, such as a liquid
fly	:	v. to move through the air with wings, like a bird or airplane; to travel in an airplane or flying vehicle
fog	:	n. a mass of wet air that is difficult to see through; a cloud close to the ground
follow	:	v. to come or go after; to accept the rule or power of; to obey
food	:	n. that which is taken in by all living things for energy, strength and growth
fool	:	v. to make someone believe something that is not true; to trick; n. a person who is tricked easily
foot	:	n. the bottom part of the leg; the part of the body that touches the ground when a person or animal walks
for	:	prep. because of ("He is famous for his work."); in exchange ("Give me one dollar for the book."); through space or time ("They travelled for one hour."); representative of ("I speak for all people."); to be employed by ("She works for a computer company.")
force	:	v. to make someone do something or make something happen by using power; n. power, strength; strength used against a person or object; military power of a nation; a military group
foreign	:	ad. of, about or from another nation; not from one's own place or country
forest	:	n. a place of many trees
forget	:	v. to not remember
forgive	:	v. to pardon; to excuse; to remove guilt
form	:	v. to make; to start; to shape ("They formed a swim team."); n. a kind ("Swimming is a form of exercise.")
former	:	ad. earlier in time; not now

forward : ad. the direction in front of; toward the front

free : v. to rele©ase; ad. not controlled by another or by outside forces; not in prison; independent; not limited by rules; without cost

freedom : n. the condition of being free

freeze : v. to cause or to become very cold; to make or to become hard by cold

fresh : ad. newly made or gathered; recent

friend : n. a person one likes and trusts

frighten : v. to cause great fear

from : prep. having a person, place or thing as a beginning or cause ("It is a message from the president."); at a place distant, not near ("The school is five kilometres from my home."); because of ("He is suffering from cancer.")

front : n. the forward part; the opposite of back; the beginning; the first part

fruit : n. food from trees and plants

fuel : n. any substance burned to create heat or power

full : ad. containing as much as a person or thing can hold; complete

fun : n. anything that is pleasing and causes happiness

funeral : n. a ceremony held in connection with the burial or burning of the dead

future : n. time after now ("We can talk about it in the future."); ad. in the time to come ("All future meetings will be held in this room.")

gain : v. to get possession of; to get more; to increase

game : n. an activity with rules in which people or teams play or compete, usually sports

gas : n. any substance that is not solid or liquid; any substance that burns to provide heat,

		light or power
gather	:	v. to bring or come together into a group or place; to collect
general	:	n. a high military leader; ad. without details; affecting or including all or almost all
gentle	:	ad. soft; kind; not rough or violent
get	:	v. to receive; to gain; to go and bring back; to become; to become the owner of
gift	:	n. something given without cost
girl	:	n. a young female person
give	:	v. to present to another to keep without receiving payment
glass	:	n. a hard, clear material that is easily broken, used most often for windows or for containers to hold liquids
go	:	v. to move from one place to another; to leave
goal	:	n. that toward which an effort is directed; that which is aimed at; the end of a trip or race
god	:	n. the spirit that is honoured as creator of all things ("They believe in God."); a spirit or being believed in many religions to have special powers
gold	:	n. a highly valued yellow metal
good	:	ad. pleasing; helpful; kind; correct; not bad
goods	:	n. things owned or made to be sold
govern	:	v. to control; to rule by military or political power
government	:	n. a system of governing; the organization of people that rules a country, city or area
grain	:	n. the seed of grass plants used for food, such as wheat, rice and corn; those plants that produce the seeds
granddaughter	:	n. the daughter of a person's daughter or son
grandfather	:	n. the father of a person's father or mother
grandmother	:	n. the mother of a person's father or mother
grandson	:	n. the son of a person's daughter or son

grass : n. a plant with long, narrow, green leaves
gray : ad. having the colour like that made by mixing black and white
great : ad. very large or more than usual in size or number; very good; important
green : ad. having the colour like that made by mixing yellow and blue; having the colour like that of growing leaves and grass
grind : v. to reduce to small pieces by crushing
ground : n. land; the earth's surface; soil
group : n. a number of people or things together; a gathering of people working for a common purpose
grow : v. to develop or become bigger; to increase in size or amount
guarantee : v. to promise a result; to promise that something will happen
guard : v. to watch and protect a person, place or thing ("He guards the president."); n. a person or thing that watches or protects ("He is a prison guard.")
guerrilla : n. a person who fights as part of an unofficial army, usually against an official army or police
guide : v. to lead to; to show the way; n. one who shows the way
guilty : ad. having done something wrong or in violation of a law; responsible for a bad action
gun : n. a weapon that shoots bullets
hair : n. the fine material that grows from the skin, especially from the head
half : n. one of two equal parts of something
halt : v. to come or cause to come to a stop; to stop
hang : v. to place something so the highest part is supported and the lower part is not; to kill by hanging
happen : v. to become a fact or event; to take place

happy	:	ad. pleased; satisfied; feeling good; not sad
hard	:	ad. not easily cut or broken; solid; difficult to do or understand; needing much effort or force
harm	:	v. to injure; to damage; n. damage; hurt
harvest	:	v. to gather crops; n. the crop after it is gathered
hat	:	n. a head cover
hate	:	v. to have strong emotions against; to consider as an enemy; opposite love
have	:	v. to possess; to own; to hold
he	:	pro. the boy or man who is being spoken about
head	:	v. to lead; to command; n. leader; chief; the top part of something; the highest position
headquarter	:	n. the centre from which orders are given; the main offices of a business or organization
heal	:	v. to return to good health; to cure; to become well
health	:	n. the general condition of the body and mind; the condition of being free from sickness or disease
hear	:	v. to receive sound through the ears; to receive news about
heat	:	v. to make hot or warm; n. great warmth; that which is produced by burning fuel; energy from the sun
heavy	:	ad. having much weight; not easy to lift; of great amount or force
helicopter	:	n. a machine without wings that can fly up or down or remain in one place above the ground
help	:	v. to give support; to assist; to make easier; n. support; aid
here	:	ad. in, to or at this place
hero	:	n. a person honoured for being brave or wise
hide	:	v. to prevent from being seen or found; to make secret

high : ad. tall; far up; far above the ground; important; above others

hijack : v. to seize or take control of a vehicle by force

hill : n. a small mountain

history : n. the written record or description of past events; the study of the past

hit : v. to strike; to touch with force

hold : v. to carry or support, usually in the hands or arms; to keep in one position; to keep as a prisoner; to contain; to possess; to occupy; to organize and be involved in ("The two sides hold talks this week.")

hole : n. an opening; a torn or broken place in something

holiday : n. a day when one does not work; a day on which no work is done to honour or remember a person or event

holy : ad. greatly honoured in religion

home : n. the building where a person lives, especially with family; the place where one was born or comes from; the area or country where one lives

honest : ad. truthful; able to be trusted

honour : v. to obey; to show strong, good feelings for ("to honour one's parents"); n. an award; an act of giving special recognition ("He received many honours for his efforts to help others.")

hope : v. to expect; to believe there is a good chance that something will happen as wanted; to want something to happen

horrible : ad. causing great fear; terrible

horse : n. a large animal often used for racing, riding or farm work

hospital : n. a place where sick or injured people are given medical care

hostage : n. a person captured and held as a guarantee

		that a demand or promise will be honoured
hostile	:	ad. ready to fight; ready for war
hot	:	ad. having or feeling great heat or a high temperature
hotel	:	n. a building with rooms, and often food, for travellers
hour	:	n. a measure of time; sixty minutes
house	:	n. a building in which people live; a country's parliament or lawmaking group ("House of Representatives")
how	:	ad. in what way; to what amount
however	:	conj. yet; but
huge	:	ad. very big; of great size
human	:	ad. of or about people
humour	:	n. the ability to understand, enjoy or express what makes people laugh
hunger	:	n. the need for food
hunt	:	v. to search for animals to capture or kill them; to seek; to try to find
hurry	:	v. to do or go fast
hurt	:	v. to cause pain, injury or damage
husband	:	n. a man who is married
I	:	pro. the person speaking
ice	:	n. frozen water
idea	:	n. a thought or picture in the mind; a belief
identify	:	v. to recognize someone or something and to say who or what they are
if	:	conj. on condition; provided that ("I will go if you go.")
illegal	:	ad. not legal; in violation of a law
imagine	:	v. to make a picture in the mind; to form an idea
immediate	:	ad. without delay; very near in time or place
import	:	v. to bring from another country; n. something brought from another country, usually for sale

important : ad. having great meaning, value or power
improve : v. to make better; to become better
in : prep. inside; held by; contained by; surrounded by; during
incident : n. an event or something that happens
incite : v. to urge or cause an action or emotion, usually something bad or violent
include : v. to have; to make a part of
increase : v. to make more in size or amount
independent : ad. not influenced by or controlled by another or others; free; separate
individual : n. one person
industry : n. any business that produces goods or provides services; the work and related activity in factories and offices; all organizations involved in manufacturing
infect : v. to make sick with something that causes disease
inflation : n. a continuing rise in prices while the value of money goes down
influence : v. to have an effect on someone or something; to cause change
inform : v. to tell; to give knowledge to
information : n. knowledge; facts
inject : v. to force a fluid into, such as putting medicine or drugs into the body through the skin
injure : v. to cause harm or damage to a person or animal
innocent : ad. not guilty of a crime; not responsible for a bad action
insane : ad. mentally sick
insect : n. a very small creature, usually with many legs and sometimes with wings
inspect : v. to look at something carefully; to examine, especially by an expert
instead : ad. in the place of; taking the place of
instrument : n. a tool or device designed to do something

or to make something

insult : v. to say something or to do something that makes another person angry or dishonoured

intelligence : n. the ability to think or learn; information gathered by spying

intelligent : ad. quick to understand or learn

intense : ad. very strong; extremely serious

interest : n. what is important to someone ("He acted to protect his interests." "She had a great interest in painting."); a share in owning a business; money paid for the use of money borrowed

interfere : v. to get in the way of; to work against; to take part in the activities of others, especially when not asked to do so

international : ad. of or about more than one nation or many nations; of the whole world

intervene : v. to come between; to come between in order to settle or solve

invade : v. to enter an area or country by force with an army

invent : v. to plan and make something never made before; to create a new thing or way of doing something

invest : v. to give money to a business or organization with the hope of making more money

investigate : v. to study or examine all information about an event, situation or charge; to search for the truth

invite : v. to ask someone to take part in or join an event, organization or gathering

involve : v. to take part in; to become a part of; to include

iron : n. a strong, hard metal used to make machines and tools

island : n. a land area with water all around it

issue : n. an important problem or subject that

people are discussing or arguing about

it : pro. a thing, place, event or idea that is being spoken about ("The sky is blue, but it also has a few white clouds.")

jail : n. a prison for those waiting to be tried for a crime or for those serving sentences for crimes that are not serious

jewel : n. a valuable stone, such as a diamond or emerald

job : n. the work that one does to earn money

join : v. to put together or come together; to become part of or a member of

joint : ad. shared by two or more

joke : n. something done or said to cause others to laugh

judge : v. to form an opinion about; to decide a question, especially a legal one; n. a public official who decides problems of law in a court

jump : v. to push down on the feet and move up quickly into the air

jury : n. a group of people chosen to decide what is true in a trial

just : ad. only ("Help me for just a minute."); very shortly before or after the present ("He just left."); at the same time ("He left just as I came in."); what is right or fair ("The law is just, in my opinion.")

keep : v. to possess; to have for oneself

kick : v. to hit with the foot

kidnap : v. to seize and take away by force

kill : v. to make dead; to cause to die

kind : n. sort ("What kind of dog is that?"); ad. gentle; caring; helpful

kiss : v. to touch with the mouth to show love or honour

knife : n. a tool or weapon used to cut

know : v. to understand something as correct; to

		have the facts about; to recognize someone because you have met and talked together before
knowledge	:	n. that which is known; learning or understanding
labour	:	n. work; workers as a group
labouratory	:	n. a room or place where experiments in science are done
lack	:	v. to be without; n. the condition of needing, wanting or not having
lake	:	n. a large area of fresh water surrounded by land
land	:	v. to come to the earth from the air ("Airplanes land at airports."); n. the part of the earth not covered by water; the ground
language	:	n. words and their use; what people speak in a country, nation or group
large	:	ad. big; being of more than usual size, amount or number; opposite small
last	:	v. to continue ("The talks will last three days."); ad. after all others; the only one remaining ("She is the last person in line.")
late	:	ad. after the correct time; near the end; opposite early
laugh	:	v. to make sounds to express pleasure or happy feelings
launch	:	v. to put into operation; to begin; to send into the air or space
law	:	n. all or any rules made by a government
lead	:	v. to show the way; to command; to control; to go first
leak	:	v. to come out of or to escape through a small opening or hole (usually a gas or liquid)
learn	:	v. to get knowledge about; to come to know a fact or facts
leave	:	v. to go away from; to let something stay where it is
left	:	ad. on the side that is toward the west when

one is facing north; opposite right

legal : ad. of or in agreement with the law

legislature : n. a government lawmaking group

lend : v. to permit someone to use a thing temporarily; to make a loan of money

less : ad. smaller in amount; not as much

let : v. to permit to do or to be; to make possible

letter : n. a message written on paper; a communication in writing sent to another person

level : n. the amount or height that something reaches or rises to; the position of something or someone

liberal : ad. one who usually supports social progress or change

lie : v. to have one's body on the ground or other surface; to say something that one knows is not true

life : n. the time between being born and dying; opposite death; all living things

lift : v. to take or bring up to a higher place or level

light : n. a form of energy that affects the eyes so that one is able to see; anything that produces light; ad. bright; clear; not heavy

lightning : n. light produced by electricity in the air, usually during a storm

like : v. to be pleased with; to have good feelings for someone or something; ad. in the same way as; similar to

limit : v. to restrict to a number or amount; n. the greatest amount or number permitted

line : n. a long, thin mark on a surface; a number of people or things organized; one after another; the edge of an area protected by military forces

link : v. to connect; to unite one thing or event with

another; n. a relation between two or more things, situations or events

liquid : n. a substance that is not a solid or gas, and can move freely, like water

list : v. to put in writing a number of names of people or things; n. a written series of names or things

listen : v. to try to hear

literature : n. all the poems, stories and writings of a period of time or of a country

little : ad. not tall or big; a small amount

live : v. to have life; to exist; ad. having life; alive

load : v. to put objects on or into a vehicle or container; n. that which is carried

loan : n. money borrowed that usually must be returned with interest payments; something borrowed

local : ad. about or having to do with one place

lonely : ad. feeling alone and wanting friends; visited by few or no people ("a lonely man")

long : ad. not short; measuring from beginning to end; measuring much; for much time

look : v. to turn the eyes toward so as to see; to search or hunt for; to seem to be

lose : v. to have no longer; to not find; to fail to keep; to be defeated

loud : ad. having a strong sound; full of sound or noise

love : v. to like very much; to feel a strong, kind emotion (sometimes involving sex); n. a strong, kind emotion for someone or something; opposite hate

low : ad. not high or tall; below the normal height; close to the ground

loyal : ad. showing strong friendship and support for someone or something

luck : n. something that happens by chance

machine : n. a device with moving parts used to do work

magazine : n. a publication of news, stories, pictures or other information

mail : n. letters, papers and other things sent through an official system, such as a post office

main : ad. the most important or largest

major : ad. great in size, importance or amount

majority : n. the greater number; more than half

make : v. to produce; to create; to build; to do something or to carry out an action; to cause to be or to become

male : n. a man or boy; the sex that is the father of children; ad. of or about men

man : n. an adult male human

manufacture : v. to make goods in large amounts

many : ad. a large number or amount of

map : n. a picture of the earth's surface or a part of it

march : v. to walk in a group like soldiers; to walk together in a large group to protest about something

mark : v. to make a sign or cut on something

market : n. a place or area where goods are sold, bought or traded; an economic system in which the prices of things are decided by how many there are and how much money people are willing to pay for them

marry : v. to join a man and woman together as husband and wife; to become husband and wife (usually in a religious or civil ceremony)

mass : n. an amount of matter having no special form and usually of a large size

mate : v. to bring together a male and a female to create another creature

material : n. the substance, substances or matter of which something is made or from which something can be made, such as wood, cloth or stone; anything that can be made into something else

mathematics : n. the science dealing with amounts, sizes and shapes, as explained by numbers and signs

matter : n. anything that can be seen or felt; what things are made of

may : v. a word used with an action word to mean permit or possible ("May I go?" "They may leave tomorrow.")

mayor : n. the chief official of a city or town government

meal : n. food eaten to satisfy hunger, such as dinner

mean : v. to want to; to give the idea of; to have the idea of

measure : v. to learn the amount, size or distance of something; n. an action taken; a legislative proposal

meat : n. the part of a dead animal used for food

media : n. all public information organizations, including newspapers, television and radio

medicine : n. a substance or drug used to treat disease or pain; the science or study of treating and curing disease or improving health

meet : v. to come together with someone or something at the same time and place

melt : v. to make a solid into a liquid by heating it

member : n. one of a group

memorial : n. something done or made to honour the memory of a person or event

memory : n. a picture in the mind of past events; the ability to remember; a thing remembered

mental : ad. about or having to do with the mind

mercy : n. kindness toward those who should be punished; the power to be kind or to pardon

message : n. written or spoken news or information; a note from one person to another person or group
metal : n. a hard substance such as iron, steel or gold
method : n. the way something is done
microscope : n. a device used to make very small things look larger so they can be studied
middle : n. the centre; a place or time of equal distance from both sides or ends; ad. in the centre
militant : n. someone active in trying to cause political change, often by the use of force or violence
military : n. the armed forces of a nation or group; ad. of or about the armed forces
milk : n. the white liquid produced by female animals to feed their young
mind : n. the thinking, feeling part of a person
mine : v. to dig useful or valuable substances out of the earth; n. a place in the earth where such substances are found; a bomb placed under the ground or under water so it cannot be seen
mineral : n. a substance found in nature that is not an animal or a plant, such as coal or salt
minister : n. a member of a cabinet; a high government official ("prime minister,"foreign minister")
minor : ad. small in size; of little importance
minority : n. the smaller number; opposite majority
minute : n. a measure of time; one of the sixty equal parts of an hour; sixty seconds
miss : v. to fail to hit, see, reach or meet
missile : n. any weapon that can be thrown or fired through the air and explodes when it reaches its target
missing : ad. lost; not found
mistake : n. a wrong action or decision; an action done without the knowledge that it was wrong

mix	:	v. to put different things together to make one thing
mob	:	n. a large group of wild or angry people
model	:	n. an example; something, usually small, made to show how something will look or work
moderate	:	ad. not extreme
modern	:	ad. of the present or very recent time; the most improved
money	:	n. pieces of metal or paper used to pay for things
month	:	n. one of the twelve periods of time into which a year is divided
moon	:	n. the bright object often seen in the night sky that orbits the earth about every twenty-nine days
moral	:	ad. concerning what is right or wrong in someone's actions
more	:	ad. greater in size or amount
morning	:	n. the early part of the day, from sunrise until noon
most	:	ad. greatest in size or amount
mother	:	n. the female parent; a woman who has a child or children
motion	:	n. a movement; a continuing change of position or place
mountain	:	n. a part of the earth's surface that rises high above the area around it
mourn	:	v. to express or feel sadness
move	:	v. to change position; to put or keep in motion; to go
movement	:	n. the act of moving or a way of moving; a series of acts or efforts to reach a goal
movie	:	n. a motion picture; a film
much	:	ad. great in amount
murder	:	v. to kill another person illegally; n. the crime of killing another person
music	:	n. the making of sounds by singing or using

a musical instrument

must : v. a word used with an action word to mean necessary ("You must go to school.")

mystery : n. something that is not or cannot be explained or understood; a secret

name : v. to appoint; to nominate; to give a name to; n. a word by which a person, animal or thing is known or called

narrow : ad. limited in size or amount; not wide; having a short distance from one side to the other

nation : n. a country, together with its social and political systems

native : n. someone who was born in a place, not one who moved there

natural : ad. of or about nature; normal; common to its kind

nature : n. all the plants, animals and other things on earth not created by humans; events or processes not caused by humans

navy : n. the part of a country's military force trained to fight at sea

near : ad. not far; close to

necessary : ad. needed to get a result or effect; required

need : v. to require; to want; to be necessary to have or to do

negotiate : v. to talk about a problem or situation to find a common solution

neither : ad. not one or the other of two

neutral : ad. not supporting one side or the other in a dispute

never : ad. at no time; not ever

new : ad. not existing before; not known before; recently made, built, bought or grown; another; different

news : n. information about any recent events, especially as reported by the media

next	:	ad. coming immediately after; nearest
nice	:	ad. pleasing; good; kind
night	:	n. the time between when the sun goes down and when it rises, when there is little or no light
no	:	ad. used to reject or to refuse; not any; not at all
noise	:	n. sound, especially when loud
nominate	:	v. to name someone as a candidate for an election; to propose a person for an office or position
noon	:	n. the middle of the day; twelve o'clock in the daytime
normal	:	n. the usual condition, amount or form; ad. usual; what is expected
north	:	n. the direction to the left of a person facing the rising sun
not	:	ad. a word showing that something is denied or untrue ("She is not going.")
note	:	v. to talk about something already known; n. a word or words written to help a person remember; a short letter
nothing	:	n. not anything; no thing
now	:	ad. at this time; immediately
nowhere	:	ad. not in, to or at any place
nuclear	:	ad. of or about the energy produced by splitting atoms or bringing them together; of or about weapons that explode by using energy from atoms
number	:	n. a word or sign used to show the order or amount of things
obey	:	v. to act as one is ordered to act
object	:	v. to show that one does not like or approve; to protest; n. something not alive that can be seen or touched
observe	:	v. to watch; to look at carefully; to celebrate or honour something ("They will observe the anniversary of the day she was born.")

occupy	:	v. to take and hold or to control by force
ocean	:	n. the area of salt water that covers almost seventy-five per cent of the earth's surface; any of the five main divisions of this water
of	:	prep. made from; belonging to; about; connected to; included among
off	:	ad. away; at a distance; condition when something is no longer operating or continuing; not on; not connected
offensive	:	n. a military campaign of attack; ad. having to do with attacking
offer	:	v. to present or propose; n. the act of presenting or proposing; that which is presented or proposed
office	:	n. a room or building where business or work is done; a public position to which one is elected or appointed
officer	:	n. a person in the military who commands others; any person who is a member of a police force
official	:	n. a person with power in an organization; a representative of an organization or government; ad. of or about an office; approved by the government or someone in power
often	:	ad. many times
oil	:	n. a thick liquid that does not mix with water and that burns easily; a black liquid taken from the ground and used as fuel
old	:	ad. not young or new; having lived or existed for many years
on	:	prep. above and held up by; touching the upper surface of ("The book is on the table."); supported by ("He is on his feet."); about ("The report on the meeting is ready."); at the time of ("He left on Wednesday.")
once	:	ad. one time only
only	:	ad. being the single one or ones; no more

		than ("We have only two dollars.")
open	:	v. to start ("They opened talks."); ad. not closed; not secret
operate	:	v. to do work or a job; to cut into the body for medical reasons
opinion	:	n. a belief based on one's own ideas and thinking
oppose	:	v. to be against; to fight against
opposite	:	ad. different as possible; completely different from; exactly the other way ("North is the opposite direction from south.")
oppress	:	v. to make others suffer; to control by the use of unjust and cruel force or power
or	:	conj. giving another of two choices; giving the last of several choices
orbit	:	v. to travel in space around a planet or other object; n. the path or way an object travels in space around another object or planet
order	:	v. to give a command; to tell someone what to do; n. a command; the correct or normal way things are organized; a peaceful situation in which people obey laws
organize	:	v. to put in order; to put together into a system
other	:	ad. different; of another kind; the remaining one or ones of two or more ("That man is short; the other is tall.")
our	:	ad. of or belonging to us
oust	:	v. to force to leave; to remove by force
out	:	ad. away from the inside; opposite of in
over	:	conj. above; covering; across, in or on every part of ("all over the world")
overthrow	:	v. to remove from power; to defeat or end by force
owe	:	v. to pay or have to repay (usually money) in return for something received
own	:	v. to have or possess for oneself
pain	:	n. a hurt or suffering somewhere in the body

paint : v. to cover with a liquid colour; to make a picture with liquid colours; n. a coloured liquid used to cover or protect a surface

pan : n. a metal container used for cooking

paper : n. a thin, flat material made from plants or cloth often used for writing

parachute : n. a device that permits a person or thing to fall slowly from an airplane or helicopter to the ground

parade : n. a group of people and vehicles moving together to celebrate a special event or anniversary

pardon : v. to forgive for a crime and release from punishment

parent : n. a father or mother

parliament : n. a government lawmaking group

part : n. something less than the whole; not all of something

party : n. a group of people working together for a political purpose; a group of people or friends gathered together for enjoyment

pass : v. to go by or move around something; to move along; to cause or permit to go

passenger : n. a person travelling by airplane, train, boat or car who is not the pilot or driver

passport : n. a document permitting a person to travel to another country

past : n. the time gone by; the time before; ad. recent; immediately before; former

path : n. a narrow way for walking; a way along which something moves

patient : n. a person being treated by a doctor for a health problem

pay : v. to give money for work done or for something bought

peace : n. the condition of freedom from war, fighting or noise; rest; quiet

people : n. any group of persons; all the persons of a

group, race, religion or nation ("the American people")

per cent : n. a part of every hundred ("Ten is ten per cent of one hundred.")

perfect : ad. complete or correct in every way; completely right or good; without mistakes

perform : v. to speak, dance or sing in front of others

period : n. an amount of time within events, restrictions or conditions

permanent : ad. never changing; lasting for a very long time or for all time

permit : v. to let; to make possible

person : n. a man, woman or child

physical : ad. of the body

physics : n. the study of motion, matter and energy

picture : n. something that shows what another thing looks like; an idea or representation of something as seen by the eye; a painting; what is made with a camera

piece : n. a part of something larger

pig : n. a farm animal used for its meat

pilot : n. one who guides or flies an airplane or helicopter

pipe : n. a long, round piece of material used to move liquid or gas

place : v. to put something somewhere; n. an area or a part of an area; space where a person or thing is; any room, building, town or country

plan : v. to organize or develop an idea or method of acting or doing something ">("They plan to have a party."); n. an organized or developed idea or method ("The plan will not work.")

planet : n. a large object in space that orbits the sun ("Earth is a planet.")

plant : v. to put into the ground to grow; n. a living growth from the ground which gets its food

		from air, water and earth
plastic	:	n. a material made from chemicals that can be formed and made into things
play	:	v. to have fun; to not work; to take part in a sport; to make music on an instrument; n. a story acted in a theater
please	:	v. to make one happy; to give enjoyment
plenty	:	n. all that is needed; a large enough amount
plot	:	v. to make secret plans; n. a secret plan to do something wrong or illegal
poem	:	n. words and their sounds organized in a special way to express emotions
point	:	v. to aim one's finger toward; to aim; n. the sharp end of something
poison	:	n. a substance that can destroy life or damage health
police	:	n. a government agency responsible for guarding the public, keeping order, and making sure people obey the law; members of that agency
policy	:	n. an established set of plans or goals used to develop and make decisions in politics, economics or business
politics	:	n. the activities of government and of those who are in public office
pollute	:	v. to release dangerous or unpleasant substances into the air, soil or water
poor	:	n. people with little or no money; ad. lacking money or goods; of bad quality
popular	:	ad. liked by many people; generally approved by the public
population	:	n. all the people in a place, city or country
port	:	n. a city where ships load or unload goods; a place on a coast where ships can be safe from a storm
position	:	n. a place; the way of holding the body; the way a thing is set or placed; a job (or level of

		a job) in an organization
possess	:	v. to have; to own; to control or be controlled by
possible	:	ad. able to be done; can happen or is expected to happen
postpone	:	v. to delay action until a later time
pour	:	v. to flow; to cause to flow
power	:	n. the ability to control or direct others; control; strength; ruling force; force or energy used to do work ("Water power turns the wheel.")
praise	:	v. to say good things about; to approve
pray	:	v. to make a request to a god or spirit; to praise a god or spirit
pregnant	:	ad. carrying a child within the body before it is born; expecting to give birth to a baby
present	:	v. to offer for consideration ("We will present our idea to the committee."); n. a gift ("I gave them a present for their anniversary."); now ("The present time is a good time."); ad. to be at a place ("I was present at school yesterday.")
president	:	n. the chief official of a country that is a republic; the leader of an organization
press	:	v. to urge strongly; n. newspapers, magazines and other publications
pressure	:	n. the force produced when something is pushed down or against something else
prevent	:	v. to keep or stop from going or happening
price	:	n. the amount of money for which anything is bought, sold or offered for sale
prison	:	n. a place where a person is kept as punishment for a crime
private	:	ad. of or about a person or group that is secret; opposite public
prize	:	n. something offered or won in a competition; something of value that one must work hard

for to get

probably : ad. a good chance of taking place; a little more than possible

problem : n. a difficult question or situation with an unknown or unclear answer

process : n. an operation or series of changes leading to a desired result

produce : v. to make; to create; to cause something to be; to manufacture

profession : n. a job that requires special training

professor : n. a teacher at a college or university

profit : n. money gained from a business activity after paying all costs of that activity

programme : n. a plan of action; the different events or parts of a meeting or show

progress : n. movement forward or toward improvement or a goal

project : n. a planned effort to do something

propaganda : n. ideas or information used to influence opinions

property : n. anything owned by someone such as land, buildings or goods

propose : v. to present or offer for consideration

protect : v. to guard; to defend; to prevent from being harmed or damaged

protest : v. to speak against; to object

prove : v. to show to be true

provide : v. to give something needed or wanted

public : ad. of or about all the people in a community or country; opposite private

publication : n. something that is published such as a book, newspaper or magazine

publish : v. to make public something that is written; to include something in a book, newspaper or magazine

pull : v. to use force to move something toward the person or thing using the force; opposite push

pump : v. to force a gas or liquid up, into or through

punish : v. to cause pain, suffering or loss for doing something bad or illegal

purchase : v. to buy with money or with something of equal value; n. that which is bought

pure : ad. free from anything that is different or that reduces value; clean

purpose : n. the reason or desired effect for doing something; goal

push : v. to use force to move something away from the person or thing using the force; opposite pull

put : v. to place; to set in position

quality : n. that which something is known to have or be ("An important quality of steel is its strength."); amount of value or excellence ("Their goods are of the highest quality.")

question : v. to ask; to express wonder or disbelief; n. a sentence or word used in asking for information; a problem; an issue to be discussed

quick : ad. fast

quiet : ad. with little or no noise; having little or no movement; calm

race : v. to run; to take part in a competition to decide who or what can move fastest; to take part in a campaign for political office; n. one of the major groups that humans can be divided into because of a common physical similarity, such as skin colour

radar : n. a device that uses radio signals to learn the position or speed of objects that may be too far away to be seen

radiation : n. waves of energy from something that produces heat or light; energy from a nuclear substance, which can be dangerous

radio : n. the system of sending and receiving

signals or sounds through the air without wires

raid : v. to make a sudden attack; n. a sudden attack carried out as an act of war, or for the purpose of seizing or stealing something

railroad : n. a road for trains; a company that operates such a road and its stations and equipment

rain : n. water falling from the sky

rare : ad. not common; not usual; not often

rate : n. speed; a measure of how quickly or how often something happens; the price of any thing or service that is bought or sold

reach : v. to put a hand toward; to arrive at; to come to

react : v. to act as a result of or in answer to

read : v. to look at and understand the meaning of written words or numbers

ready : ad. prepared; completed; organized; willing

real : ad. true; truly existing; not false

realistic : ad. in agreement with the way things are

reason : n. the cause for a belief or act; purpose; something that explains

reasonable : ad. ready to listen to reasons or ideas; not extreme; ready or willing to compromise

rebel : v. to act against a government or power, often with force; to refuse to obey; n. one who opposes or fights against the government of his or her country

receive : v. to get or accept something given, offered or sent

recent : ad. a short time ago

recession : n. a temporary reduction in economic activity, when industries produce less and many workers lose their jobs

recognize : v. to know or remember something or someone that was known, known about or seen before; to accept another nation as independent and establish diplomatic ties

		with its government
record	:	v. to write something in order to have it for future use; to put sound or pictures in a form that can be kept and heard or seen again; n. a writing that shows proof or facts about something
recover	:	v. to get again something that was lost, stolen or taken away ("The police recovered the stolen money."); to return to normal health or normal conditions She is expected to recover from the operation.")
red	:	ad. having the colour like that of blood
reduce	:	v. to make less or smaller in number, size or amount; to cut
reform	:	v. to make better by changing; to improve; n. a change to a better condition
refúgee	:	n. a person who has been forced to flee because of unjust treatment, danger or war
refuse	:	v. to reject; to not accept, give or do something
regret	:	n. a feeling of sadness or sorrow about something that is done or that happens
reject	:	v. to refuse to accept, use or believe
relation	:	n. understandings or ties between nations; members of the same family; people connected by marriage or family ties
release	:	v. to free; to permit to go; to permit to be known or made public
religion	:	n. a belief in, or the honouring of, a god or gods
remain	:	v. to stay in a place after others leave; to stay the same
remains	:	n. a dead body
remember	:	v. to think about the past; opposite forget
remove	:	v. to take away or take off; to put an end to; to take out of a position or office
repair	:	n. work done to fix something
repeat	:	v. to say or do again

report	:	v. to tell about; to give the results of a study or investigation; n. the story about an event; the results of a study or investigation; a statement in which the facts may not be confirmed
represent	:	v. to act in the place of someone else; to substitute for; to serve as an example
repress	:	v. to control or to restrict freedoms by force
request	:	v. to ask for; n. the act of asking for
require	:	v. to need or demand as necessary
rescue	:	v. to free from danger or evil
research	:	n. a careful study to discover correct information
resign	:	v. to leave a position, job or office
resist	:	v. to oppose; to fight to prevent
resolution	:	n. an official statement of agreement by a group of people, usually reached by voting
resource	:	n. anything of value that can be used or sold
responsible	:	ad. having a duty or job to do ("He is responsible for preparing the report."); being the cause of ("They were responsible for the accident.")
rest	:	v. to sit, lie down or sleep to regain strength; n. that which remains; the others
restrain	:	v. to keep controlled; to limit action by a person or group
restrict	:	v. to limit; to prevent from increasing or becoming larger
result	:	v. to happen from a cause; n. that which follows or is produced by a cause; effect
retire	:	v. to leave a job or position because one is old or in poor health
return	:	v. to go or come back; to bring, give, take or send back
revolt	:	v. to protest violently; to fight for a change, especially of government
rice	:	n. a food grain
rich	:	ad. having much money or goods; having

plenty of something

ride : v. to sit on or in and be carried along; to travel by animal, wheeled vehicle, airplane or boat

right : n. what a person legally and morally should be able to do or have ("It is their right to vote."); ad. agreeing with the facts; good; correct; opposite wrong; on the side that is toward the east when one is facing north; opposite left

riot : v. to act with many others in a violent way in a public place; n. a violent action by a large group of people

rise : v. to go up; to go higher; to increase; to go from a position of sitting or lying to a position of standing

risk : n. the chance of loss, damage or injury

river : n. a large amount of water that flows across land into another river, a lake or an ocean

road : n. a long piece of hard ground built between two places so people can walk, drive or ride easily from one place to the other

rob : v. to take money or property secretly or by force; to steal

rock : n. a hard piece of mineral matter

rocket : n. a device shaped like a tube that moves through air or space by burning gases and letting them escape from the back or bottom, sometimes used as a weapon

roll : v. to turn over and over; to move like a ball

room : n. a separate area within a building with its own walls

root : n. the part of a plant that is under the ground and takes nutrients from the soil

rope : n. a long, thick piece of material made from thinner pieces of material, used for tying

rough : ad. not flat or smooth; having an uneven surface; violent; not made well

round : ad. having the shape of a ball or circle
rub : v. to move something over the surface of another thing
rubber : n. a substance made from the liquid of trees with the same name, or a similar substance made from chemicals
ruin : v. to damage severely; to destroy
rule : v. to govern or control; to decide; n. a statement or an order that says how something must be done
run : v. to move quickly by steps faster than those used for walking
sabotage : v. to damage or destroy as an act against an organization or nation ("The rebels sabotaged the railroad.")
sacrifice : v. to do without something or to suffer a loss for a belief, idea, goal or another person
sad : ad. not happy
safe : ad. away from harm or danger
sail : v. to travel by boat or ship
sailor : n. a person involved in sailing a boat or ship
salt : n. a white substance found in sea water and in the ground, used to affect the taste of food
same : ad. not different; not changed; like another or others
sand : n. extremely small pieces of crushed rock found in large amounts in deserts and on coasts
satellite : n. a small object in space that moves around a larger object; an object placed in orbit around the earth
satisfy : v. to give or provide what is desired, needed or demanded
save : v. to make safe; to remove from harm; to keep for future use
say : v. to speak; to express in words
school : n. a place for education; a place where people go to learn

science	:	n. the study of nature and the actions of natural things, and the knowledge gained about them
sea	:	n. a large area of salt water, usually part of an ocean
search	:	v. to look for carefully
season	:	n. one of the four periods of the year that is based on the earth's position toward the sun (spring, summer, autumn, winter); a period of time based on different weather conditions ("dry season", "rainy season"); a period during the year when something usually happens ("baseball season")
seat	:	n. a thing to sit on; a place to sit or the right to sit there ("a seat in parliament")
second	:	ad. the one that comes after the first
secret	:	n. something known only to a few and kept from general knowledge; ad. hidden from others; known only to a few
security	:	n. freedom from danger or harm; protection; measures necessary to protect a person or place ("Security was increased in the city.")
see	:	v. to know or sense through the eyes; to understand or know
seed	:	n. the part of a plant from which new plants grow
seek	:	v. to search for ("They are seeking a cure for cancer."); to try to get ("She is seeking election to public office."); to plan to do ("Electric power companies are seeking to reduce their use of coal.")
seem	:	v. to appear to be ("She seems to be in good health.")
seize	:	v. to take quickly by force; to take control of quickly; to arrest
self X	:	n. all that which makes one person different from others
sell	:	v. to give something in exchange for money

Senate	:	n. the smaller of the two groups in the governments of some countries, such as in the United States Congress
send	:	v. to cause to go; to permit to go; to cause to be carried, taken or directed to or away from a place
sense	:	v. to come to know about by feeling, believing or understanding; n. any of the abilities to see, hear, taste, smell or feel
sentence	:	v. to declare the punishment for a crime; n. the punishment for a crime
separate	:	v. to set or keep people, things or ideas away from or independent from others; ad. not together or connected; different
series	:	n. a number of similar things or events that follow one after another in time, position or order
serious	:	ad. important; needing careful consideration; dangerous
serve	:	v. to work as an official; to be employed by the government; to assist or help
service	:	n. an organization or system that provides something for the public ("Schools and roads are services paid for by taxes."); a job that an organization or business can do for money; military organizations such as an army, navy or air force; a religious ceremony
set	:	v. to put in place or position; to establish a time, price or limit
settle	:	v. to end (a dispute); to agree about (a problem); to make a home in a new place
several	:	ad. three or more, but not many
severe	:	ad. not gentle; causing much pain, sadness or damage
sex	:	n. either the male or female group into which all people and animals are divided because of their actions in producing young; the physical activity by which humans and

		animals can produce young
shake	:	v. to move or cause to move in short, quick movements
shape	:	v. to give form to; n. the form of something, especially how it looks
share	:	v. to give part of something to another or others; n. a part belonging to, given to or owned by a single person or a group; any one of the equal parts of ownership of a business or company
sharp	:	ad. having a thin edge or small point that can cut or hurt; causing hurt or pain
she	:	pro. the girl or woman who is being spoken about
sheep	:	n. a farm animal used for its meat and hair
shell	:	v. to fire artillery; n. a metal container that is fired from a large gun and explodes when it reaches its target; a hard outside cover
shelter	:	v. to protect or give protection to; n. something that gives protection; a place of safety
shine	:	v. to aim a light; to give bright light; to be bright; to clean to make bright
ship	:	v. to transport; n. a large boat
shock	:	v. to cause to feel sudden surprise or fear; n. something that greatly affects the mind or emotions; a powerful shake, as from an earthquake
shoe	:	n. a covering for the foot
shoot	:	v. to cause a gun or other weapon to send out an object designed to kill; to use a gun
short	:	ad. lasting only for a small period of time; not long; opposite tall
should	:	v. used with another verb (action word) to show responsibility ("We should study."), probability ("The talks should begin soon."), or that something is believed to be a good

idea ("Criminals should be punished.")

shout : v. to speak very loudly

show : v. to make something be seen; to make known; n. a play or story presented in a theater, or broadcast on radio or television, for enjoyment or education; something organized to be seen by the public

shrink : v. to make or become less in size, weight or value

sick : ad. suffering physically or mentally with a disease or other problem; not in good health

sickness : n. the condition of being in bad health

side : n. the outer surfaces of an object that are not the top or bottom; parts away from the middle; either the right or left half of the body

sign : v. to write one's name; n. a mark or shape used to mean something; evidence that something exists or will happen; a flat piece of material with writing that gives information

signal : v. to send a message by signs; n. an action or movement that sends a message

silence : v. to make quiet; to stop from speaking or making noise; n. a lack of noise or sound

silver : n. a valued white metal

similar : ad. like something else but not exactly the same

simple : ad. easy to understand or do; not difficult or complex

since : prep. from a time in the past until now ("I have known her since we went to school together.")

sing : v. to make music sounds with the voice

single : ad. one only

sink : v. to go down into water or other liquid

sister : n. a female with the same father or mother as

another person

sit : v. to rest on the lower part of the body without the support of the legs; to become seated

situation : n. the way things are during a period of time

size : n. the space occupied by something; how long, wide or high something is

skeleton : n. all the bones of a human or other animal together in their normal positions

skill : n. the ability gained from training or experience

skin : n. the outer covering of humans and most animals

sky : n. the space above the earth

slave : n. a person owned or controlled by another

sleep : v. to rest the body and mind with the eyes closed

slide : v. to move smoothly over a surface

slow : v. to reduce the speed of; ad. not fast in moving, talking or other activities

small : ad. little in size or amount; few in number; not important; opposite large

smash : v. to break or be broken into small pieces by force; to hit or move with >force

smell : v. to sense through the nose; n. something sensed by the nose ("the smell of food cooking")

snow : n. soft, white pieces of frozen water that fall from the sky, usually in winter or when the air temperature is very cold

so : ad. in such a way that ("He held the flag so all could see it."); also; too ("She left early, and so did we."); very ("I am so sick."); as a result ("They were sick, so they could not come."); conj. in order that; for the purpose of ("Come early so we can discuss the plans.")

social : ad. of or about people or a group

soft : ad. not hard; easily shaped; pleasing to

touch; not loud

soil : n. earth in which plants grow

soldier : n. a person in the army

solid : ad. having a hard shape with no empty spaces inside; strong; not in the form of a liquid or gas

solve : v. to find an answer; to settle

some : ad. of an amount or number or part not stated; not all

son : n. a person's male child

soon : ad. not long after the present time; quickly

sort : n. any group of people or things that are the same or are similar in some way; a kind of something

sound : n. fast-moving waves of energy that affect the ear and result in hearing; that which is heard

south : n. the direction to the right of a person facing the rising sun

space : n. the area outside the earth's atmosphere where the sun, moon, planets and stars are; the area between or inside things

speak : v. to talk; to say words with the mouth; to express one's thoughts to others and exchange ideas; to give a speech to a group

special : ad. of a different or unusual kind; not for general use; better or more important than others of the same kind

speech : n. a talk given to a group of people

speed : v. to make something go or move faster; n. the rate at which something moves or travels; the rate at which something happens or is done

spend : v. to give as payment; to use ("He spends much time studying.")

spill : v. to cause or permit liquid to flow out, usually by accident

spirit : n. the part of a human that is not physical

and is connected to thoughts and emotions; the part of a person that is believed to remain alive after death

split : v. to separate into two or more parts; to divide or break into parts

sport : n. any game or activity of competition involving physical effort or skill

spread : v. to become longer or wider; to make or become widely known

spring : n. the time of the year between winter and summer

spy : v. to steal or get information secretly; n. one who watches others secretly; a person employed by a government to get secret information about another country

square : n. a flat shape having four equal sides

stab : v. to cut or push into or through with a pointed weapon

stand : v. to move into or be in a position in which only the feet are on a surface; to be in one position or place

star : n. a mass of gas that usually appears as a small light in the sky at night, but is not a planet; a famous person, usually an actor or singer

start : v. to begin; to make something begin

starve : v. to suffer or die from a lack of food

state : v. to say; to declare; n. a political part of a nation

station : n. a place of special work or purpose ("a police station"); a place where passengers get on or off trains or buses; a place for radio or television broadcasts

statue : n. a form of a human, animal or other creature usually made of stone, wood or metal

stay : v. to continue to be where one is; to remain; to not leave; to live for a time ("They stayed

		in New York for two years.")
steal	:	v. to take without permission or paying
steam	:	n. the gas that comes from hot water
steel	:	n. iron made harder and stronger by mixing it with other substances
step	:	v. to move by lifting one foot and placing it in a new position; n. the act of stepping; one of a series of actions designed to reach a goal
stick	:	v. to attach something to another thing using a substance that will hold them together; to become fixed in one position so that movement is difficult ("Something is making the door stick."); n. a thin piece of wood
still	:	ad. not moving ("The man was standing still."); until the present or a stated time ("Was he still there?"); even so; although ("The job was difficult, but she still wanted to do it.")
stone	:	n. a small piece of rock
stop	:	v. to prevent any more movement or action; to come or bring to an end
store	:	v. to keep or put away for future use; n. a place where people buy things
storm	:	n. violent weather, including strong winds and rain or snow
story	:	n. the telling or writing of an event, either real or imagined
stove	:	n. a heating device used for cooking
straight	:	ad. continuing in one direction without turns
street	:	n. a road in a city, town or village
stretch	:	v. to extend for a distance; to pull on to make longer or wider
strike	:	v. to hit with force; to stop work as a way to seek better conditions, more pay or to make other demands
strong	:	ad. having much power; not easily broken, damaged or destroyed
structure	:	n. the way something is built, made or

organized; a system that is formed or organized in a special way; a building

struggle : v. to try with much effort; to fight with; n. a great effort; a fight

study : v. to make an effort to gain knowledge by using the mind; to examine carefully

stupid : ad. not able to learn much; not intelligent

subject : n. the person or thing being discussed, studied or written about

submarine : n. an underwater ship

substance : n. the material of which something is made (a solid, liquid or gas)

substitute : v. to put or use in place of another; n. a person or thing put or used in place of another

subversion : n. an attempt to weaken or destroy a political system or government, usually secretly

succeed : v. to reach a goal or thing desired; to produce a planned result

such : ad. of this or that kind; of the same kind as; similar to

sudden : ad. not expected; without warning; done or carried out quickly or without preparation

suffer : v. to feel pain in the body or mind; to receive or experience hurt or sadness

sugar : n. a sweet substance made from liquids taken from plants

suggest : v. to offer or propose something to think about or consider

summer : n. the warmest time of the year, between spring and autumn

sun : n. the huge star in the sky that provides heat and light to earth

supply : v. to give; to provide; n. the amount of something that can be given or sold to others

support : v. to carry the weight of; to hold up or in position; to agree with others and help them reach a goal; to approve

suppose	:	v. to believe, think or imagine ("I suppose you are right."); to expect ("It is supposed to rain tonight.")
suppress	:	v. to put down or to keep down by force; to prevent information from being known publicly
sure	:	ad. very probable; with good reason to believe; true without question
surface	:	n. the outer side or top of something ("The rocket landed on the surface of the moon.")
surplus	:	n. an amount that is more than is needed; extra; ("That country has a trade surplus. It exports more than it imports.")
surprise	:	v. to cause a feeling of wonder because something is not expected; n. something not expected; the feeling caused by something not expected
surrender	:	v. to give control of oneself or one's property to another or others; to stop fighting and admit defeat
surround	:	v. to form a circle around; to be in positions all around someone or something
survive	:	v. to remain alive during or after a dangerous situation
suspect	:	v. to imagine or believe that a person is guilty of something bad or illegal; n. a person believed to be guilty
suspend	:	v. to cause to stop for a period of time
swallow	:	v. to take into the stomach through the mouth
swear in	:	v. to put an official into office by having him or her promise to carry out the duties of that office ("The chief justice will swear in the president.")
sweet	:	ad. tasting pleasant, like sugar
swim	:	v. to move through water by making motions with the arms and legs
sympathy	:	n. a sharing of feelings or emotions with

another person, usually feelings of sadness

system : n. a method of organizing or doing something by following rules or a plan; a group of connected things or parts working together for a common purpose or goal

take : v. to put a hand or hands around something and hold it, often to move it to another place; to carry something; to seize; to capture; to begin to be in control ("The president takes office tomorrow.")

talk : v. to express thoughts in spoken words; n. a meeting for discussion

tall : ad. higher than others; opposite short

tank : n. a large container for holding liquids; a heavy military vehicle with guns

target : n. any person or object aimed at or fired at

taste : v. to sense through the mouth ("The fruit tastes sweet.")

tax : n. the money a person or business must pay to the government so the government can provide services

tea : n. a drink made from the plant of the same name

teach : v. to show how to do something; to provide knowledge; to cause to understand

team : n. a group organized for some purpose, often for sports

tear : v. to pull apart, often by force

tears : n. the fluid that comes out of the eyes while crying

technical : ad. involving machines, processes and materials in industry, transportation and communications; of or about a very special kind of subject or thing ("You need technical knowledge to understand how this system works.")

technology : n. the use of scientific knowledge and methods to produce goods and services

telephone	:	n. a device or system for sending sounds, especially the voice, over distances
telescope	:	n. a device for making objects that are far away appear closer and larger
television	:	n. a device that receives electronic signals and makes them into pictures and sounds; the system of sending pictures and sounds by electronic signals over a distance so others can see and hear them on a receiver
tell	:	v. to give information; to make known by speaking; to order; to command
temporary	:	ad. lasting only a short time
tense	:	ad. having fear or concern; dangerous; opposite calm
term	:	n. a limited period of time during which someone does a job or carries out a responsibility ("He served two terms in Congress."); the conditions of an agreement that have been accepted by those involved in it
terrible	:	ad. very bad; causing terror or fear
territory	:	n. a large area of land
terror	:	n. extreme fear; that which causes great fear
terrorist	:	n. a person who carries out acts of extreme violence as a protest or a way to influence a government
test	:	v. to attempt to learn or prove what something is like or how it will act by studying or doing ("The scientists will test the new engine soon."); n. an attempt to learn or prove what something is like or how it will act by studying or doing ("The test of the new engine takes place today."); a group of questions or problems used to find out a person's knowledge ("The students did well on the language test.")
than	:	conj. connecting word used to link things that may be similar, but are not equal ("My

sister is taller than I am.")

thank : v. to say that one has a good feeling toward another because that person did something kind ("I want to thank you for helping me.")

that : ad. showing the person, place or thing being spoken about ("That man is a soldier."); pro. the person, place or thing being spoken about ("The building that I saw was very large.")

the : pro. used in front of a name word to show that it is a person or thing that is known about or is being spoken about

theater : n. a place where movies are shown or plays are performed

them : pro. other people being spoken about

then : ad. at that time; existing; and so

there : ad. in that place or position; to or toward that place

these : pro. of or about the people, places or things nearby that have been spoken about already

they : pro. those ones being spoken about

thick : ad. having a large distance between two opposite surfaces ("The wall is two metres thick."); having many parts close together ("The forest is very thick."); almost solid, such as a liquid that does not flow easily; opposite thin

thin : ad. having a small distance between two opposite surfaces; not fat; not wide; opposite thick

thing : n. any object

think : v. to produce thoughts; to form ideas in the mind; to consider; to believe

third : ad. coming after two others

this : pro. of or about the person, place or thing nearby that has been spoken about already

threaten : v. to warn that one will do harm or cause damage

through : prep. in at one end and out at the other; from front to back; from top to bottom; with the help of; by

throw : v. to cause to go through the air by a movement of the arm

tie : v. to join or hold together with some material; n. anything that joins or unites; links or connections ("The two nations have strong trade ties.")

time : n. that which is measured in minutes, hours, days and years; a period that can be identified in hours and minutes and is shown on a clock; a period when an event should or will take place

tired : ad. having less strength because of work or exercise; needing sleep or rest

to : prep. showing the direction of an action; showing the person or place toward which an action is directed; showing a goal or purpose

today : n. this day

together : ad. in one group; at the same time or place; in cooperation

tomorrow : n. the day after today

tonight : n. this night

too : ad. also; as well as; more than is necessary

tool : n. any instrument or device designed to help one do work

top : n. the upper edge or surface; the highest part; the cover of something

torture : v. to cause severe pain; n. the act of causing severe pain in order to harm, to punish or to get information from

total : n. the complete amount

touch : v. to put the hand or fingers on

toward : prep. in the direction of; leading to

town : n. a centre where people live, larger than a village but not as large as a city

trade : v. to buy and sell or exchange products or services; n. the activity of buying, selling or exchanging products or services

tradition : n. a ceremony, activity or belief that has existed for a long time

traffic : n. the movement of people, vehicles or ships along a street, road or waterway

tragic : ad. extremely sad; terrible

train : v. to teach or learn how to do something; to prepare for an activity; n. an engine and the cars connected to it that move along a railroad

transport : v. to move goods or people from one place to another

transportation : n. the act or business of moving goods or people

trap : v. to catch or be caught by being tricked; to be unable to move or escape; n. a device used to catch animals

travel : v. to go from one place to another, usually for a long distance

treason : n. the act of fighting against one's own country or of helping its enemies

treasure : n. a large collection of money, jewels or other things of great value

treat : v. to deal with; to act toward in a special way; to try to cure

treatment : n. the act of treating; the use of medicine to try to cure or make better

treaty : n. a written agreement between two or more nations

tree : n. a very tall plant that is mostly wood, except for its leaves

trial : n. an examination in a court of a question or dispute to decide if a charge is true

tribe : n. a group of families ruled by a common chief or leader

trick : v. to cheat; to fool a person so as to get

something or make him or her do something

trip : n. a movement from one place to another, usually a long distance

troop : n. a number of soldiers in a large controlled group

trouble : n. that which causes concern, fear, difficulty or problems

truce : n. a temporary halt in fighting agreed to by all sides involved

truck : n. a heavy vehicle used to carry goods

true : ad. correct; not false

trust : v. to believe that someone is honest and will not cause harm

try : v. to make an effort; to take court action against a person to decide if he or she is guilty or innocent of a crime

tube : n. a long, round structure through which liquids or gases can flow; a long, thin container in which they can be kept

turn : v. to change direction; to move into a different position; to change colour, form or shape

under : prep. below; below the surface of; less than; as called for by a law, agreement or system ("The river flows under the bridge." "Such action is not permitted under the law.")

understand : v. to know what is meant; to have knowledge of

unite : v. to join together

universe : n. all of space, including planets and stars

university : n. a place of education that usually includes several colleges and research organizations

unless : conj. except if it happens; on condition that ("I will not go, unless the rain stops.")

until : conj. up to a time; before

up : ad. to, in or at a higher position or value

urge : v. to advise strongly; to make a great effort to get someone to do something

urgent : ad. needing an immediate decision or action
us : pro. the form of the word "we" used after a preposition ("He said he would write to us.") or used as an object of a verb ("They saw us yesterday.")
usual : ad. as is normal or common; as is most often done, seen or heard
valley : n. a long area of land between higher areas of land
value : n. the quality of being useful, important or desired; the amount of money that could be received if something is sold
vegetable : n. a plant grown for food
very : ad. extremely ("He was very late.")
veto : v. to reject or refuse to approve
vicious : ad. bad; dangerous; showing harm or hate
victim : n. someone or something that is injured, killed or made to suffer; someone who is tricked
victory : n. a success in a fight or competition
village : n. a very small town
violate : v. to fail to obey or honour; to break (an agreement)
violence : n. the use of force to cause injury, death or damage
visit : v. to go to or come to a place for a short time for friendly or business reasons
voice : n. the sound made by creatures, especially humans, for speaking
volcano : n. a hill or mountain around a hole in the earth's surface that can explode, sending hot, melted rock and ash into the air
wage : n. money received for work done
wait : v. to delay acting; to postpone
walk : v. to move by putting one foot in front of the other
wall : n. the side of a room or building formed by wood, stone or other material; a structure

		sometimes used to separate areas of land
want	:	v. to desire; to wish for; to need
war	:	n. fighting between nations, or groups in a nation, using weapons
warm	:	ad. almost hot; having or feeling some heat
warn	:	v. to tell of possible danger; to advise or inform about something bad that may happen
wash	:	v. to make clean, usually with water
water	:	n. the liquid that falls from the sky as rain or is found in lakes, rivers and oceans
way	:	n. a path on land or sea or in the air; how something is done; method
wealth	:	n. a large amount of possessions, money or other things of value
weapon	:	n. anything used to cause injury or to kill during an attack, fight or war
wear	:	v. to have on the body, as clothes
weather	:	n. the condition of the atmosphere resulting from sun, wind, rain, heat or cold
week	:	n. a period of time equal to seven days
weigh	:	v. to measure how heavy someone or something is
welcome	:	v. to express happiness or pleasure when someone arrives or something develops
what	:	pro. used to ask about something or to ask for information about something ("What is this?"); ad. which or which kind ("He wants to know what you would like to drink.")
which	:	pro. used to ask about what one or what ones of a group of things or people ("Which programme do you like best?" "Which students will take the test?")
while	:	n. a space of time ("Please come to my house for a while."); conj. at or during the same time ("It may not be a good idea to eat while you are running.")
white	:	ad. having the colour like that of milk or

snow

who : pro. what or which person or persons that ("Who wants to go?"); the person or persons ("They are the ones who want to go.")

whole : ad. the complete amount; all together; not divided; not cut into pieces

wife : n. a woman who is married

wild : ad. living and growing in natural conditions and not organized or supervised by humans; angry; uncontrolled

will : v. a word used with action words to show future action ("They will hold talks tomorrow.")

willing : ad. being ready or having a desire to ("They are willing to talk about the problem.")

win : v. to gain a victory; to defeat another or others in a competition, election or battle

wind : n. a strong movement of air

window : n. an opening in a wall to let in light and air, usually filled with glass

winter : n. the coldest time of year, between autumn and spring

wire : n. a long, thin piece of metal used to hang objects or to carry electricity or electronic communications from one place to another

wise : ad. having much knowledge and understanding; able to use knowledge and understanding to make good or correct decisions

wish : v. to want; to express a desire for

with : prep. along or by the side of; together; using ("He fixed it with a tool."); having ("the house with the red door")

withdraw : v. to take or move out, away or back; to remove

without : prep. with no; not having or using; free from; not doing

woman : n. an adult female human

wonder	:	v. to ask oneself; to question ("She wonders if it is true."); n. a feeling of surprise
wonderful	:	ad. causing wonder; especially good
wood	:	n. the solid material of which trees are made
word	:	n. one or more connected sounds that form a single part of a language
work	:	v. to use physical or mental effort to make or do something; n. the effort used to make or to do something; that which needs effort; the job one does to earn money
world	:	n. the earth; the people who live on the earth
worry	:	v. to be concerned; to continue thinking that something, possibly bad, can happen
worse	:	ad. more bad than
worth	:	n. value measured in money
wound	:	v. to injure; to hurt; to cause physical damage to a person or animal; n. an injury to the body of a human or animal in which the skin is usually cut or broken
wreck	:	v. to damage greatly; to destroy; n. anything that has been badly damaged or broken
wreckage	:	n. what remains of something severely damaged or destroyed
write	:	v. to use an instrument to make words appear on a surface, such as paper
wrong	:	ad. not correct; bad; not legal; opposite right
year	:	n. a period of time equal to twelve months
yellow	:	ad. having the colour like that of gold or the sun
yes	:	ad. used to express agreement or to permit
yesterday	:	n. the day before today
you	:	pro. the person or persons being spoken to
young	:	ad. in the early years of life; not old
zero	:	n. the number meaning none or nothing
zoo	:	n. a place where animals are kept for the public to look at and study

Chapter 3

Pronuncing Idioms

abide by (something)

- To follow the rules of something

  The cleaning staff must abide by the rules of the school.

able to breathe easily again

- To be able to relax and recover from a stressful time or event

  My friend was able to breathe easily again when his company did not go bankrupt.

able to do (something) blindfolded

- To be able to do something easily and quickly

  The car was easy to fix and we were able to do it blindfolded.

able to do (something) standing on one's head

- To be able to do something easily and quickly

  The boy is good at fixing his bicycle. He can do it standing on his head.

able to take a joke

- To be able to let others laugh and joke about you

  Our boss is not able to take a joke. We must be careful what we say to him.

about time

- To be something that should have happened earlier

  "It is about time that you returned that book to me."

about to (do something)

- To be on the point of doing something

  I was about to leave my house when the phone rang.

above all else

- Most importantly of all

  Above all else, I plan to go to the Natural History Museum when I visit the city.

above and beyond

- To be more than is required

  The work that the man did on our house was above and beyond what was required.

above reproach

- To be not deserving of blame or criticism

  The actions of the police officer were above reproach.

above suspicion

- To be very honest so that nobody will suspect you

  The man's actions are always above suspicion.

absent-minded

- To be forgetful

  My grandfather is very absent-minded and he often forgets his keys.

according to Hoyle

- Doing something strictly by the rules, doing something the usual and correct way

  "According to Hoyle, we should not use this room but probably nobody will complain if we do use it."

according to (someone or something)

- As said or told by someone, in agreement with something, in the order of something, in proportion to something

According to our teacher, there will be no class next week.

We did everything according to the terms of our agreement.

back and forth

- Backwards and forwards, first one way and then the other way

  The argument went back and forth before the judge made a decision.

back down (from someone or something)

- To fail to carry through on a threat to do something

  The government backed down from their plan to sell the national airline.

back in circulation

- To be available to the public again (a library book)

  The books were back in circulation after we returned them to the library.

back in circulation

- To be socially active again (after the breakup of a relationship between two people)

  My friend stopped seeing his girlfriend and he is now back in circulation.

back of beyond

- Somewhere very remote

  Every summer we go to the back of beyond for a camping trip.

back off

- To retreat or move away (from a fight or argument or an object)

  The man wanted to start an argument but finally he backed off.

back on one's feet

- To return to good financial or physical health

My friend is back on his feet after his company went out of business.

back out (of something)

- To withdraw from an agreement or promise

  The company backed out of the agreement with the foreign firm.

back the wrong horse

- To support someone or something that cannot win or succeed

  We backed the wrong horse in the election and our candidate lost badly.

back-to-back

- Something follows immediately after something else, two people touching backs

  There were two back-to-back games today because of the rain last week.

back to square one

- To go back to the beginning of something

  The city was back to square one in their effort to build a new bridge.

back to the drawing board

- To go back and start a project or idea from the beginning

  The boss does not like our idea so we must go back to the drawing board.

back to the salt mines

- To return to work or return to something else that you do not want to do

  We finished our lunch and went back to the salt mines.

back up (someone or something)

- To support someone or something

The doctor made a mistake and the hospital refused to back him up.

bad blood (between people)

- Unpleasant feelings between people

  There was much bad blood between the three brothers.

bad-mouth (someone or something)

- To say bad things about someone or something

  The supervisor has the habit of bad-mouthing her boss.

bag of tricks

- A collection of special techniques or methods

  The teacher has a bag of tricks to keep her students occupied.

bail out (of something)

- To abandon a situation, to jump out of an airplane

  The plan to buy a summer home with our friends was becoming too expensive so we decided to bail out.

bail (someone) out

- To pay a sum of money that allows someone to get out of jail while waiting for a trial

  The singer had to pay much money to bail himself out of prison.

bail (someone or something) out

- To help or rescue someone or something

  The government decided to bail out the troubled bank.

balance the books

- To check that all the money in a business is accounted for

  The accountant spent several days trying to balance the books of his company.

ball of fire

- An active and energetic person

  The woman is a ball of fire and is always busy doing something.

bang/beat one's head against the wall

- To try to do something that is hopeless

  I am banging my head against the wall when I try to ask my boss for something.

bank on (someone or something)

- To be sure of someone or something, to count on someone or something

  You can bank on my sister to help you.

baptism of fire

- A first experience of something (often difficult or unpleasant)

  We went through a baptism of fire when we had to learn how to operate the small business.

bargain for (something)

- To anticipate something, to take something into account

  The difficulty of the job was more than I had bargained for.

bargain on (something)

- To plan or expect something

  We did not bargain on having heavy rain during our summer birthday party.

barge in on (someone or something)

- To interrupt someone or something, to intrude on someone or something

  My sister often barges in on me when I am with my friends.

bark is worse than one's bite

- Someone is not as bad as they sound

"Don't worry if the boss gets angry - his bark is worse than his bite."

bark up the wrong tree

- To make a wrong assumption about something

  The police are barking up the wrong tree in their investigation of the criminal.

call out to (someone)

- To shout to someone

  We called out to our friend at the concert but she did not hear us.

call (someone) in

- To ask someone for help, to call for special advice

  We called in a special doctor to look at the patient.

call (someone or something) into question

- To dispute or cast doubt upon someone or something

  The lawyer called the man's statement about his neighbour into question.

call (someone) names

- To call a person unpleasant names

  The children began to call the new student names.

call (someone) on the carpet

- To call someone before an authority to be scolded or reprimanded

  The salesman was called on the carpet by his boss for losing the big sale.

call (someone's) bluff

- To challenge someone to prove that what they are saying is true

  I decided to call the man's bluff and I asked him to show me the evidence.

call (something) in

- To collect something for payment, to withdraw

something from circulation

The bank decided to call in the business loan.

call the shots

- To be in charge, to give orders

  The vice-president is now calling the shots and is in control of the company.

call up (someone)

- To telephone someone

  My friend said that he will call up his parents tomorrow night.

calm down

- To relax

  The woman finally calmed down after the accident.

cancel (something) out

- To destroy the effect of something

  The overeating by the girl cancelled out the benefits of her exercise.

can of worms

- A complicated situation or problem

  The lawsuit opened up a can of worms for the company.

can't do anything with (someone or something)

- To be unable to manage or control someone or something

  My sister is always complaining that she can't do anything with her daughter.

can't see the forest for the trees

- To be unable to understand the whole picture of something because you are only looking at small parts of it

  He has no understanding of most problems because he can't see the forest for the trees.

can't stand/stomach (someone or something)

- To dislike someone or something very much

  My uncle cannot stand his daughter's boyfriend.

card up one's sleeve

- A plan or argument that is kept back to be used later if needed

  I think that our boss has a card up his sleeve and he will be able to help us later.

cards are stacked against (someone)

- Luck is against someone

  The cards have been stacked against the young boy since he was born.

(in) care of (someone)

- (Send something) to one person at the address of another person

  I sent the parcel to my sister in care of her friend at the university.

carrot and stick

- A reward or a threat of punishment at the same time

  The trade negotiators took a carrot-and-stick approach to the automobile talks.

carried away

- To lose one's control or judgement due to strong feelings

  I got carried away and yelled at my friend for losing my textbook.

carry a lot of weight with (someone or something)

- To be very influential with someone or a group of people

  The man's education and experience carry a lot of weight in the university.

carry a tune

- To be able to sing accurately, to have musical ability

  The girl in the music class cannot carry a tune.

carry coals to Newcastle

- To bring something of which there is plenty, to duplicate something (Newcastle is a town in England where there is a lot of coal)

  Bringing extra food to the farmer's picnic was like bringing coals to Newcastle.

carry on

- To continue, to keep doing something as before

  We were permitted to carry on with the party after we talked to the apartment manager.

carry out (something)

- To do something, to put something (a plan) into action, to accomplish something

  We were able to carry out the move with no problems.

carry over (something)

- To save for another time or location

  The store will carry over the sale until next week.

carry the ball

- To be in charge of something

  The vice-president was forced to carry the ball while the president was away.

carry the day

- To win or be successful

  His fine performance in our company carried the day for us.

carry the torch

- To show loyalty to a cause or a person

  The man has been carrying the torch for the candidate for a long time.

carry the weight of the world on one's shoulders

- To appear to be burdened by all the problems of the world

  My aunt feels that she is working too hard and that she is carrying the weight of the world on her shoulders.

carry through with (something)

- To put a plan into action

  The company carried through with its plan to open a new factory.

a case in point

- An example that proves something or helps to make something clear

  What the man said is a case in point about what I have been saying all year.

a case of mistaken identity

- An incorrect identification of someone

  It was a case of mistaken identity when the police arrested the wrong person.

cash-and-carry

- A system where you pay cash for some goods and then carry them away

  The supermarkets in our city always operate on a cash-and-carry basis.

cash cow

- A good source of money

  His new business is a cash cow and he is making much money.

cash in (something)

- To exchange something for money

  We decided to cash in the coupons because we needed some money.

cash in on (something)

- To make a lot of money at something

  The small city cashed in on their success after the winter Olympics.

cash on the barrelhead

- To pay cash to buy something

  It was cash only at the store and we were forced to pay cash on the barrelhead for everything.

cast around/about for (someone or something)

- To look for someone or something

  We have been casting around for a new file clerk in our company.

cast aspersions on (someone)

- To make insulting remarks about someone

  The woman is always casting aspersions on her colleagues at work.

cast doubts on (someone or something)

- To cause someone or something to be doubted

  The first witness at the trial cast doubts on the testimony of the main witness.

cast in the same mold

- To be very similar

  The two sisters were cast in the same mold and were almost identical.

cast one's lot in with (someone)

- To join with someone and accept whatever happens

  The woman cast her lot in with the company and worked hard to keep the business going.

cast one's vote

- To vote

  We arrived early to cast our vote in the election.

cast pearls before swine

- To waste something valuable on someone who does not appreciate it

  Giving the woman the gold earrings was like casting pearls before swine.

cast the first stone

- To be the first to blame someone

  The man was the one to cast the first stone and now he is fighting with his neighbour.

castles in the air

- Daydreams

  My sister is always building castles in the air and is very unrealistic.

cat burglar

- A burglar who enters a building by climbing a wall etc.

  Our stereo was stolen when a cat burglar entered our apartment.

cat gets one's tongue

- The inability to say something

  I think that the cat got our supervisor's tongue. She has not said anything since the meeting started.

catch-22

- A situation which contradicts itself, a paradoxical situation

  It was a catch-22 situation and if I went to work there would be problems but if I did not go to work there would also be problems.

catch a cold

- To become sick with a cold

  I caught a cold because of the rain and the cold weather.

catch-as-catch-can

- In any way possible

  We are in the middle of moving house so our meals are catch-as-catch-can.

catch fire

- To begin to burn

  We were very careful that the wooden house would not catch fire.

dare (someone) to do (something)

- To challenge someone to do something

  The little boy dared his friend to throw a rock at the window.

dark horse

- A political candidate who is little known to the general public

  The woman candidate was a dark horse but she won the election easily.

darken (someone's) door

- To visit someone or somewhere

  The man has never darkened the door of the library in his town.

dash off

- To leave quickly

  We dashed off as soon as the concert ended.

dash (something) off

- To write or finish something quickly

  I plan to dash off a letter before I go to work.

date back to (a previous time)

- To go back to a previous time

  The old building dates back to 1850.

Davy Jone's locker

- The bottom of the sea (as a grave)

When the boat sank all of the crew members went to Davy Jone's locker.

dawn on (someone)

- To become clear or occur to someone

  It finally dawned on me why my friend was angry.

day after day

- Everyday

  Day after day the woman goes to the school to meet her child.

day and night

- All of the time

  We worked day and night to finish the project before the end of the month.

day in and day out

- Regularly, all of the time

  My father goes to that restaurant for lunch day in and day out and he never gets tired of it.

day-to-day

- Daily, everyday

  The president was not involved in the day-to-day running of the university.

daylight robbery

- The extreme overcharging of money for something

  The amount of money which they charged for the gasoline was daylight robbery.

days running

- Several days in a row

  There were concerts at the auditorium for six days running.

dead ahead

- To be directly ahead

There was a truck dead ahead so we put on the car brakes suddenly.

dead as a doornail

- To be very dead

  The man was as dead as a doornail after the car accident.

dead centre

- The exact middle

  I easily hit the target dead centre.

dead duck

- A person or a thing in a hopeless situation

  The man is a dead duck and he has no hope of recovering his former position.

dead end

- The end of a road, an impasse

  The negotiations between the players and the owners have come to a dead end.

dead in one's/its tracks

- To be stopped exactly where someone or something is at the moment

  The police stopped the robber dead in his tracks.

dead letter

- A piece of mail that cannot be delivered or returned to the sender

  The letter with no return address went back to the post office as a dead letter.

dead loss

- A total loss

  The money that I gave to my friend is a dead loss and none of it will be returned.

dead on one's feet

- To be exhausted

I was dead on my feet after working all day in my garden.

dead set against (something)

- To be determined not to do something

  The parents are dead set against their son going to Europe for a year.

dead tired

- To be very tired, to be exhausted

  I was dead tired so I went to bed when I got home.

dead to the world

- To be sleeping soundly

  The little boy was dead to the world when his father took him out of the car.

dead wrong

- To be totally wrong

  I was dead wrong in my calculations to build the table.

deadbeat

- A person who never pays his debts

  There is a new government policy to penalize deadbeat fathers.

deadpan

- An expressionless or emotionless face

  My friend had a deadpan expression when he told us the story.

deaf and dumb

- To be unable to hear or speak

  The man was deaf and dumb and could not communicate with the woman on the train.

deal in (something)

- To buy and sell something

  The man has been dealing in antiques for many years.

deal with (someone)

- To act in a specific way toward someone, to do business with someone

  The company is planning to deal with the late employee soon.

deal with (something)

- To be concerned with something, to take action about something

  We will deal with the boxes tomorrow.

decide in favour of (someone or something)

- To determine the winner of something, to decide who is right

  The city decided in favour of building a new bridge over the river.

decked out

- To be dressed in fancy clothes

  My sister was decked out in her best clothes for the party.

deem it to be necessary

- To believe that something is necessary

  The judge deemed it to be necessary to postpone the trial for a week.

deep-six (something)

- To throw away something, to dispose of something

  I decided to deep-six the videos as I did not want them any longer.

deep water

- Serious trouble or difficulty

  The boy will be in deep water if he does not tell us where he spent the money.

deliver the goods

- To do a good or successful job of something

He is the best manager that we have had. He knows how to deliver the goods.

desert a sinking ship

- To leave a situation or place when things become difficult or unpleasant

  Many employees decided to desert a sinking ship when their company began to have problems.

devil of a job

- A very difficult job

  Everybody thought that unloading the truck was a devil of a job.

devil-may-care attitude

- An unworried attitude, an attitude where one does not care what happens

  The man has a devil-may-care attitude to his job and nothing bothers him.

diamond in the rough

- A good person or thing that is hidden by a rough exterior

  The man is a diamond in the rough and a very gentle person under his harsh exterior.

die down

- To come slowly to an end, to grow weaker

  When the sound of the music died down we were able to go to sleep.

die in one's boots

- To die fighting

  The soldiers died in their boots after fighting very hard.

the die is cast

- Something has been decided and you cannot change the decision

The die is cast and now that we have sold our house we must move.

die laughing

- To laugh very loud and hard

  We almost died laughing when we saw the comedy at the theater.

die off

- To die one after another until the number is small

  The house plants began to die off as soon as we moved to a new apartment.

easier said than done

- To be easier to talk about than to do

  I would like to change jobs but it is easier said than done.

easy come, easy go

- Something that you get easily can be lost easily

  My cousin does not care if he loses his job or not. For him everything is easy come, easy go.

easy does it

- Doing something slowly or without sudden movements

  "Easy does it," I said as we moved the large piano.

easy-going

- To be tolerant and relaxed

  Our boss has a very easy-going management style.

easy to come by

- To be easy to find

  Money is not easy to come by for many people with no education.

eat and run

- To eat a meal quickly and then leave

  We had to eat and run in order to arrive at the soccer field early.

eat away at (someone)

- To bother someone, to worry someone

  Money problems have been eating away at the man recently.

eat away at (something)

- To rot/destroy something

  The mildew has been eating away at the window frame all year.

eat crow

- To admit that one is mistaken or defeated

  Our boss was forced to eat crow when the figures that he presented at the meeting were wrong.

eat dirt

- To accept another's insults or bad treatment

  The accountant had to eat dirt because of the problems that he had caused.

eat humble pie

- To admit one's error and apologize

  The boy had to eat humble pie when his friends discovered his mistake.

eat like a bird

- To eat very little

  He eats like a bird. That is why he cannot gain enough weight to join the football team.

eat like a horse

- To eat a lot

  My friend eats like a horse but he never gains any weight.

eat one's cake and have it too

- To use or spend something but still keep it

  The man wants to eat his cake and have it too and he will never give up anything.

eat one's heart out

- To be envious, to be very sad

  "You can eat your heart out. I am going to Hawaii for three weeks!"

eat one's words

- To admit being wrong in something that one has said

  The worker was forced to eat his words after his boss proved that he was wrong.

eat out

- To eat in a restaurant

  I eat out three or four times a week.

eat out of (someone's) hand

- To do what someone else wants

  The secretary had her boss eating out of her hand and she could do whatever she wanted.

eat (someone) out of house and home

- To eat much food in someone's home

  The two teenage boys were eating their parents out of house and home.

eat (something) up

- To enjoy something, to absorb something

  The children ate up the stories that the teacher was telling.

eating someone

- To be bothering or worrying someone

  I do not know what is eating my friend but she is not in a good mood today.

ebb and flow

- The decrease and increase of something like the tide

  The ebb and flow of the singer's popularity was always a topic of conversation.

edge (someone) out

- To win a competition against someone and get a job or position

  I was able to edge out the other applicants to get the job.

egg (someone) on

- To urge or push someone to do something

  The boy is always egging his friend on to do stupid things.

either feast or famine

- To be/have either too much or not enough of something

  It is either feast or famine for the woman. Sometimes she has lots of money and sometimes she has none.

eke out (a living)

- To earn one's living with difficulty

  My uncle was unable to eke out a living on the farm so he sold it.

elbow grease

- The effort and strength to clean something

  We will have to use a lot of elbow grease to clean the kitchen.

elbow room

- Enough space to be comfortable

  The couple moved to the country in order to have more elbow room.

elbow (someone) out of (somewhere)

- To pressure someone out of somewhere

  The woman elbowed the other shoppers out of the way so that she could buy some shoes.

eleventh-hour decision

- A decision that is made at the last possible minute

The government made an eleventh-hour decision to save the hospital.

an end in itself

- Something that one wants for itself alone and not as a way to get/do something else

  For many people travelling is an end in itself and the destination is not important.

end of one's rope

- The last of one's ability or ideas about how to do something

  I am at the end of my rope regarding what to do about my job.

end up (doing something)

- To do something that one had not planned to do

  I ended up studying rather than going to a movie last night.

end up (going somewhere)

- To go somewhere where you had not planned to go

  We ended up going to a restaurant after the movie last night.

end up (somewhere)

- To finish at a certain place

  We ended up at a small coffee shop near the restaurant.

engage in small talk

- To talk about minor things rather than more important things

  The sale staff engaged in small talk before the meeting.

enough to go around

- To be enough of something to serve everyone

  There was enough cake to go around and everybody had a piece.

enter one's mind

- To come into one's consciousness (an idea)

  It never entered my mind to make a reservation at the restaurant.

equal to (something)

- To be able to deal with something

  The apartment manager was more than equal to the task of managing the building.

escape (someone's) notice

- To go unnoticed

  The fact that my library books were overdue escaped my notice.

even so

- Nevertheless, however

  My friend always works but even so he has no money saved.

even steven

- Even with (someone or something)

  Both teams were even steven by the middle of the game.

every cloud has a silver lining

- There is something good in every bad thing

  Every cloud has a silver lining and although I lost my job other good things have happened.

every dog has his day

- Everyone will have a chance for success someday

  You should be patient and wait until you get a chance. Remember every dog has his day.

every inch a (something)

- Completely, in every way

  Jack was every inch a sailor and loved to go out on the ocean with his boat.

every last one

- Every single one

  Every last one of the children received a certificate from the swimming club.

every living soul

- Everybody

  We gave a free newspaper to every living soul in the apartment building.

every minute counts

- Time is very important

  Every minute counts when the fire department goes to fight a fire.

every nook and cranny

- Every small hiding place where you can put something

  I looked in every nook and cranny of my apartment but I could not find my house keys.

every other

- Every second one

  I have to work every other Saturday evening.

every so often

- Occasionally

  You should stand up every so often when you are on a long plane trip.

every time one turns around

- Frequently

  Every time I turn around my little boy asks me a question.

every Tom, Dick and Harry

- The average person

  The man said that he is not the same as every Tom, Dick and Harry.

every which way

- In all directions

  The small children at the birthday party were running every which way.

face down (someone)

- To confront someone boldly, to defy someone

  We decided to face down our competitors and were able to stay in business.

face the music

- To accept the consequences of something

  The boy must face the music for his actions very soon.

face to face

- In person

  I had a face-to-face meeting with my supervisor to talk about my job performance.

face up to (something)

- To accept something that is not easy to accept

  My friend must face up to the fact that he will never have enough money to buy a car.

face value

- The value or price printed on a stamp/bond/paper money etc.

  I sold the postage stamps for their face value.

face value

- The truth of something on the surface

  The woman is a very nice person but you must take what she says at face value.

facts of life

- The facts about sex/marriage/birth that one should know

  The boy seems to be too young to know about the facts of life.

fair and impartial

- Fair and unbiased

  The criminal was given a fair and impartial trial by the court.

fair and square

- Completely fair, honestly

  The British team won the game fair and square.

fair game

- Someone or something that you feel you can easily attack

  Our company is fair game as a takeover target by other companies.

fair play

- Justice, equal and right action

  The boy believes in fair play and is a good person to have on our team.

a fair shake

- Honest treatment

  The woman was not given a fair shake at the inquiry into her behaviour.

fair to middling

- A little better than acceptable, so-so

  I said that I was feeling fair to middling when my friend asked me how I was.

fair-weather friend

- A person who is a friend only during good times

  He is a fair-weather friend and you cannot rely on him if you have a problem.

fall apart

- To become to not work properly

  The equipment fell apart soon after I bought it.

fall apart at the seams

- To break into pieces, to fall apart

  My backpack was falling apart at the seams so I bought a new one.

fall asleep

- To go to sleep

  I fell asleep as soon as I arrived home.

fall back

- To move back, to go back

  The runner fell back from the other runners during the race.

fall back on (someone or something)

- To seek help when other things have failed

  The woman had to fall back on her father when her business began to have problems.

fall behind

- To fail to keep up with work/studies/payments etc.

  I fell behind with my homework at the beginning of the term and had problems throughout the year.

fall by the wayside

- To give up or fail before the end of something

  The man fell by the wayside and could no longer compete in the design competition.

fall down on the job

- To fail to do something properly

  The man fell down on the job so they replaced him with another worker.

fall flat (on one's face)

- To be unsuccessful, to fail

  My attempt at humour fell flat and now the girl does not like me.

fall for (someone or something)

- To begin to like or love someone or something

  The man fell for the woman at the bank but was afraid to ask her for a date.

fall from grace

- To lose approval

  The politician fell from grace with the public during the money scandal.

fall head over heels

- To fall down

  The little boy fell head over heels down the hillside.

fall head over heels in love with (someone)

- To fall deeply in love with someone

  My sister fell head over heels in love with a boy in her English class.

fall ill

- To become ill

  My father fell ill with a cold last week.

fall in love (with someone or something)

- To begin to love someone or something

  I fell in love with the girl the first time that I saw her at the restaurant.

  We fell in love with the house when we first saw it.

fall in with (a group of people)

- To become associated with a bad group of people

  The boy fell in with a bad group of friends and began to have problems at school.

fall into a trap

- To become caught in someone's scheme

  The criminals fell into a trap that the police had prepared for them.

fall into line

- To stand properly in a row (like soldiers)

  The soldiers fell into line as they waited for the inspection.

fall into line

- To conform to a certain course of action

  The players fell into line after the coach became more strict during practice.

fall into place

- To fit together, to become organized

  Everything fell into place and we were able to prepare for our trip to Brazil.

fall off

- To decrease

  The number of tourists to the island is falling off.

fall off the wagon

- To return to use alcohol or drugs after stopping for awhile

  The man fell off the wagon after he had stopped drinking for three years.

fall on deaf ears

- To ignore something that is intended for you

  My complaints to my boss always fall on deaf ears.

fall on hard times

- To meet many troubles

  The town fell on hard times after the computer company moved to another town.

fall out of use

- To be no longer used

  Video recorders have fallen out of use recently.

fall out with (someone) over (something)

- To disagree or quarrel with someone about something

I fell out with my roommate over who should clean the bathroom.

fall over backwards (to do something)

- To do everything possible to do something to please someone

  The teacher fell over backwards to help his students.

fall over oneself to do something

- To be extremely eager to do something or please someone

  The couple fell over themselves in their effort to please their host.

fall short of (one's expectations)

- To be not be as good as one expected

  The new movie fell short of people's expectations and attendance is very low.

fall short of (something)

- To not have enough of something

  The campaign fell short of the amount of money that it had hoped to gather.

fall through

- To fail, to not happen

  My plan to go abroad fell through when my father refused to lend me some money.

fall to (someone) to do (something)

- To become the responsibility of someone

  It usually falls to me to tell my roommates to be quiet.

fall upon/on (someone or something)

- To attack someone or something

  The wolves fell upon the deer and quickly killed it.

a falling-out (with someone)

- A disagreement or quarrel with someone

  We had a falling-out during our holiday and we have not spoken since.

familiar with (someone or something)

- To have knowledge of someone or something

  My friend is familiar with the streets in the city and can drive there easily.

fan the flames of (something)

- To make a situation worse

  The speech by the labour leader fanned the flames of the protesting workers.

far and away the best

- Without doubt the best

  The basketball player is far and away the best player on the team.

far and wide

- Everywhere, in all directions

  We looked far and wide for the book but could not find it.

far be it from (someone) to do (something)

- It is not really someone's place to do something

  Far be it from me to tell the cleaning lady how to do her job.

a far cry from (something)

- Something very different from something

  The man's statement is a far cry from what he told me over the telephone.

far from it

- Not at all

  "Far from it," I answered when the supervisor asked me if I was finished my work.

far into the night

- Late into the night

  I studied far into the night because I had a big test the next day.

far out

- To be strange

  The man's sense of humour was far out and nobody understood him.

gain ground

- To go forward, to make progress

  The toy company is gaining ground in their effort to sell more products.

game that two can play

- A good or bad strategy that two competing sides can both use

  The insults from my friend are a game that two can play and if she wants to continue then so can I.

gang up on (someone)

- To attack someone in a group

  The children tried to gang up on the boy but he ran away.

gas up

- To fill up a gas tank

  We must gas up before we leave on our holiday tomorrow.

gear up for (something)

- To prepare for something

  The city is gearing up for the Olympic games.

gee whiz

- Used as an exclamation to show surprise or other strong feelings

"Gee whiz! Are we really going to go to France for our holiday?"

generous to a fault

- To be too generous

  My friend is generous to a fault and he sometimes gives too much to his friends.

get a bang out of (someone or something)

- To receive special pleasure from someone or something

  My father gets a bang out of the funny birthday cards that we send him.

get a break

- To get an opportunity or good deal

  I got a break when my friend sold me his car for a cheap price.

get a bright idea

- To have a clever thought or idea occur to you (often used as sarcasm)

  My father got the bright idea that he should buy a motorcycle.

get a checkup

- To receive a physical examination by a doctor

  I go to the doctor every year to get a checkup.

get a clean bill of health

- To be pronounced healthy by a doctor

  I got a clean bill of health when I went to see the doctor.

get a dirty look from (someone)

- To receive a frown from someone

  I got a dirty look from the man who was sitting next to my crying child.

get a feel for (something)

- To become accustomed to something and learn how it works, to learn how to do something

I am beginning to get a feel for my new job.

get a fix on (something)

- To receive a reading of a distant object by electronic means

  We were able to get a fix on the island and took the boat safely to the harbor.

get a foothold (somewhere)

- To find a starting point somewhere

  The new political party is beginning to get a foothold in the big cities.

get a grasp of (something)

- To begin to understand something

  I am beginning to get a grasp of how to operate the new computer system.

get a grip of oneself

- To take control of one's feelings

  The man got a grip of himself and calmed down.

get a head start (on someone or something)

- To start earlier than someone or something, to start earlier than usual

  We tried to get a head start on our holiday.

get a kick out of (someone or something)

- To enjoy someone or something

  My father got a kick out of seeing his old school friend.

get a load of (someone or something)

- To take a good look at someone or something

  "Get a load of that man over there with the four dogs."

get a load off one's feet

- To sit down and relax

  I sat down and tried to get a load off my feet.

get a load off one's mind

- To express what one is thinking or worried about

  I talked with my supervisor and was able to get a load off my mind regarding our recent conflict.

get a lot of mileage out of (something)

- To get much use from something (like a car)

  I hope to get a lot of mileage out of the new sneakers that I bought last week.

get a lump in one's throat

- To feel like there is something in one's throat (like you are going to cry)

  My sister got a lump in her throat when she watched her daughter's graduation.

get a move on

- To hurry up

  "Please get a move on. We are already three hours late."

get a raw deal

- To receive unfair or bad treatment

  The secretary got a raw deal when she was forced to work late everyday.

get a rise out of (someone)

- To tease or have fun with someone by making him or her angry or annoyed

  We got a rise out of the teacher when we opened the window in the cold weather.

get a slap on the wrist

- To receive a light punishment for doing something wrong

  The judge gave the boy a slap on the wrist and decided not to punish him severely for his crime.

get a suntan

- To make your skin browner/darker by exposing it to the rays of the sun

The girl went to the beach to get a suntan.

get a toehold (somewhere)

- To find a starting point somewhere

  The new political party is beginning to get a toehold in rural areas.

get a whiff of (something)

- To learn a little about something (almost by chance)

  Whenever the reporters get a whiff of a scandal they become excited and start asking questions.

get a wiggle on

- To hurry up, to get going

  "Get a wiggle on. I want to arrive at the party before the other guests."

get a word in

- To find a chance to say something when others are talking

  The customer could not get a word in while talking to the salesman.

get a word in edgewise

- To manage to join a conversation

  I could not get a word in edgewise so I left the meeting.

get across (something) to (someone)

- To explain or say something so that someone can understand it

  It was difficult to get across the importance of the school safety rules to the children.

get after (someone) to do (something)

- To urge someone to do something that he or she should do but has neglected

  I will get after the repairman to fix the computer as soon as he returns.

get ahead

- To advance or be successful

  The woman works hard at her job in order to get ahead.

get ahead of (oneself)

- To do or say something sooner than you should

  I was getting ahead of myself when I started asking questions about the job that I did not have.

get ahold of (someone or something)

- To make contact with someone, to obtain something

  I have been trying very hard to get ahold of my old high school teacher.

get along

- To leave

  It's late so I must get along now.

get along in years

- To grow older

  My parents are getting along in years but they are still very healthy.

get along on (something)

- To manage to survive or do well with something

  My friend is able to get along on very little money.

  The young woman gets along on her good looks very well.

get along on a shoestring

- To manage with very little money

  I had to get along on a shoestring during university.

get along (with someone)

- To have a good relationship with someone

  I get along with everybody at my company.

get an earful

- To hear much talk/criticism/complaints about something

  Our boss got an earful when he asked the employees if they had any complaints.

get around

- To go to different places, to move about

  My friend gets around and has been to many different cities.

get around to (do something)

- To finally find time to do something

  The apartment manager finally got around to fixing our bath.

get at (someone or something)

- To attack or hit someone or something

  Our dog tried to get at the other dog.

get at (something)

- To mean something

  I do not know what the man was trying to get at during the meeting.

get away

- To succeed in leaving, to escape

  I was able to get away from work early so I went shopping.

get away from it all

- To go on a holiday

  We want to get away from it all this summer and relax somewhere.

get away with murder

- To do something very bad without being caught or punished

  The students were able to get away with murder while the substitute teacher was in the school.

get away with (something)

- To do something that one should not do and not get caught

  The criminal got away with stealing the money and was never caught.

get back

- To return

  We got back from London early yesterday afternoon.

get back at (someone)

- To do something bad to someone who has done something bad to you

  The girl is angry at her boyfriend and she is getting back at him by not answering the telephone.

get back to (someone)

- To communicate something to someone at a later time, to contact someone later

  We were very careful that our complaints did not get back to the school principal.

get back to (something)

- To return to something

  I needed a rest before I could get back to my work.

get back together (with someone)

- To resume a relationship or marriage after separating

  The couple got back together after separating for three months.

get behind

- To fail to maintain a desired pace or level of progress, to become late

  If you get behind with your homework you will never pass many courses.

get behind (a person or idea)

- To support/help someone or something

  Many people decided to get behind the candidate who promised to cut taxes.

get better

- To improve one's skill at doing something, to improve one's health

  The little boy is getting better at riding his bicycle.

hand over fist

- Quickly

  His new company is making money hand over fist.

hand over (someone or something) to (someone)

- Give control or possession of something to someone, give something to another person

  The criminals were forced to hand over the stolen money to the police.

hand (something) down to (someone)

- Give something to a younger person

  The girl always handed her old clothes down to her younger sister.

hand (something) to (someone) on a silver platter

- Give a person something that has not been earned

  The man handed a job to his son on a silver platter and he never had to make any effort at all.

(live) **hand-to-mouth**

- Have only enough money for basic living

  He was living a hand-to-mouth existence until he was finally able to find a job.

(one's) **hands are tied**

- One is unable to help

  I am sorry that I can't help you but my hands are tied at the moment.

hands down

- Easy, unopposed

  They won the game hands down over the other team.

hands off

- Leave alone, don't interfere

  The government decided to take a hands-off approach to the teachers during the strike.

handle with kid gloves

- Be very careful handling someone or something

  He is very sensitive so you have to handle him with kid gloves when you speak to him.

the handwriting is on the wall

- A sign that something bad or significant will happen

  The handwriting is on the wall. Business conditions are bad so nobody will get a pay raise this year.

handy

- Can easily fix things

  He is very handy around the house and is always fixing or building something.

hang a left

- Turn to the left

  We drove to the end of the block and hung a left there.

hang a right

- Turn to the right

  We decided to hang a right when we came to the main street.

hang around

- Pass time or stay someplace without any real purpose or aim

We decided to stay home and hang around rather than go to the game.

hang back

- Stay some distance behind or away, hesitate or be unwilling to do something

  He lacks self-confidence and always hangs back when his boss asks for volunteers.

hang by a thread/hair

- Be in doubt, depend on a very small thing

  The outcome of the election was hanging by a thread until late at night.

hang in the balance

- Have two equally possible results, be uncertain

  After the opposition party won the election whether or not the new highway will be built hangs in the balance.

hang in (there)

- Persevere, don't give up

  "You should hang in there and not quit your job even if you hate the supervisor."

Hang it!

- A rather old expression used to express annoyance or disappointment

  "Hang it", the man said when he hit his finger with the hammer.

hang loose

- Relax, remain calm

  I want to stay at home this weekend and hang loose.

hang on

- Continue

  Although conditions were very bad he decided to hang on and fight to keep his business going.

hang on

- Wait, continue listening on the telephone

  "Hang on for a minute while I go and get some paper and a pen."

hang on (someone's) every word

- Listen with complete attention to everything someone says

  The audience hung on every word of the speaker.

hang on to (something)

- Hold tightly, keep firmly

  "Please hang on to your hats or the strong wind will blow them off."

hang one on

- Get very drunk

  He hung one on last night after he heard about his promotion.

hang one's hat (somewhere)

- Live or take up residence somewhere

  I want to move and hang my hat in a small town somewhere.

hang out one's shingle

- Notify the public of the opening of an office - especially an office of a doctor, lawyer or other professional

  He has decided to hang out his shingle now that he has graduated from law school.

hang out (somewhere/with someone)

- Spend one's time with no great purpose, spend leisure time with friends

  Recently my friend has been hanging out with a group of people who are not a good influence on him.

hang (someone) in effigy

- Hang a dummy of a hated person

The demonstrators hung the dishonest politician in effigy.

hang tough

- Stick to one's position

  I decided to hang tough and stop negotiating with the lawyer.

hang up (something)

- Place something on a hook/peg/hangar

  Everyone was forced to hang up their jackets before they entered the room.

hang up (the telephone)

- Place a telephone receiver back on the telephone and end the call

  After I hung up the telephone I left home to go to work.

a hang-up

- A delay in some process

  There was a hang-up in the construction of the office tower because of the fire.

a hang-up

- An inhibition, a neurotic reaction to some life situation

  The girl has a serious hang-up about the dark and is afraid to go out at night.

happen upon (someone or something)

- Meet someone or find something unexpectedly

  I happened upon a very valuable book when I was cleaning up my grandfather's house.

happy hour

- A time in bars or restaurants when drinks are served at a discount

  We stopped at the restaurant during happy hour and had a drink.

a hard-and-fast rule

- A rule that cannot be altered to fit special cases

  There is no hard-and-fast rule that says you can't use a cellular phone in the train.

as hard as nails

- Physically very fit and strong, rough

  He is as hard as nails and is not a good person to have an argument with.

hard feelings

- Angry or bitter feelings

  I don't have any hard feelings toward my boss even though he fired me.

hard-nosed

- Not weak or soft, stubborn - especially in a fight or contest or negotiations

  The company had a hard-nosed attitude while bargaining with the union.

a hard nut to crack

- A person or thing not easily understood or influenced

  He is a hard nut to crack and is not close to many people.

hard of hearing

- Unable to hear well

  The man is hard of hearing so you must speak loudly when talking to him.

hard on (someone or something)

- Treat someone or something roughly

  His son is very hard on shoes.

(to be) hard on (someone's) heels

- To be following someone very closely

  The police officer was hard on the heels of the criminal.

hard-pressed

- Burdened with urgent business

  "I am hard-pressed for time. Can we meet later?"

a hard sell

- An attitude where you pressure someone to buy something

  The car dealer gave me a hard sell on the new car so I went to another dealer.

be hard up

- Be short of money

  I am hard up for money at the moment so I can't go to the movie.

harken back to (something)

- Have started out as something

  The new building harkens back to a style that appeared over 100 years ago.

to harp on (something)

- To talk repeatedly and tediously about something

  He has been harping on his lack of money for several weeks now.

hash (something) over

- Discuss something in great detail

  We stayed after school to hash over the new contract.

a hassle

- A bothersome thing

  It is a hassle to have to report to my boss two times a day.

a hatchet man

- A politician whose job it is to say negative things about the opposition, a person in a company who must fire extra workers or cut other expenses.

  He is acting as a hatchet man for the leader but I don't think that he really believes what he is saying.

hate (someone's) guts

- Feel very strong dislike for someone

  I absolutely hate the apartment manager's guts after she caused me so many problems.

haul (someone) in

- Take someone to the police station, arrest someone

  The police hauled the man in because he was drinking while driving.

have a ball

- Have a good time

  She had a ball at the party last night.

have a bee in one's bonnet

- Have an idea or thought that stays in one's mind

  My sister has a bee in her bonnet about going to Mexico to teach.

have a big mouth

- Be a person who gossips or tells secrets

  My friend has a big mouth so I don't like to tell him any secrets.

have a blowout

- Have a big wild party or sale

  The university students had a big blowout on their graduation day.

have a blowout

- One's car tire bursts

  Our car had a blowout on the road up the mountain.

have a bone to pick with (someone)

- Have a disagreement to discuss with someone

  I have a bone to pick with my boss because of his criticism of me.

have a brush with (the law or something)

- Have a brief experience with the law or something

  I had a brush with the law when my car was stopped for speeding.

have a case (against someone)

- Have much evidence that can be used against someone

  The police have a very good case against the man who is selling the stolen cars.

have a change of heart

- Change one's attitude or decision (usually from negative to positive)

  I had a change of heart and will let my friend use my car tomorrow.

if looks could kill

- Used when someone makes an unfriendly look or frowns at someone

  If looks could kill then the horrible way that the woman looked at me would have killed me instantly.

if so

- If that is the case

  The lawyer said that he wants to meet us this afternoon but if so then we will not have any documents ready to discuss.

if the shoe fits, wear it

- If something that is said describes you then it probably is meant for you as well

  He was complaining that many workers at his company were lazy. However, his friend looked at him and said that if the shoe fits, wear it.

if worst comes to worst

- If the worst possible thing happens

If worst comes to worst we can cancel our holiday and go next year.

ill at ease

- Nervous/uncomfortable

  He appeared to be ill at ease during the interview.

ill-disposed to (do something)

- Not friendly or favourable to something

  Our company is ill-disposed to begin working on the project with the other company.

ill-gotten gains

- Money or other goods acquired illegally or dishonestly

  The man used his ill-gotten gains from the sale of the stolen car to go on a holiday.

ill will

- Hostile feelings or intentions

  There is much ill will between the two departments in our company.

implicate (someone) in (something)

- Suggest that someone is involved in something

  The man was implicated in the scheme to sell the illegal shares in the company.

in a bad mood

- Sad, depressed

  I was in a bad mood after I wrote the university exam.

in a bad way

- In a bad or critical state

  The woman is in a bad way after her recent car accident.

in a bind

- In trouble

They will really be in a bind if they can't sell their house by next month.

in a coon's age

- In a very long time

  I have not seen my friend in a coon's age.

in a family way

- Pregnant, going to have a baby

  Our new secretary is in a family way and plans to take a few months off from work soon.

in a flash

- quickly

  I was finished with the job interview in a flash.

in a fog (haze)

- Confused, not sure what is happening

  He is always in a fog and never seems to know what is going on.

in a fool's paradise

- Seem to be happy but in a situation that will not last

  The couple were living in a fool's paradise with their temporary jobs and the high salaries.

in a hole

- In some trouble, in an embarrassing or difficult position

  He is really in a hole now that he has problems both at work and at home.

in a huff

- In an angry or offended manner

  The head of our department left the meeting in a huff.

in a hurry

- Moving or acting quickly

  He is very busy and always in a hurry.

in a jam

- In trouble, in a difficult situation

  He is in a jam now that his car is not working properly.

in a jiffy

- Very fast, very soon

  I promised that I would be finished with the phone in a jiffy.

in a kind/sort of way

- To a certain extent, a little, somewhat

  In a kind of way I want to buy a new car but in other ways I don't think that I really need one.

in a lather

- Excited and agitated

  My friend was in a lather when she heard that she would be transferring to another department.

in a little bit

- Soon

  "I will give you back your dictionary in a little bit."

in a mad rush

- In a hurry, frantically

  The woman was in a mad rush to finish her shopping and return home.

in a month of Sundays

- In a very long time

  I have not been to the shopping mall in a month of Sundays.

in a nutshell

- Briefly

  I tried to explain the problem to him in a nutshell but there still wasn't enough time.

in a pickle/in a pretty pickle

- In a mess, in trouble

My friend is in a pickle now that she has lost her job.

in a pig's eye

- Hardly, unlikely, never

  In a pig's eye will I let him borrow my car next weekend.

in a pinch

- Okay when nothing else is available

  The other tool will do in a pinch if we can't find the correct one.

in a quandary

- Confused and uncertain about what to do

  I am in a quandary about where I should go on my vacation next month.

in a rush

- In a hurry

  They did the job in a rush so I am a little worried about the quality.

in a rut

- Always doing the same thing

  She feels that she is in a rut after doing the same job for seven years.

in a sense

- In a way, sort of

  In a sense I can understand what my friend's problem is about but still it is difficult to imagine what he wants to say.

in a snit

- In a fit of anger or irritation

  My friend was in a snit because I forgot to phone her on Saturday.

in a split second

- In just an instant

The car accident happened in a split second before anyone could do anything to prevent it.

in a spot

- In some trouble, in an embarrassing or difficult position

  She is in a spot right now as she was unable to enter university and also has no job.

in a stew (about someone or something)

- Upset or bothered about someone or something

  The woman's husband is in a stew because he lost his car keys.

in a stupor

- In a dazed condition

  I was in a stupor after I wrote my last exam.

in a tight spot

- In a difficult situation

  The man was in a tight spot after he lost his job.

in a tizzy

- In an excited and confused condition

  The girl was in a tizzy all morning as she got ready for her friend's wedding.

in a way

- To a certain extent, a little, somewhat

  In a way I want to go to the restaurant but basically I don't care.

in a word

- Briefly, to sum up

  In a word, the problem with the car is that it needs a new motor.

in a world of one's own

- In deep thought or concentration, not caring about other people

He is always in a world of his own and doesn't notice what other people say or think.

in abeyance

- The temporary suspension of an activity or a ruling

  The final estate settlement was in abeyance while the lawyers looked at the will in more detail.

in accordance with (something)

- In agreement with (something)

  In accordance with the wishes of my grandfather we did not sell the family farm.

in addition to (something)

- Additionally, further

  In addition to a degree in history my friend also has a degree in economics.

in advance

- Ahead of time

  They bought the tickets in advance so that they could get a good seat.

in agreement

- In harmony, agreeing

  All of the members of the team were in agreement regarding the training schedule of the coach.

in all one's born days

- In all one's life

  In all my born days I have never met a more stubborn person.

in all probability

- Very likely

  In all probability I will be unable to attend my classes during the next two weeks.

in and of itself

- Considering one thing alone

In and of itself there is no problem having a large number of people at the dinner. However, the fire regulations do not allow so many people to be in the building

in and out

- Coming in and going out often

  He has been in and out all day but I don't know where he is at the moment.

in any case/event

- No matter what happens, surely, without fail

  I may not be able to meet you next week but in any case I will still give you the books before then.

in arms

- Armed, angry and ready to fight

  The workers are in arms since they found out about the wage decrease.

in arrears

- Overdue (bills or money), late

  I have never been in arrears with my bill payments.

in awe of (someone or something)

- Fearful and respectful of someone or something

  All of the children were in awe of the firemen who came to visit the school.

in bad faith

- With bad or dishonest intent

  The man was bargaining in bad faith when he tried to buy the car.

in bad/poor taste

- Rude, vulgar

  The jokes that the man told at the dinner were in very bad taste.

in between

- Located in the middle of two things/states

My friend is in between jobs at the moment.

in black and white

- In writing

  I want to get the information in black and white before I go to the meeting.

in bloom/blossom

- A flower/tree at the peak of blooming

  All of the flowers are in bloom in our garden now.

in brief

- Briefly

  I explained in brief what the new supervisor was supposed to do while I was on vacation.

in broad daylight

- Publicly visible in the daytime

  The robbery of the store took place in broad daylight.

in bulk

- In large quantities or amounts

  We usually buy some of our food in bulk.

in cahoots with (someone)

- In secret agreement or partnership with someone

  The supermarket was in cahoots with the vegetable producer to try and keep the prices high.

in care of (someone)

- Send something to one person at the address of another person

  My income tax refund was sent to me in care of my company.

in case

- If, if something should happen

  I will take my umbrella in case it rains.

in case of

- In the event of, if there should be, as a precaution

In case of fire we keep our computer backup files in a fireproof safe.

in character

- As usual, typical, in the way that a person usually behaves

  Supporting the members of her staff is in character with the way our manager does business.

in charge of (someone or something)

- In control or authority, responsible for someone or something

  He is in charge of the sales department at his company.

in check

- Under control, kept quiet

  The violence was kept in check by the police department and the army.

in clover

- Rich or successful, having a pleasant or easy life

  They are in clover now that they have sold their business and retired.

in cold blood

- Without feeling or pity, cooly and deliberately

  The family was murdered in cold blood by the criminal gang.

in common

- Shared together or equally, in use or ownership by all

  I had nothing in common with the other members of the class.

in concert (with someone)

- With the aide of someone

  We made the presentation in concert with members of another company.

join the fray

- Join a fight or argument

  I did not want to join the fray and argue with the other members of the group.

jolt to a stop

- Stop moving suddenly which causes a jolt

  The train jolted to a stop when the engineer put the brakes on.

judge (someone or something) on its own merits

- Judge or evaluate someone or something on its own good points and achievements

  Our company always judges each employee on his or her own merits.

judging by (something)

- Considering something

  Judging by the weather, I don't think that we will be able to go to the festival today.

jump all over (someone)

- Criticize/scold/blame someone

  As soon as I began to talk about my plans for the summer my boss jumped all over me.

jump at (something)

- Seize the opportunity to do something

  He jumped at the chance to go to France on company business.

jump bail

- Run away and fail to come to trial and therefore give up the money that you have already paid to the court

  The man jumped bail and went to live in a foreign country.

jump down (someone's) throat

- Criticize or become angry with someone

As soon as I reached the office my boss jumped down my throat over the missing file.

jump on (someone)

- Scold/criticize/blame someone

  Everybody jumped on the supervisor because they were angry about the new schedules.

jump/climb/get on the bandwagon

- Join a popular activity/campaign

  Everybody jumped on the bandwagon to try and stop smoking in the workplace.

jump out of one's skin

- Be badly frightened

  I nearly jumped out of my skin when I saw the man at the window.

jump the gun

- Start before you should

  He jumped the gun and started selling the tickets before he should have.

kangaroo court

- An illegal court formed by a group of people to settle a dispute among themselves

  The men were convicted by a kangaroo court in the town and nobody agreed with the decision.

Katie bar the door

- Get ready for trouble, a desperate situation is at hand

  The gang arrived at the hotel and were ready to come in and fight. "Katie bar the door."

keel over

- Fall over and faint

  Three of the members of the band keeled over because of the heat.

keel over

- Turn upside down, tip over

The boat keeled over in the middle of the lake but everybody was safe.

keen on (someone or something)

- Be enthusiastic about someone or something

  My girlfriend is keen on going to a movie this weekend.

keep a civil tongue

- Speak decently and politely

  The angry customer was asked to keep a civil tongue when talking with the sales clerk.

keep a close watch on (someone or something)

- Monitor or observe someone or something

  The woman always keeps a close watch on her child when she is at the shopping centre.

keep a close watch over (someone or something)

- Guard or care for someone or something

  I kept a close watch over the soup as it was cooking.

keep a secret

- To not tell a secret to others

  I have been trying to keep a secret about my friend's boyfriend for a long time now.

keep a stiff upper lip

- Be brave, face trouble bravely

  The storm victims tried hard to keep a stiff upper lip in spite of the hardships of their situation.

keep a straight face

- Stop oneself from smiling or laughing

  It was difficult to keep a straight face when the man fell off his chair into the grass.

keep a tight/close rein on (someone or something)

- Strictly watch and control someone or something

Our principal keeps a tight rein on what is being taught in the classrooms.

keep abreast (of something)

- Keep informed about something

  I read the newspaper regularly so that I can keep abreast of current events.

keep after/at (someone)

- Remind someone over and over about something

  I always have to keep after my friend to do her job properly.

keep an eye on (someone or something)

- Watch and take care of something (but not just look at something)

  "Will you keep an eye on the baby while I go to the store."

keep an eye out for (someone or something)

- Watch for the arrival or appearance of someone or something

  I kept an eye out for a nice restaurant after I arrived in the small town.

keep at (something)

- Persist with something

  He has decided to keep at his studies and I am sure that he will succeed.

keep body and soul together

- Keep alive, survive

  It was very cold during the winter but somehow she was able to keep body and soul together and survived.

keep books

- Keep records of money gained and spent, do the work of a bookkeeper

  My first job was to keep books for a small company in my hometown.

keep company (with someone)

- Associate with or spend much time with someone

  I like to keep company with my friends from university.

keep cool

- Stay calm

  The police officers were trained to keep cool in difficult situations.

keep down (something)

- Keep from progressing or growing, keep within limits, control

  The students were told to keep down the noise as some of the other classes were having exams.

keep from (doing something)

- Prevent/refrain from doing something

  I love ice cream and couldn't keep from eating three bowls.

keep good time

- Work accurately (used for a clock or watch)

  My watch has not been keeping good time lately.

keep harping on (something)

- Continue to talk or complain about something

  The boy's father keeps harping on the fact that his son never does his homework.

keep house

- Look after a house or a household

  She has been keeping house for her father while he is sick.

keep in touch (with someone)

- Talk or write to someone

  I have always tried to keep in touch with my friends from high school.

keep late hours

- Stay up or stay out until very late

  My friend keeps late hours now that he is working for the newspaper.

keep off (something)

- Stay off someone's land or other property

  The students were asked to keep off the grass which was being replanted.

keep on (doing something)

- Continue

  She is careless and keeps on making the same mistakes over and over.

keep on an even keel

- Remain cool and calm

  I was very busy with my job and school but I tried very hard to keep on an even keel and get everything done.

keep on one's toes

- Stay alert and watchful

  I try to keep on my toes during a class where the teacher may ask me a question.

keep one's chin up

- Be brave, be determined

  "Try and keep your chin up. Things will get better in the future."

keep one's cool

- To stay/remain calm

  I tried to keep my cool during the argument with my neighbour.

keep one's distance from (someone or something)

- Maintain a certain distance from someone or something

The girl always keeps her distance from the other students in the class.

keep one's eye on the ball

- Be watchful and ready for something

  "You should keep your eye on the ball or you will make a mistake."

keep one's eyes open

- Remain alert and watchful for someone or something

  "Please keep your eyes open for a good place to eat so that we can have lunch."

keep one's feet on the ground

- Remain firmly established

  My friend lost his job but he is trying hard to keep his feet on the ground.

keep one's fingers crossed

- Wish for good results in something one is doing

  "Please keep your fingers crossed that I will pass my exam."

keep one's hand in (something)

- Retain some control of something

  My uncle sold his business but he is still trying to keep his hand in some of its operations.

a labour of love

- Something done for personal pleasure and not for money

  The man's book is a labour of love and he doesn't expect to make any money from it.

lace into (someone)

- Attack or scold someone

  The mother laced into her child when he came home late from the movie.

lace into (something)

- Devour/eat food

We laced into our dinner as soon as we entered the house.

lady killer

- A man who some women find very charming and attractive

  The man in the movie was a lady killer who broke the hearts of many women.

lady's man

- A man who is popular with women

  He is a lady's man and always seems to have a woman interested in him.

laid-back

- Relaxed, not worried by things

  Our teacher has a very laid-back attitude about how long we should spend preparing for our class.

be laid up

- Be confined to bed or unfit for work

  He has been laid up for a few days because of a cold.

a lame duck

- A public official who has a short time left to serve in office and therefore has less power than before

  He was a lame-duck leader so it was difficult for him to accomplish some things.

land of Nod

- Sleep

  I entered the land of Nod as soon as my head hit the pillow.

land on one's feet/both feet

- Come out of a bad situation successfully

  My friend always manages to land on his feet no matter how difficult the situation is.

land up (somewhere or in some situation)

- Come to be in a certain place or situation

We landed up in the suburbs although we were trying to go downtown.

landslide victory

- A very substantial victory (usually in an election)

  My favourite candidate won a landslide victory in the election.

lap up (something)

- To eat or drink something with the tongue (as a dog or cat would)

  The dog lapped up the milk that his owner had given him.

lap up (something)

- Eagerly take in or accept some information/praise

  He lapped up the praise that his boss gave him for the recently completed project.

lapse into a coma

- Go into a coma

  The woman lapsed into a coma soon after the accident.

lash out (at someone)

- Attack someone with words

  They were walking along the beach when the girl suddenly lashed out in anger at her boyfriend.

lash out (at someone)

- Suddenly try to hit someone

  The boy suddenly lashed out and hit the man who was sitting beside him.

last but not least

- In the last place but not the least important

  Last but not least the boy came up to the front of the class to receive his report card.

a last-ditch effort

- A final effort

The government made a last-ditch effort to prevent a strike by the teachers.

the last person

- The most unlikely person to do something or to be seen somewhere

  My friend is the last person that you would expect to see in a clothing store buying clothes.

the last straw

- The last insult or mistake that one can endure and which then causes some reaction

  The fourth time that the girl came to work late was the last straw and we finally fired her.

last will and testament

- One's will (especially its latest version)

  After my grandfather's funeral my uncle read out his last will and testament.

the last word

- The last remark in an argument, the final say in deciding something

  She always expects to have the last word when she and her husband go shopping together.

late in life

- When one is older

  Some very great painters never started painting until rather late in life.

late in the day

- Far along in a project or activity

  We received some new instructions for our marketing effort but it was a little late in the day to change our plans.

laugh all the way to the bank

- Make money in a way that other people think is impossible

I was laughing all the way to the bank with the money that I made from selling drinks at the sports stadium.

laugh off (something)

- To not take something seriously

  The man laughed off the attempt by his boss to make him come to work on time.

laugh out of the other side of one's mouth

- Change from being happy to being sad

  My friend was laughing out of the other side of his mouth when he learned that he would get a ticket for parking his car in the wrong place.

laugh (something) out of court

- Dismiss (a legal case) as being ridiculous

  They laughed the case out of court when the woman tried to sue the dog's owner after the dog ate her flowers.

laugh up one's sleeve

- Laugh quietly to oneself

  I was laughing up my sleeve when I learned that my friend would have to clean the bathroom at work and not me.

launch forth (on something)

- Start out on something

  Our boss launched forth on a long criticism of how we were doing our jobs.

a law unto oneself

- One who makes one's own laws or rules

  The city council member thought that she was a law unto herself until she resigned because of a scandal.

not lay a finger/hand on (someone)

- Not touch someone, not do something to someone

The man was told by the police never to lay a finger on his wife again.

lay an egg

- Fail to win the interest or favour of an audience

  Although the magician was supposed to be good, his performance was terrible and it laid an egg with the audience.

lay away (something)

- Save something

  The couple are trying to lay away some money for their holiday next year.

lay down one's life (for someone or something)

- Sacrifice one's life for someone or something

  The young man layed down his life trying to protect the property of his company.

lay down the law

- Tell someone what to do by using your power or influence

  The new manager plans to lay down the law to the workers regarding long lunch breaks.

lay eyes on (someone or something)

- See someone or something

  I have never laid eyes on a more beautiful dog in my life.

lay hold of (something)

- Get possession of something

  If I can lay hold of some tools I will help you fix your toilet.

lay in (something)

- Store up a supply of something, get and store something for future use

  They are trying to lay in as much food as possible before winter comes.

mad as a hatter

- Crazy

  My neighbour is mad as a hatter and we never know what she will do next.

mad as a hornet

- Very angry

  Our boss was mad as a hornet when we saw him at the meeting yesterday.

made for each other

- Two people are very well suited romantically

  The young couple are made for each other and seem to be very happy.

made to measure

- Made especially to fit the measurements of someone

  When I was working in Hong Kong I purchased several suits that were made to measure.

made to order

- Put together on request

  My father decided to buy a new computer desk that was made to order.

maiden voyage

- The first voyage of a ship or boat

  The maiden voyage of the new cruise ship was popular with many people.

the main drag

- The most important street in a town

  We spent Saturday evening driving up and down the main drag of the town.

make a bed

- Arrange the sheets and blankets of a bed neatly

  My mother always told me to make my bed when I was a child.

make a beeline for (someone or something)

- Hurry directly toward someone or something

  When I enter the cafeteria I always make a beeline for the dessert section.

make a big deal about (something)

- Exaggerate the seriousness of something

  I wish that my friend would not make a big deal about every small problem.

make a break for (something/somewhere)

- Move or run quickly to something or somewhere

  The audience made a break for the doors as soon as the concert was over.

make a bundle/pile

- Make a lot of money

  My father made a bundle on the stock market several years ago.

make a check out (to someone)

- Write a check to give to someone with their name on it

  I made a check out to the animal hospital after they cared for our dog.

make a clean breast of (something)

- Confess something bad that you have done in order not to feel guilty/bad

  The woman made a clean breast of things and worked hard to start over.

make a clean sweep of (something)

- Do something completely or thoroughly

  The new political party made a clean sweep of the large cities during the election.

make a comeback

- Return to one's former (successful) career

The boxer has been training very hard in his attempt to make a comeback.

make a day of it

- Do something all day

  We decided to make a day of it and spend the day at the beach.

make a dent in (something)

- Make progress doing something

  We worked hard all day but we didn't make a dent in the amount of work left to do.

make a difference

- Cause a change in a situation

  It doesn't make a difference whether he comes to the meeting or not.

make a face (at someone)

- Make a strange face to ridicule someone

  The little girl made a face at the boy in her class.

make a fast/quick buck

- Make money with little effort

  The two men tried to make a fast buck during the construction boom.

make a fool out of (someone)

- Make someone look foolish

  The secretary made a fool out of her boss when she argued with him at the meeting.

make a fuss (over someone or something)

- Worry about or make a bother about someone or something

  My grandmother always makes a fuss over me when I go to visit her.

make a go of (something)

- Succeed at something, produce good results

Although he tried hard he was never able to make a go of his business.

make a great show of (something)

- Do something in a showy fashion

The woman made a great show of telling everybody about her new and rich boyfriend.

make a hit

- Be successful

Her cake made a hit at the party.

make a killing

- Make a large amount of money

Her mother made a killing on the real estate market before she retired.

make a laughingstock of (someone)

- Do something that makes people laugh at someone

I made a laughingstock of myself when I dropped the plate of crackers at the party.

make a living

- Earn enough money to live

He cannot make a living by only doing a part-time job.

make a long story short

- Bring a story to an end by omitting some details

I had to make a long story short in order to finish my story and leave to catch my train home.

make a meal of (something)

- Eat one main dish/food as an entire meal

We were able to make a meal of the chicken that my mother gave us last night.

make a mistake

- Make an error

I made a mistake on the math test.

make a mountain out of a molehill

- Make a big problem out of a small problem

  He is making a mountain out of a molehill by worrying about his son's problem.

make a name for oneself

- Become well-known or famous

  He has made a name for himself in the field of computers.

make a night/evening of (doing something)

- Do something for the entire night/evening

  We decided to stay home and make a night of playing cards.

make a note of (something)

- To write something on a piece of paper

  I made a note of the people that I was going to phone on the weekend.

make a nuisance of oneself

- Be a constant bother

  I didn't phone the apartment manager to complain about the sink because I didn't want to make a nuisance of myself.

make a pass at (someone)

- Make romantic advances to someone

  The man was fired because he made a pass at one of the women who he works with.

make a pitch (for someone or something)

- Attempt to promote/sell/advance someone or something

  The city made a pitch for more money from other levels of government to help build a new sports stadium.

make a play for (someone)

- Try to make someone romantically interested in you

I workèd hard all term to make a play for a woman in my computer class.

make a point

- State something important

  The speaker used some good examples in order to make a point during his speech.

nail down (someone or something)

- To make certain/sure of something

  I am trying to nail down the exact time that we can meet with our supplier.

a nail in (someone's) coffin

- Something that will harm someone

  Fighting with his boss was a nail in my friend's coffin. He will not get a promotion now.

naked eye

- The human eye (with no binoculars etc.)

  It was difficult to see the bird with the naked eye.

one's name is mud

- A person's reputation is bad

  His name is mud now that he has been charged by the police with stealing money from his company.

the name of the game

- The main part of a matter

  The name of the game is selling cars and not worrying about other things.

name (someone) after (someone or something)

- To give someone the name of another person/place/thing

  My cousin was named after his mother's grandfather.

a narrow escape

- An escape with little chance of error

He had a narrow escape when he almost fell from his bicycle.

near at hand

- To be close or handy (to someone)

  I looked for a pair of scissors that were near at hand.

neck and neck

- To be equal or nearly equal in a race or contest

  The two teams were neck and neck in the race to win the national championship.

neck of the woods

- An area or part of the country

  He has never been to my neck of the woods since he was a child.

need (something) like (one needs) a hole in the head

- To not need something at all

  My friend needs a new computer like he needs a hole in the head.

need (something) yesterday

- To need something in a very big hurry

  I need a new computer yesterday.

a needle in a haystack

- Something that is very hard to find

  Looking for the lost receipt among the thousands of other receipts was like looking for a needle in a haystack.

neither fish nor fowl

- Something that does not belong to a definite group

  The man's opinions were neither fish nor fowl and nobody could put them into an identifiable category.

neither here nor there

- Not relevant to the thing being discussed, to be off the subject

"What you are saying is neither here nor there. We are talking about our plans this year - not five years in the future."

neither hide nor hair of (someone or something)

- No sign or indication of someone or something

  I have seen neither hide nor hair of my friend recently.

a nervous Nellie

- A timid person who lacks determination and courage

  He is a nervous Nellie and is afraid of the other students in the school.

a nest egg

- Money that someone has saved up

  He has a large nest egg and will have no financial problems if he leaves his company.

never fear

- Do not worry

  "Never fear, I will finish work and meet you in time for the movie."

never in one's life

- Not in one's experience

  I have never in my life seen such a strange person.

never mind

- Don't worry, don't bother

  "If you don't have time to pick up my laundry today, never mind, I will get it tomorrow."

never would have guessed

- Never would have thought something to be the case

  I never would have guessed that the woman on the bicycle was one of the richest women in the city.

new blood

- Fresh energy or power, someone or something that gives new life or vigour to something

She is a good employee and helped us to inject some new blood into our organization.

a new broom sweeps clean

- A new person makes many changes

  A new broom sweeps clean and when our new boss came he changed many things in our organization.

a new deal

- A complete change, a fresh start, another chance

  The player was given a new deal by the team although the previous year he had not played well.

a new hire

- A person who has recently been hired

  The man at the gas station is a new hire and is very slow at his job.

a new lease on life

- A renewed outlook on life

  I gave my car a new lease on life after I took it to the mechanic for repairs.

occur to (someone)

- To come into someone's mind (an idea or thought)

  It occurred to me that I will not be able to meet my friend on Saturday because I have to go to the airport to meet someone else.

ocean(s) of (something)

- A very large amount of something

  There was oceans of food at the party.

odd man out

- An unusual person or thing

  I always feel that I am the odd man out when I go with my coworkers to a restaurant.

(the) odd (something)

- An extra or spare something, one or two of something

We saw the odd interesting bird on our hike through the mountains.

an oddball

- A person who does not act like other people

  The man is an oddball and nobody at his company likes to work with him.

odds and ends

- A variety of small items (sometimes remnants of something)

  We made games for the children from odds and ends that we found around the house.

an odor of sanctity

- An atmosphere of excessive holiness or piety

  There was an odor of sanctity surrounding the chambers of the judge at the courthouse.

of age

- To be old enough to be allowed to do something (vote,drink etc.)

  When my cousin came of age we had a big party for him to celebrate.

of age

- To be fully developed, to be mature

  Rapid transportation came of age when the first jets were built.

of all the nerve

- How shocking!

  Of all the nerve for my friend to ask me for more money when she never repaid me what she had already borrowed.

of all things

- Imagine that!

  "Of all things," the woman said when the post office worker told her that her package was too large for delivery.

of benefit to (someone)

- To be good for someone, to be a benefit to someone

  Another meeting to solve the problem would be of no benefit to myself so I decided not to attend.

of course

- Certainly, definitely, naturally

  "Of course you can use my car if you want to."

of interest (to someone)

- To be interesting to someone

  The man who works at the gas station is of interest to the police in their investigation of the murder.

of late

- Lately

  Of late there has been almost no rain in our city.

of no avail

- With no effect, unsuccessful

  My complaints to the company were of no avail and nothing was done.

of one's own accord/free will

- By one's own choice

  The supervisor decided to leave her job of her own free will and was not fired.

of the old school

- To have attitudes from the past which are no longer popular

  Our teacher's attitudes are of the old school and are not often found these days.

off and on

- Occasionally

  My friend has been seeing a woman off and on but I do not think that their relationship is very serious.

off and running

- To be started up and already going

  The candidates are off and running in the race to become mayor of the city.

off balance

- To be not prepared for something, to be unable to meet the unexpected

  I was off balance when my boss asked me to deliver the speech instead of him.

off base

- To be inaccurate/wrong

  He was off base with his estimate of next year's budget.

off campus

- To be not on the grounds of a college or university

  The used bookstore was off campus but it was very popular with the university students.

off-centre

- To be not exactly in the centre or middle of something

  The picture was off-centre and did not look good on the wall.

the off chance

- A slight possibility

  I went to the department store on the off chance that I would find a new jacket that I liked.

off-colour

- To be in bad taste, to be not polite, to be not the exact colour

  He likes to tell off-colour jokes which most people do not like.

  We painted the walls an off-colour of white.

off duty

- To be not working

The police officer was off duty when he saw the bank robbery.

off guard

- To be not alert to the unexpected

  It caught me off guard when my friend suddenly asked me to lend her some money.

off like a shot

- To go away quickly

  The children were off like a shot when the school bell rang.

off limits

- To be forbidden

  The factory was off limits to everybody except the workers who worked there.

off one's back

- To be not bothering someone

  I wish my father would get off my back and stop asking me when I am going to look for a job.

off one's chest

- To talk about a problem to someone so that it does not bother you anymore

  I talked to my friend and I was able to get some of my problems off my chest.

off one's hands

- To no longer be in one's care or possession

  I sold my old computer and got it off my hands.

off one's high horse

- To be not acting proud and scornful, to be not acting like you are better than others

  We got our boss off his high horse when he admitted that he had made many mistakes with the new product launch.

off one's rocker

- To be crazy

He must be off his rocker if he thinks that he can spend much money and not have financial problems.

pack a punch/wallop

- To provide a burst of energy/power/excitement

  The storm packed a wallop and did much damage to the coast.

a pack of lies

- A series of lies

  Everything that the man said was a pack of lies and nobody believed him.

pack them in

- To attract a lot of people

  The new restaurant is able to pack them in with its new and exciting menu.

packed in like sardines

- To be packed very tightly

  The commuters on the train were packed in like sardines during the morning rush hour.

pad the bill

- To add false expenses to a bill

  The salesman always pads the bill when he goes on a business trip.

paddle one's own canoe

- To do something by oneself

  I was forced to paddle my own canoe when the rest of the staff went away for a seminar.

a pain in the neck/ass

- An annoying/bothersome thing or person

  Dealing with my neighbour is always a pain in the neck.

paint oneself into a corner

- To get into a bad situation that is difficult or impossible to get out of

My friend has painted himself into a corner now that he has begun to fight with his supervisor.

paint the town red

- To go out and party and have a good time

  We decided to go out and paint the town red after we passed our exams.

pal around (with someone)

- To be friends with someone

  I have begun to pal around with a friend from my evening language class.

pale around the gills

- To look sick

  My colleague was looking a little pale around the gills when he came to work today.

palm (something) off on (someone)

- To deceive someone by a trick or a lie, to sell or give something by tricking

  The man palmed off his old television set as one that was new and reliable.

pan out

- To end or finish favourably, to work out well

  "I hope that your plans to go back to school pan out."

paper over the cracks (in/of something)

- To try to hide faults or difficulties

  Our boss is trying to paper over the cracks in the office and will not deal with the problems of the staff.

par for the course

- To be just what was expected, to be nothing unusual

  That was par for the course. He always comes late when there is a lot of work to do.

paradise (on earth)

- A place on earth that is as lovely as paradise

The resort in the mountains was paradise on earth.

part and parcel of (something)

- A necessary or important part of something

  The house that we bought is part and parcel of a much larger piece of property.

part company (with someone)

- To leave someone, to depart from someone

  The two business partners decided to part company and begin their own businesses.

partake of (something)

- To eat or drink something

  I decided not to partake of the large dinner before the golf tournament.

partial to (someone or something)

- Favouring or preferring someone or something

  Our boss is partial to the new person who recently began to work in our company.

the particulars of (something)

- The specific details about something

  I have no knowledge of the particulars of my father's business dealings.

parting of the ways

- A point at which people separate and go their own ways

  I had a parting of the ways with my closest friend from high school.

party line

- The official ideas of a group (usually political) that must be followed by all members

  The members of the political party were forced to follow the party line on most issues.

the party's over

- A happy or good time has come to an end

The party's over and I must now begin to work after my long holiday.

pass away

- To die

  His father passed away when he was 96 years old.

pass for/as (someone or something)

- To succeed in being accepted as someone or something

  The young woman was trying to pass for a reporter when she went to the concert.

pass muster

- To pass a test or checkup, to measure up to a certain standard

  The player was not able to pass muster and was not included on the team.

pass off (something) as (something else)

- To sell or give something by false claims, to offer something as genuine when it is not

  The man passed off the watch as a diamond watch and received more money than it was worth.

pass on

- To die

  My grandmother passed on when she was 92 years old.

pass on (something)

- To give away something that you don't use anymore

  The girl always passes on her old clothes to her younger sister.

pass oneself off as (someone or something) else

- To claim to be someone one is not, to pretend to be someone else

  My friend passed himself off as a reporter and was able to get into the concert free.

pass out

- To faint

  Three teenage girls passed out at the rock concert.

pass the buck

- To shift responsibility to someone else

  Our supervisor always tries to pass the buck if someone tries to criticize his work.

pass the hat

- To attempt to collect money for some project

  We passed the hat in order to raise money for the movie projector.

pass the time

- To fill up time by doing something

  My grandfather usually passes the time reading and working in his garden.

quake in one's boots

- To be afraid, to shake from fear

  I was quaking in my boots when my boss told me to come to his office.

queer as a three-dollar bill

- To be very strange

  The woman is the strangest person that I have ever seen and she is as queer as a three-dollar bill.

quick and dirty

- Fast and cheap, fast and careless

  The method that the company chose to cut expenses was quick and dirty.

quick as a flash

- Very quickly

  I was able to get out of the house as quick as a flash and go to work.

quick as a wink

- Very quickly

The woman turned around and quick as a wink her purse was stolen.

quick as geased lightning

- Very quickly, very fast

  The cat climbed up the tree as quick as greased lightning.

quick on the draw

- To be quick to respond to something, to be quick to draw a gun and shoot

  The man is quick on the draw and can answer most questions immediately.

quick on the trigger

- To be quick to respond to something, to be quick to draw a gun and shoot

  The man was too quick on the trigger and should have thought more carefully about what he was going to say.

quick on the uptake

- To be quick to understand something

  The student is quick on the uptake and understands most scientific theories very quickly.

quiet as a mouse

- Very quiet, shy and silent

  The little boy was quiet as a mouse as he moved around the kitchen.

quite a bit

- Much or many

  I had quite a bit of time so I decided to go to the library.

quite a few

- Many

  The boy has quite a few DVDs at home.

quite a lot

- Much or many

There are quite a lot of chairs in the meeting hall.

quite a number

- Much or many

  Quite a number of the teachers agreed to use the new textbooks.

quite a (something)

- Definitely something

  The girl is quite a pianist and everybody loves her.

quote a price

- To state in advance the charge for doing or supplying something

  I asked the moving company to quote a price to move our furniture.

a race against time

- A rush to beat a deadline

  It was a race against time to rescue the miners who were trapped in the mine.

rack one's brains

- To try hard to think or remember something

  I have been racking my brains all day trying to remember the man's name.

racked with pain

- To be suffering from severe pain

  The man was racked with pain after he fell from the ladder.

rail at (someone) about (something)

- To complain loudly to someone about something

  The customer was railing at the clerk about the bad service.

rain cats and dogs

- To rain very hard

  It has been raining cats and dogs all morning.

a rain check

- A free ticket to an event that replaces a ticket that was cancelled because of rain or for some other reason

  We received a rain check for the concert that was suddenly cancelled.

a rain check

- A promise to repeat an invitation at a later date

  I did not have time to go to the restaurant with my friend so I decided to take a rain check.

rain on (someone's) parade

- To spoil someone's plans

  I tried not to let my friend's bad mood rain on my parade during the concert.

rain or shine

- No matter whether it rains or the sun shines

  We plan to go to the beach tomorrow rain or shine.

rain (something) out

- To spoil something by raining

  The music festival was rained out yesterday evening.

raise a fuss

- To make trouble, to cause a disturbance

  The woman at the restaurant raised a fuss when her meal arrived late.

raise a hand against (someone or something)

- To hit or threaten to hit someone or something

  If the man raises a hand against his supervisor the police will be called.

raise a stink about (something)

- To make a major issue out of something

  The small business owners began to raise a stink about the new parking tax.

raise an objection to (someone or something)

- To object to someone or something

  My friend raised an objection about including my parents in our travel plans.

raise Cain

- To create a disturbance, to cause trouble

  The boys began to raise Cain at the dance and were asked to leave.

raise eyebrows

- To cause surprise or disapproval

  It raised eyebrows when the actress appeared at the party with no invitation.

raise havoc with (someone or something)

- To create confusion or disruption for or against someone or something

  The bad weather raised havoc with our plans to clean up the area around our house.

raise hell with (someone or something)

- To make trouble, to behave wildly

  The woman began to raise hell with her supervisor after she heard about the new policy.

raise one's sights

- To set higher goals for oneself

  Our team is doing very well this year and we are now raising our sights on the city championship.

raise one's voice to (someone)

- To speak loudly or shout at someone in anger

  The teacher asked the child not to raise his voice.

to be raised in a barn

- To behave crudely like a barnyard animal

  When the boy did not shut the door his mother asked him if he had been raised in a barn.

rake in the money

- To make a lot of money

  My cousin's new pizza franchise has been raking in the money since it opened.

rake (someone) over the coals

- To scold/reprimand someone

  My boss raked me over the coals when he heard about the lost sales report.

rake (something) off

- To take money from something illegally

  The sales clerk was accused of raking money off of the daily cash sales.

rally around (someone or something)

- To come together to support someone or something

  Everybody in the small town began to rally around the mayor when he was accused of wrongdoing.

ram (something) down (someone's) throat

- To force someone to do or agree to something that is not wanted

  Our teacher always tries to ram her ideas down our throats which makes us angry.

ramble on about (someone or something)

- To talk aimlessly and endlessly about someone or something

  My friend spent the entire evening rambling on about his problems at work.

rank and file

- The members of a group and not the leaders, regular soldiers and not the officers

  The rank and file of the large union were happy with their new contract.

sack out

- To go to bed, to go to sleep

I sacked out as soon as I arrived home last evening.

a sacred cow

- Something that is never criticized or laughed at even if it sometimes deserves to be

  The medical insurance system is a sacred cow of the government and is never criticized by anyone.

sadder but wiser

- Unhappy about something but having learned something from the experience

  The man was sadder but wiser after he learned that his wallet had been stolen.

saddle (someone) with (something)

- To give someone something undesirable or difficult to deal with

  I try not to saddle my friend with the problems that I am having at work.

safe and sound

- To be safe/whole/healthy

  We arrived at our destination safe and sound after a long journey.

to be on the safe side

- To take no chances

  It may rain so to be on the safe side I think that I will bring my umbrella.

safety in numbers

- To feel safe by being surrounded by a large number of people

  There was safety in numbers when the students went to complain to the principal about their new teacher.

sage advice

- Very good and wise advice

  I waited for my friend to ask me for my sage advice regarding his problems.

sail into

- It is always the same old story with my friend. He borrows money but he never wants to pay it back.

same to you

- The same comment applies to you

  "The same to you," the boy said when his friend said that he was stupid.

sands of time

- The accumulated tiny amounts of time (like the sand in an hourglass)

  The sands of time have done much to change the woman's attitude toward her sister.

save face

- To preserve one's good reputation or dignity when something has happened to hurt it

  Our boss was very embarrassed when our company lost a lot of money. However, he was able to save face when he showed that the problems were outside of his control.

save one's breath

- To remain silent because talking will do no good

  You may as well save your breath and not talk to her as she will not believe you anyway.

save one's neck/skin

- To save oneself from danger or trouble

  The man left the scene of the fire as soon as possible in order to save his neck.

save (something) for a rainy day

- To reserve something/money for the future

  I always try to save some money for a rainy day when I get paid.

save the day

- To bring about victory or success (when defeat is likely)

The player saved the day for his team when he played his best game of the season.

save up for (something)

- To save money in order to buy something

  My friend's brother is saving up for a new digital camera.

saved by the bell

- To be rescued from a difficult situation just in time by something that brings the situation to a sudden end

  I was saved by the bell and do not have to give my presentation until tomorrow.

saving grace

- Something that saves someone or something that would otherwise be a total disaster

  The man's saving grace was his mathematical ability. His other personality traits were very strange.

say a mouthful

- To say something of great importance/meaning/length

  "You certainly said a mouthful," I said when my friend began to tell me about his complaint.

say grace

- To say a prayer of thanks before or after a meal

  The bride's father was asked to say grace before the wedding banquet.

say one's piece

- To say openly what one thinks

  I said my piece at the meeting and then left quietly by the back door.

say (something) in a roundabout way

- To say something indirectly

I had to say what I wanted to say in a roundabout way in order to make my point.

say (something) to (someone's) face

- To say something (often unpleasant) directly to someone

  My supervisor always complains about me but she is afraid to say anything to my face.

say (something) under one's breath

- To say something so softly that almost nobody can hear it

  The woman said something under her breath but I could not understand it.

say the word

- To give a sign, to show a wish

  "Just say the word and I will come and meet you at the airport."

say uncle

- To surrender, to give in

  The little boy was forced to say uncle and agree to do what the older boy wanted.

scale (something) down

- To make something smaller by a certain amount or proportion

  The government decided to scale down their plans for the sports stadium.

scare (someone) out of his or her wits

- To frighten someone very much

  The dog scared the little boy out of his wits.

table a motion

- To postpone the discussion of something during a meeting

  We tabled a motion to discuss the safety issue at another time.

tag along with (someone)

- To go with someone, to follow along with someone

  The little boy tagged along with his older brother when they went to the beach.

tail between one's legs

- Feeling ashamed or beaten

  The salesman resigned from his company with his tail between his legs after he told a lie about his expense account.

tail wagging the dog

- A situation where a small part controls the whole thing

  It is like the tail wagging the dog when the receptionist is able to control everything in the office.

take a backseat to (someone or something)

- To accept a poorer or lower position than someone, to be second to someone or something

  I had to take a backseat to my boss when we went on the business trip.

take a bath (on something)

- To come to financial ruin, to lose much money on something

  My aunt took a bath on the stock market last year and she is afraid to buy stocks now.

take a beating

- To lose money

  My father took a beating when he sold his car.

take a bow

- To bow and receive credit for a good performance

  The violinist stopped to take a bow before she went backstage with the orchestra.

take a break

- To have a short rest period in one's work

I stopped to take a break after working all morning.

take a chance/risk

- To try something where failure or bad fortune is likely

  I plan to take a chance and visit my friend without phoning first.

take a course in (something)

- To enroll in a class to study/learn something

  I am planning to take a course in photography next year.

take a crack at (something)

- To try/attempt to do something

  "Have you decided to take a crack at writing the entrance examination?"

take a dig at (someone)

- To criticize someone, to say something that will irritate someone

  The man is always taking a dig at his wife.

take a dim view of (something)

- To be against something, to disapprove of something

  Our company takes a dim view of people who do not wear a suit and tie.

take a fancy/liking to (someone or something)

- To develop a fondness or a preference for someone or something

  The woman took a fancy to the new person who she was working with.

take a gander at (someone or something)

- To examine someone or something

  I asked the car mechanic to take a gander at the steering system on my car.

take a hand in (something)

- To help plan or do something

The man is always ready to take a hand in any work that needs to be done.

take a hard line (with someone)

- To be firm with someone, to have a firm policy for dealing with someone

  The company takes a hard line with people who come to work late.

take a hint

- To understand what is hinted at and behave accordingly

  The man is unable to take a hint and does not notice when people are angry at him.

take a leaf out of (someone's) book

- To behave or do something in the way that someone else would

  We plan to take a leaf out of our competitor's book and advertise our product on the Internet.

take a leak

- To urinate

  The man stopped at the side of the road to take a leak when he was walking home last night.

take a look at (someone or something)

- To examine (usually briefly) someone or something

  I will take a look at the problem with the computer tomorrow.

take a look for (someone or something)

- To look for someone or something

  Tomorrow I will take a look for the pen which I lost.

ugly duckling

- An ugly or plain child who grows up to be attractive

  She was an ugly duckling when she was a child but now she is very beautiful.

unaccustomed to (someone or something)

- Not used to someone or something

  The man was unaccustomed to waking up early in the morning.

under a cloud

- Depressed, sad

  She has been under a cloud of depression since her cat died.

under a cloud (of suspicion)

- Not trusted, suspected of doing something wrong

  The politician has been under a cloud of suspicion over the possibility of taking bribes.

under arrest

- Arrested by the police before being charged with a crime

  The three men were under arrest for robbing a bank.

under certain circumstances/conditions

- Depending on or influenced by something

  Under certain circumstances the children were permitted to use the indoor stadium for practice.

under (close) scrutiny

- Being watched or examined closely

  The business owner was under close scrutiny after the accounting scandal.

under construction

- Being built or repaired

  The hotel was still under construction, two years after it began.

under control

- Not out of control, manageable

  The fire was under control after the fire department arrived.

under cover

- Hidden, concealed

  The police officer went under cover to look for the drug dealers.

under fire

- Being shot at or attacked, under (verbal) attack

  The owner of the company is under fire for not paying his employees a fair salary.

under oath

- Having taken an oath (solemn promise)

  The man was under oath when he spoke before the judge.

under one's belt

- In one's experience, memory or possession

  When he has more experience as a cook under his belt he will begin to look for a job.

under one's belt

- In one's stomach

  After he had a big breakfast under his belt he was ready for work.

under one's breath

- In a whisper, with a low voice

  He was talking under his breath in the movie theater and somebody complained.

under one's nose

- Within sight of someone, easily seen or found

  He found his driver's license right under his nose where he had left it.

under one's own steam

- By one's own efforts, without help

  He was able to go home under his own steam even though he was feeling very sick.

vanish into thin air

- Disappear without leaving a trace

  The university student vanished into thin air and was never seen again.

variety is the spice of life

- Life is made more interesting by doing new or different things

  My grandmother believed that variety is the spice of life and is always starting new projects.

vent one's spleen

- Get rid of one's angry feelings

  I was able to vent my spleen at the manager of our apartment for the problems that she was causing.

verge on (something)

- Come close or approach something

  The accident verged on becoming a major disaster but luckily it was not.

very last

- The end of something

  We were able to buy the very last tickets to the concert.

very thing

- The exact thing that is required

  The new sofa was the very thing that we needed to make our house comfortable.

very well

- Agreed, all right

  "Very well, if you want me to go I will go with you."

vicious circle

- Unbroken sequence of cause and effect with bad results

  He had fallen into a vicious circle of drinking too

much and then losing his job and then drinking even more.

vim and vigour

- Energy and enthusiasm

  Our great aunt is always full of vim and vigour when we see her.

vote down

- Defeat in a vote

  The proposal to extend the opening hours of nightclubs was voted down in the election.

vote of confidence

- A vote to see if a person or political party still has the majority's support

  The government received a vote of confidence when everyone supported their new proposal.

wade into

- Attack, join in

  The football player waded into the fight to help his teammate.

wait-and-see attitude

- An uncertain attitude where you wait and see what will happen

  We decided to take a wait-and-see attitude regarding what our new boss was going to do.

wait on (someone) hand and foot

- Serve someone in every possible way, do everything for someone

  He always waits on his wife hand and foot.

wait tables

- Serve food (in a restaurant etc.)

  He spent the summer waiting tables at the resort.

wait up (for someone)

- Not go to bed until someone arrives or something happens

The woman always waits up for her daughter to come home.

wait with bated breath

- Feel excited or anxious while waiting

  I waited with bated breath for the results of my exams.

waiting in the wings

- Ready to do something such as take over someone's job

  The vice-president was waiting in the wings to help the president.

wake the dead

- Be very loud and able to wake even those who have died

  Our neighbours told us that our stereo was so loud that it would wake the dead.

walk a tightrope

- Be in a situation where you must be very cautious

  The Prime Minister is walking a tightrope regarding the international trade deal.

walk all over (an opponent)

- Win a game easily

  They walked all over the other team at the soccer tournament.

walk all over (someone)

- Treat someone badly

  He tried to walk all over me when I began working but after I became used to the job he stopped.

walk away/off with (something)

- Take and go away with something, steal

  Somebody walked away with the computer from the library last night.

walk of life

- Social rank, occupation

People from every walk of life came to the concert in the park.

walk on air

- Feel happy and excited

  She has been walking on air since she heard that she passed her exams.

walk out

- Go on strike

  More than half of the workers at the factory decided to walk out on strike this morning.

walk out of (something)

- Leave suddenly

  Three people walked out of the meeting yesterday.

walk the floor

- Walk back and forth across the floor

  He spent the night walking the hospital floor while waiting for his wife to have a baby.

walk the plank

- Be forced to resign from a job

  The vice-president was forced to walk the plank when the new president joined the company.

walk the plank

- Be forced by pirates to walk a long plank from the ship out over the water to your death

  The pirates captured the small ship and forced the captain to walk the plank.

Chapter 4

Pronouncing Misused Words

CONFUSED WORDS

Accept and **except**. While they both sound the same, *except* is a preposition that means "apart from", while *accept* is a verb that means "agree with", "take in" or "receive". Except is also rarely used as a verb, meaning to leave out.

- *Standard*: We accept all major credit cards, except Diners Club.
- *Standard*: Men are fools... present company excepted! (Which means "present company excluded")
- *Non-standard*: I had trouble making friends with them; I never felt excepted.
- *Non-standard*: We all went swimming, accept for Jack.

Accept is a verb that means to "receive or take" or "to give a positive answer to a proposition or offer."

"Do you accept travellers' checks?" (receive, take)

Susan accepted his offer of a job. (gave a positive answer)

The club accepted three new members. (received)

Except as a preposition, meaning "with the exception of." (Commonly used)

"Everybody except John went to the party." (John didn't go)

Except as a verb means, "to exclude," "to keep out." (Rarely used)

The boys excepted Frank from their club.

(They did not accept him)

Expect is a verb that means, "waiting for sth to happen" or "believed to be the state of sth"

She expected her husband home from work at any minute.

"I expect you are hungry after such a long trip?"

accidently, slip, mistake

- ***Accidently*** *means to happen by chance*: I ***accidently*** dropped the cup. ***Slip*** means to reveal something uninten-tionally; as in a ***slip*** of the tongue. ***Mistake*** means to err in identifying; misjudge; misevaluate; an error in opinion, judgement, or perception due to inadequate knowledge, carelessness or the like; an act done unintentionally. This text may contain ***mistakes***.

all right/alright

- Although *alright* is widely used, it is considered nonstandard English. As the *American Heritage Dictionary* notes, it's not "all right to use alright."

all together/altogether

- *All together* is applied to people or things that are being treated as a group. "We put the pots and pans all together on the shelf." *All together* is the form that must be used if the sentence can be reworded so that *all* and *together* are separated by other words: "We put all the pots and pans together on the shelf." *Altogether* is used to mean entirely: "I am altogether pleased to be receiving this award."

allusion/illusion

- *Allusion* is a noun that means an indirect reference: "The speech made allusions to the final report." *Illusion* is a noun that means a misconception: "The policy is designed to give an illusion of reform."

alternately/alternatively

- *Alternately* is an adverb that means in turn; one after

the other: "We alternately spun the wheel in the game." *Alternatively* is an adverb that means on the other hand; one or the other: "You can choose a large bookcase or, alternatively, you can buy two small ones."

Acute and chronic

Acute means "sharp", as an acute illness is one that rapidly worsens and reaches a crisis. A chronic illness may also be a severe one, but it is long-lasting or lingering.

- *Standard*: She was rushed to hospital during an acute asthma attack.
- *Standard*: It is not a terminal illness, but it does cause chronic pain.
- *Non-standard*: I have suffered from acute asthma for twenty years.

Affect and effect

The verb *affect* means "to influence something", and the noun *effect* (noun) means "the result of". *Effect* can also be a somewhat formal verb that means "to cause to be".

- *Standard*: This poem affected me so much that I cried.
- *Standard*: Temperature has an effect on reaction spontaneity.
- *Standard*: The dynamite effected the wall's collapse.
- *Non-standard*: The rain effected our plans for the day.

Advice/Advise

Note spelling differences between British English and American English:

- ***Advise** is a verb*: The doctor advised her to quit smoking.
- ***Advice** is a noun*: She gave me some good advice.

adapt, adopt

- ***Adapt*** means suited to the purpose, therefore, ***adapt*** means to make suitable: The movie, Gone With

The Wind, was ***adapted*** from the novel by Margaret Mitchell. ***Adopt*** means to choose or to make one's own selection: Will the NFL ***adopt*** Canadian Football rules?

adverse, averse

- *Adverse means opposing*: The ***adverse*** weather made driving hazardous. ***Averse*** means disinclined, not wanting to: She was ***averse*** to my suggestion.

advert, avert

- *Advert means refe*r: The teacher ***adverted*** to an earlier examination. ***Avert*** means to ward off: The Bank of Canada narrowly ***averted*** a run on the dollar.

aggravate, irritate

- ***Aggravate*** means to make a bad situation worse: He***aggravated*** the situation by slamming the door. ***Irritate*** means to annoy: He ***irritated***the rash by rubbing it.

aid, aide

- *Aid means to assist and can be a verb*: John will ***aid*** Bill with the newsletter.***Aid*** can also be a noun: The rich should give ***aid*** to the poor. ***Aide*** is always a noun and means an assistant: The Prime Minister's ***aide*** refused to answer any more questions.

aloud, allowed

- *Aloud means to vocalize*: He read the poem ***aloud***. ***Allowed*** means to permit: He was ***allowed*** to go to the library.

All ready/Already

- **All ready** is an adjective phrase meaning "completely ready."' We were all ready to leave at eight o'clock.
- **Already**is an adverb of time meaning "by or before a specific time." They had already left by three o'clock.

He had already eaten when I arrived. (before I arrived)

allusion, illusion, delusion

- An ***allusion*** is an indirect reference to a statement by another (written or verbal): The reporter ***alluded*** to the mayor's speech. An ***illusion*** is something that appears to be real, but isn't: A magician's art is nothing more than***illusion*** because it is based on misdirection. A ***delusion*** is a false perception of self or others based on false beliefs: Jason though he was attractive to women, but it was only a ***delusion***.

Altogether/All Together

- **Altogether** is an adverb meaning "completely." "I am altogether upset with you."
- **All together** is an adjective phrase meaning "in a group." The children sang a song all together.

Among/Between

Use among when referring to three or more people/things, but only use between when you are referring to two people/things.

- *The conversation was **between** Shane and Lisa.*
- *The manager will divide the work **among** the four employees.*

ambiguous, ambivalent

- ***Ambiguous*** is a statement that can be misinterpreted because it is not clear: The politician was so ***ambiguous*** that no one new what he was promising to do. ***Ambivalent*** means to have mixed feelings about a person or an idea: Jayne's ***ambivalence*** over choosing what to order for lunch was annoying.

amend, emend

- ***Amend*** means to alter for the better: The minutes were ***amended*** to show the correct number of members present. ***Emend*** means to remove errors from text: Philip spent hours ***emending*** the grammatical errors in his essay.

amiable, amicable

- Amiable is used to describe people who are kind, friendly and gentle: The amiable, old man wrapped the sobbing child in his embrace. Amicable is used to describe peaceful settlements or arrangements between two parties: Management and strikers came to an amicable agreement over the contract.

among, between

- ***Among*** is used in connection with more than two: His will divided his assets equally ***among*** all of his children.
- ***Between*** is used with two people or things: The candy was divided ***between*** Alice and Mary.

Exceptions: If more than two are united in a situation, ***between*** is used: They ran fifty miles in one hour ***between*** the ten of them. If a comparison or opposition is involved, ***between*** is used: He could not choose ***between*** the grey suit or the black one. There are vast cultural differences ***between*** the ten Canadian provinces.

Assure/Ensure

Assure means **to eliminate uncertainty, fear or something troubling a person.** Ensure should be used express a guarantee of an outcome.

- *The doctor **assured** the patient that nothing was wrong with her.*
- *A college degree does not **ensure** a job good after graduation, but it helps a lot.*

Averse/Adverse

Averse means **opposed to.** Adverse means **bad or unfavourable**, such as the weather conditions.

- *I am **averse** to the death penalty.*

- *Classes were cancelled because of* ***adverse*** *weather conditions.*

Admission/Admittance

- I went to the U.S. Consulate but was refused admittance. No admission will be charged at the school concert. There is no admittance into that country without a visa.

Air/Airs

- There was air pollution near the factories. I don't like people who put on airs. There was an air of excitement when the match began.

allude/elude

- To ***"allude"*** to something is to make an indirect reference to it. ***"Elude"*** means "to avoid" or "to escape." The police report **alluded** to Jim's unusually strong sense of smell.
- Harry **eluded** Snape, thanks to his invisibility cloak.
- Daniel **alluded** to the Tollan's advanced technology.
- Merry and Pippin **eluded** the Orcs for a while.

all right/alright

Traditionally, ***"all right"*** has been properly written as two words, and many people still think that that's the only correct way. "All right" is usually an adjective, and the two-word form fits with the adjectives "all ready" and "all together," as opposed to the adverbs "already" and "altogether." However, "alright" is used fairly frequently, and many dictionaries say that it's correct. Just be aware that if you use "alright," some of your readers will be grinding their teeth, correct or not.

Alone/Lonely

- "Leave me alone", shouted John. John felt lonely when he remained alone in the house.

alter/altar

- An ***"altar"*** is a place or a table that's involved in

religious rites. Any usage besides that should be *"alter."*

- Daniel was intrigued by the hieroglyphs at the base of the **altar**.
- Qui-Gon needed to have his robes **altered**.

Almost/Most/Mostly

- She is the most intelligent student in the class. The people in Hong-Kong are mostly Chinese. Most of the students wish to have a rest after long hours of work.

anal/annals

- *"Anal"* is an adjective that means "referring to the anus." Colloquially, it can also be shorthand for "anal-retentive" and mean "parsimonious, meticulous; stick-in-the-mud." *"Annals"* is a plural noun that means "a record of events arranged in a yearly sequence; chronicles." Annals is always plural.
- Boromir had never had **anal** sex before.
- The War of The Ring was recorded in the **annals** of Gondorian history.
- Han thought Threepio was rather **anal**.

ante-/anti-

"Ante-" is a prefix meaning "before" or "front." *"Anti-"* is a prefix meaning "against" or "opposite."

- **Antebellum**: before the war (esp. the U.S. Civil War)
- **Anteroom**: a small room that leads into a larger room
- **Antediluvian**: antiquated or old-fashioned
- **Antibiotic**: a medicine that destroys micro-organisms
- **Antisocial**: antagonistic or hostile to others
- **Antiquate**: to make obsolete
- **As a whole/On the whole**

Let us take the whole incident into consideration as a whole. Jack is on the whole an industrious student.

Assure/Ensure/Insure

- The manager assures us that the recorder would be repaired properly. The owner of the goldsmith wants to insure against robbery. You must check your work carefully to ensure that you do not make any mistakes.

amount, number

- ***Amount*** *refers to quantity*: A large ***amount*** of money is wasted by the government. ***Number*** refers to things which are thought of a individual units: She bought a large ***number*** of oranges, pears, grapes and apples. Words following ***amount*** are usually singular, those following ***number*** are usually plural.

and/or

- ***And/or*** is a legal term that is quickly becoming common in current English. It is a fad best to be avoided. The word ***or*** carries the same meaning (in most cases) and does not draw attention to itself.

ante-, anti-

- These prefixes, though similar, are very different in meaning: ***Ante*** means before, as in: ***ante***chamber (a small room that comes before a larger one) ***Anti*** means against or opposed to, as in: ***Anti*** Christ, ***anti***toxin.

appraise, apprise

- ***Appraise*** *means to give value to*: The goldsmith ***appraised*** the necklace at over one thousand dollars. ***Apprise*** means to tell or inform: Joan went in to shock when ***apprised*** of the necklace's value.

apt, likely, liable

- ***Apt*** *refers to a habit*: Because of his big feet, he was ***apt*** to trip over the stairs. ***Liable*** infers the probability of something unfortunate: The President is***liable*** to lose the next election. ***Likely*** means possible: It is ***likely*** to rain tomorrow.

as, like

- When used as a preposition, ***like*** should never begin a clause: **NOT** ***like*** I said. When introducing a clause, ***as*** is used: ***As*** he said yesterday...

ascent, assent

Ascent is a noun referring to climbing or upward movement:The***ascent*** to the peak was delayed by the weather. ***Assent*** is a noun or verb having to do with agreement: The senate gave their ***assent*** to the President's budget.

averse/adverse

- *"**Averse**"* means "having an active feeling of repugnance or distaste."
- Harry was **averse** to Potions.
- Snape is **averse** to washing his hair.
- *"**Adverse**"* means "acting against or in a contrary direction" or "opposed to one's interests."
- Harry hated playing Quidditch in **adverse** weather.
- Jim's testimony was **adverse** to the DA's position.

Besides/Beside

- The preposition **besides** means "except."
- Everyone besides Jane went to the party.
- The preposition **beside** means "next to."
- Jane was standing beside me."

Not: Besides me)

Beside is a preposition that means next to: "Stand here beside me." *Besides* is an adverb that means also: "Besides, I need to tell you about the new products my company offers."

bimonthly/semimonthly

- *Bimonthly* is an adjective that means every two

months: "I brought the cake for the bimonthly office party." *Bimonthly* is also a noun that means a publication issued every two months: "The company publishes several popular bimonthlies." *Semimonthly* is an adjective that means happening twice a month: "We have semimonthly meetings on the 1st and the 15th."

Bad/Badly

Bad should be used as an adjective, and badly should be used as an adverb. More specifically, you can not feel badly about something, unless you are referring specifically to your sense of feeling, say in your fingertips.

- *I feel **bad** about missing your birthday party.* (bad is an adjective modifying the pronoun "I")
- *The football team played **badly** last Saturday.* (badly is an adverb describing how the team played)

Bare/Bear

Bare means **uncovered, naked or without supplies**. Bear is of course an animal, but it also means **to carry, to put up with or to undertake a burden.**

- *Do you believe Americans should have the right to **bear** arms?* (to carry)
- *I can't **bear** the thought of walking up at 6 a.m.* (put up with)
- ***Bears** aren't as cuddly as they may seem.* (the animal)
- *Her **bare** arms were cold.* (naked)
- *She knew it was time to go shopping because her cupboards were **bare.*** (without supplies)
- *We all **bear** the burden of paying taxes.* (to undertake a burden)

blond/blonde

"Blond" and "blonde" both refer to people with light-coloured hair. Traditionally, blond has been used for men, blonde for women. However, it's becoming more common to use "blond" to refer to someone of either gender, and you can safely use "blond" to refer to hair, regardless of the gender of its owner. I highly recommend reading ***Bartleby discussion*** of this issue, which describes the pros and cons of differentiating between the two forms. ***"Brunet"*** and "brunette" fall into the same category, although they don't seem to be used as frequently.

- Lucius Malfoy is **blond**.
- Cassie Wells is **blonde**.
- Cassie Wells has **blond** hair.

boarder/border

- A ***"boarder"*** is someone who pays for lodging that includes meals. That's it. Otherwise, use ***"border."***
- Martha had to take in **boarders** after Jonathan died.
- Harry stopped at the **border** of the Forbidden Forest.
- Daniel's love of coffee **borders** on a fixation.

borne/born

"Borne" and ***"born"*** are both past participle forms of ***"bear."*** According to dictionary, "Traditionally, born is used only in passive constructions referring to birth: *I was born in Chicago*. For all other uses, including active constructions referring to birth, borne is the standard form: *She has borne both her children at home. I have borne his insolence with the patience of a saint."*

- Lucius Malfoy was a **born** leader.
- Harry was **borne** up by his broom.
- The petals were **borne** on the wind.
- Blair was **born** in 1969.
- Jim didn't want Brackett to release the air-**borne** virus.

Bring/Take

Put simply: Use bring when you mean carrying/leading something toward something/someone and use take when you mean carrying/leading something away from something/someone.

- *Are you going to **bring** me dinner after work?*
- *Are you going to **take** this paper to her office?*

breach/breech

- *"Breeches"* are, in the US, anyway, pants that come down to the knees. In addition, a baby can be "breeched," that is, coming out legs first. That's it for "breech."
- A *"breach"* is a break of some sort. "Breach" can also be a verb, meaning "to form a breach."
- The whale **breached** the water.
- The Asgard **breached** their agreement with the SGC.
- Draco's behaviour was a **breach** of Quidditch protocol.
- Once more unto the **breach**, dear friends.

breath/breathe

- *"Breath"* is a noun and is pronounced with a soft th (like with). Most of the time it means the air one takes into and pushes out of one's lungs. It can also mean "spirit" or "suggestion," as in "the faintest breath of scandal." *"Breathe"*is a verb and is pronounced with a hard th (like father). It means, mostly, "to respire" or "to pause and rest before continuing."
- Harry used Gillyweed to **breathe** underwater during the Tri-Wizard Tournament. Obi-Wan watched as Qui-Gon drew his last **breath.**

broach/brooch

A *"brooch"* is "an ornament that is held by a pin or clasp and is worn at or near the neck." *"Broach"* is usually adverb; it can mean "to pierce," "to open up" or "to make known for the first time." If you "broach" a subject, there's a definite connotation of its being a difficult discussion. "Broach" has other, less common meanings as well, but it's never a piece of jewelry.

This is another case where British English is more strict than U.S. English—in the U.S. you can get away with using "broach" for "brooch," but anyone speaking British English would say that's incorrect.

- Hermione pinned the **brooch** to her collar.
- Obi-Wan was afraid to **broach** the subject of Anakin.
- Sam **broached** the cask of beer.

Burglary/Robbery

Burglary is a crime that involves breaking and entering to steal something, but without the confrontation between the criminal and the victim. Conversely, robbery is a crime where force or a threat is used to steal something from someone. The difference is whether or not confrontation was involved.

- *There was a **burglary** last night on Maple Street while the residents were on vacation.*
- *There was a **robbery** last night in which three people were shot.*

capital/capitol

The city or town that is the seat of government is called the *capital*; the building in which the legislative assembly meets is the *capitol*. The term *capital* can also refer to an accumulation of wealth or to a capital letter.

cite/site

Cite is a verb that means to quote as an authority or example: "I cited several eminent scholars in my study of water resources." It also means to recognize formally: "The public official was cited for service to the city." It can also mean to summon before a court of law: "Last year the company was cited for pollution violations." *Site* is a noun meaning location: "They chose a new site for the factory just outside town."

complement/compliment

Complement is a noun or verb that means something that completes or makes up a whole: "The red sweater is a perfect complement to the outfit." *Compliment* is a noun or verb that means an expression of praise or admiration: "I received compliments about my new outfit."

comprise/compose

According to the traditional rule, the whole comprises the

parts, and the parts compose the whole. Thus, the board comprises five members, whereas five members compose (or make up) the board. It is also correct to say that the board is composed (not comprised) of five members.

cannon/canon

A ***"cannon"*** is a very large gun. ***"Canon"***, in fandom, is usually used to mean the characterizations and events that are taken directly from the source. In the dictionary, "canon" means "an accepted principle or rule." (It can also refer to the accepted list of books of the Bible, or to a song like "Row, Row, Row Your Boat.") In fandom, you almost always want to use "canon," even though it seems like no one else does. They're all wrong.

concurrent/consecutive

Concurrent is an adjective that means simultaneous or happening at the same time as something else: "The concurrent strikes of several unions crippled the economy. "*Consecutive* means successive or following one after the other: "The union called three consecutive strikes in one year."

choose/chose/chosen

- ***"Choose"*** - present tense "Chose" - past tense "Chosen" - past participle
- I **choose** not to go on the roller coaster. (present)
- Qui-Gon **chose** Obi-Wan as his padawan. (past)
- Jim was **chosen** Detective of the Year. (past participle)

connote/denote

Connote is a verb that means to imply or suggest: "The word 'espionage' connotes mystery and intrigue." *Denote* is a verb that means to indicate or refer to specifically: "The symbol for 'pi' denotes the number 3.14159."

convince/persuade

Strictly speaking, one convinces a person that something is true but persuades a person to do something. "Pointing out that I was overworked, my friends persuaded [not convinced] me to take a vacation. Now that I'm relaxing on the beach with my book, I am convinced [not persuaded] that they were right." Following this rule, *convince* should not be used with an infinitive.

council/councilor/counsel/counselor

A *councilor* is a member of a *council,* which is an assembly called together for discussion or deliberation. A *counselor* is one who gives *counsel,* which is advice or guidance. More specifically, a *counselor* can be an attorney or a supervisor at camp.

compliment/complement

- A ***"compliment"*** is when someone says something nice to you. Plural, it means best wishes, as in "**compliments** of the season." As a verb, "compliment" means "to pay a compliment to." Everything else is ***"complement"***. It usually has to do with something that makes a thing complete, or the number required to make something complete.
- Jack **complimented** Daniel on his translating skills.
- "Was that a **compliment** I just got from Jack?" Daniel wondered.
- Harry's dress robes **complemented** his eyes.
- The ship's entire complement disembarked for shore leave.

congratulations/congradulations

It's spelled ***congratulations***. With a "t". This is one that drives me absolutely up the wall.

conscious/conscience/conscientious/unconscionable

- *"Conscious"* is an adjective with several meanings, mostly relating to being awake and aware.
- *"Conscientious"* is also an adjective, but it means "governed by or conforming to the dictates of conscience," or scrupulous, meticulous or careful.

- ***"Unconscionable"*** is another adjective. It means "not guided or controlled by conscience: unscrupulous."
- Finally, ***"conscience"*** is a noun that means, well, Jiminy Cricket. It's that little voice that tells you whether you're behaving.

It's tough keeping all these words straight, because they're all related, but it's important. People who know the difference will be very jarred if you get them wrong.

- Harry's **conscience** nagged him after he snuck into Hogsmeade without permission.
- Blair became **conscious** in the ambulance
- Obi-Wan was **conscious** of Qui-Gon's anger.
- Hermione is very **conscientious** in Potions class.
- Leaving Anakin in slavery would have been **unconscionable**.

couldn't care less/could care less

The phrase ***"couldn't care less"*** means that one has the lowest possible level of interest in something. Taken literally, "could care less" means just the opposite—that one does have some sort of interest. However, people do say they *could* care less when they really mean they *couldn't,* and some American sources say this is accepted usage. In writing, using "could" instead of "couldn't" tends to lead to confusion. "Could care less" is much more informal; some characters might use it in dialogue, but, in general, it's safer to stick with "couldn't care less," which can't be misunderstood.

Note that ***using "could care less" is an American thing***. British characters would use the proper phrase, "couldn't care less." And British readers will probably think you made a mistake if you use "could care less."

Cloth/Clothes

- **Cloth** is a noun (usually as a non-count noun) that means "material or fabric." She bought some cloth to make a new dress.
- **Clothes** is a plural count noun meaning "garments used to cover the body."

She bought a lot of clothes in Paris.
I feel nice when I wear new clothes.

Can/May

Can is used when meaning ability and may is used when meaning permission.

- ***May** I please leave class early?*
- ***Can** you do 15 pushups?*

Cant and can't.

There are several meanings for the word *cant* (without an apostrophe); however, none of them is "unable to". One meaning of *cant* is "a kind of slang or jargon spoken by a particular group of people". *Can't* is a contraction of *cannot.*

- *Standard*: I can't understand the dialogue in this book because it's written in cant.
- *Non-standard*: I cant swim; I've never taken lessons.

Compose/Comprise

The rule is that parts compose the whole, while the whole is composed of the parts.

- *Peanut butter, jelly and bread* **compose** *a peanut butter and jelly sandwich.*
- *A peanut butter and jelly sandwich is* **comprised** *of peanut butter, jelly and bread.*

Complimentary/Complementary

- Complimentary is an adjective which means "given freely, or giving praise" The teacher was very **complimentary** about my work. Complementary is an adjective, which means, "supplying needs"
- The **complementary** relationship of the bee and the flower is quite remarkable.

Cause/Reason

What are the causes of their quarrel?
What is your reason for studying in this school?

Charge/Cost/Price/Value/Worth

- These books cost a lot of money.
- These books are worth a lot of money.
- The price of the books has been raised recently.
- An antique has no value if it is broken.
- We did not need to pay any service charge after using the hall.

censure, criticize

- To ***censure*** always expresses disapproval. To ***criticize*** may be neutral, expressing approval of some parts and disapproval of others.

cents, scents, sense

- ***Cents*** refers to money, usually small coins I have a few ***cents***in my pocket.. ***Scents*** refers to smell, or odors: The ***scents*** of roses and wood smoke dominated the evening breeze.***Sense*** refers to one of the five senses; to feel something: I ***sensed*** his approach even though I could not see him

chose, choose

- ***Chose*** in legal terms means an incorporeal right enforceable by legal action, as in a franchise. ***Chose*** is also used to indicate someone has made a choice: He chose the red truck. The ***Choose*** means to select from a number, or in preference to another or others. Choose one of the following: Red, Blue, Green, or Yellow.

cite, site, sight

- To ***cite*** is to make a reference to a specific original source. The noun***site*** refers to a specific piece of ground where a building is or will be erected: The ***site*** of the new playground. ***Sight*** refers to: vision, a field of vision, something worth seeing, a shocking or spectacular event, an observation from surveying instruments or sextants, the guides on a firearm.

claim, assert

- *Claim* refers to a legal or justified demand: He *claimed* the first piece of cake. ***Assert*** means to come forward and assume one's rights: The President*asserted* that he was innocent of all charges.

compare to, compare with

- ***Compare to*** is used to indicate a definite resemblance: Compared ***to*** last year, this year's sales are better. ***Compare with*** is used to indicate an examination of similarities and dissimilarities: He compared Bill Gates ***with*** Socrates.

complement, compliment

- ***Complement*** is something that fills up or completes: Black Forest Cake is a decadent ***complenent*** to any meal! A***compliment*** is an expression of praise: He ***complimented*** her new hair style.

comprehensible, comprehensive

- ***Comprehensible*** means able to be understood: Although the manual contained technical language, it was ***comprehensible***. ***Comprehensive*** means to include all, or covering a wide range: The ***comprehensive*** study of the art of writing does not necessarily lead to a best selling novel.

compulsion, compunction

- ***Compulsion*** means forced to comply or a strong, irresistible impulse to carry out an act: She was ***compelled*** to eat the cherries.***Compunction*** (noun) means to feel shame, unhappiness, guilt, or regret for one's actions: He filled with ***compunction*** at the thought of cheating on his wife.

confidant, confident

A *confidant* (*confidante,* if female) is a trusted friend.

Confident means you are certain: You were ***confident*** that your story would sell.

congenital, congenial

- ***Congenital*** means existing in an individual from birth.***Congenial*** refers to a person who is agreeable, pleasing, compatible, or sympathetic.

connotation, denotation

- ***Denotation*** refers to the exact meaning of a word as found in a dictionary. ***Connotation*** refers to what the word suggests beyond it's dictionary meaning: Damsel ***denotes*** a young woman, but ***connotes*** a a beautiful maiden from the centre ages who is usually in distress.

consensus

- ***Consensus*** means a general agreement or majority of opinion. Many of today's respected newspapers misspell the word as concensus. Note: The phrase: ***Concensus of opinion*** is redundant and should NOT be used.

contemptible, contemptuous

- ***Contemptible*** means worthy of contempt; deserving scorn or disdain; mean; vile: When Jason punched his wife, his actions were ***contemptible***. ***Contemptuous*** means to express contempt or disdain; scornful: He stared at the politician with a ***contemptuous*** frown.

continual, continuous

- A ***continual*** action is one that occurs over a long period of time, with pauses or intermissions: He ***continually*** called attention to her poor posture. A ***continuous*** action occurs without the the pauses: The tap leaked in a***continuous*** stream. **council, counsel** To ***counsel*** is to give advice: He ***counselled*** her to wait for the bylaw to be passed. As a noun, ***counsel*** means advice: I sought legal ***counsel*** after the car accident. ***Council*** is a group of people who act in an advisory capacity, or meet for discussions or decision making: They submitted their proposal to the mayor's ***council***

credible, credulous

- ***Credible*** means capable of being believed: He gave a***credible*** rendition of Elvis' love song, Love Me Tender. ***Credulous*** means willing to believe without sufficient evidence, easily deceived, gullible: a con man's ***credulous***victim

councilor, counselor

- A ***councilor*** is a member of a council. A ***counselor*** is one who gives advice.

Clash/Crash

- What a pity that the two meetings clash.
- He saw a bus crash into the lamp post.
- Ann and Mary often quarrel because their ideas often clash.

Cloth/Clothing/Clothes

- John cleaned the table with a cloth.
- He laid a cloth on the ground and put down some clothes.
- Her clothes got wet after the rain.
- I don't like wearing thick clothing in winter.

Compose/Comprise/Consist

- The class club committee comprises eight members.
- The class club committee consists of eight members.
- The committee is composed of teachers and students.

Compare to/Compare with

- You may compare your work with David's and see which is better.

- Your work is nothing compared with David's.
- Many poets like to compare life to morning dew.

Concern/Concerning/Concern

- All the classmates are concerned about his health.
- The topic is concerned with careless driving.
- They are discussing something concerning the youth problem.

Continual/Continuous

- The continual rain made us feel bored.
- They enjoyed a continuous performance till midnight.

Copy/Imitate

- You should not copy your neighbour's answers.
- The teacher advised his students not to imitate him.

Credible/Credulous/Incredible

- That is really an incredible story. I don't think it's real one.
- He is such a credulous man that he often believes what you say.
- Did the committee find his statement credible?

cue/queue

A ***"queue"*** is a line of people or things. To "queue," or "queue up," means to get in line, or to form a line. (A queue can, incidentally, also be a braid, but it's not used that way very often—unless you're in an Age of Sail fandom.)

As a verb, ***"cue"*** means "to prompt" or "to position in readiness for playing" or "to insert into a continuous performance." A "cue" is a signal or a hint, or the stick you use to play pool with.

These get kind of tricky sometimes. You could queue a list of songs on your iPod, but most likely you cue a song. When a director brings in an instrument, he's cuing.

Damage/Injure/Hurt/Wound

- He hurt his leg after jumping down from a tree.

- Many huts are damaged by the fire.
- A tall man hurt him with an axe.
- Many fire victims were injured and taken to hospital.

defuse/diffuse

"Defuse" means "to remove the fuse from," or "to make less harmful, potent, or tense." ***"Diffuse,"*** as a verb, refers to spreading out or thinning.

When Harry and Draco pulled out their wands, Dumbledore stepped in to **defuse** the situation.

The nerve gas **diffused** throughout the room.

desert/dessert

A ***"dessert"*** is a sweet course or a fruit course served at the end of a meal. So far so good.

"Desert" can be a verb, in which case the accent is on the second syllable, and it means "to leave in the lurch" or "to abandon," especially in the military. As a noun, "desert" is usually pronounced with the accent on the first syllable, and it means "an arid land with sparse vegetation," or "a desolate or forbidding area."

However, "desert" has another meaning that most people aren't aware of. As a noun, it can be pronounced with the accent on the second syllable, like "dessert," and in that case it means "a deserved reward or punishment." So it's actually "just deserts," *not* "just desserts."

When Malfoy ended up in the infirmary, Hermione thought he had got his just **deserts**.

Jack was tired of having pie for **dessert**.

Most of "Lawrence of Arabia" takes place in the **desert**.

The soldier was court-martialed for **deserting** his unit.

deduce, deduct

Deduce means to draw a conclusion from something known or assumed: That may be *deduced* from the statistics. *Deduct* means to subtract, or infer: *Deduct* my contribution from my pay check.

deprecate, depreciate

- *Deprecate* means to plead or argue against; express strong disapproval: His ***deprecatory*** speech had the audience in an uproar. ***Depreciate*** means to bring down the price or value of: The accountant ***depreciated*** the value of the truck.

desert, dessert

- This is usually a spelling error. ***Desert*** means a region of rock or sand that receives very little or no precipitation. ***Dessert*** means something (usually sweet) that is served after the main course.

detract, distract

- ***Detract*** means to take away a part or lessen: Her gaudy clothes***detract*** from her beauty. ***Distract*** means to divert, confound, or harass; to provide a diversion: Her attention was ***distracted*** by the birds in the feeder.

different from

- ***Different from*** is the correct idiom, NOT ***different than.***

differ from, differ with

- ***Differ from*** applies to differences between one person or things and others: My stove ***differs from*** hers because it is self-cleaning. ***Differ with*** means to have a difference in opinion: His views on politics ***differed with*** mine.

discover, invent

- To ***discover*** is to find or uncover something already in existence, but unknown: Franklin ***discovered*** electricity. To ***invent*** is to create something new: Edison ***invented*** the light bulb.

discreet, discrete

- *Discreet* means prudent in conduct; cautious; heedful;

guarded: He was ***discreet*** with his money. ***Discrete*** means separate or distinct from others: Each grain of rice was ***discrete,*** not clinging to the rest in a sticky pile.

disinterested, uninterested

Disinterested means impartial; unconcerned: He was ***disinterested*** with the weather report. ***Uninterested*** means not interested; indifferent; not personally concerned: He sat like a lump, ***uninterested*** in the world around him.

Disinterested/Uninterested

A disinterested judge is said to make a fair judgment.
He is uninterested in dancing.

discreet/discrete

- *Discreet* is an adjective that means prudent, circumspect, or modest: "Her discreet handling of the touchy situation put him at ease." *Discrete* is an adjective that means separate or individually distinct: "Each company in the conglomerate operates as a discrete entity."

disinterested/uninterested

- *Disinterested* is an adjective that means unbiased or impartial: "We appealed to the disinterested mediator to facilitate the negotiations." *Uninterested* is an adjective that means not interested or indifferent: "They seemed uninterested in our offer."

Divide/Share

John shared the books among themselves.
The teacher divided the students into four groups.

Desert/Dessert

- A **desert** is "a dry area with little vegetation and rainfall." The Sahara desert in Africa is the largest in the world.

- A **dessert** is "sweet food usually eaten after a meal." We had chocolate cake and ice cream for dessert.

Different from/Different than

Different from is a preposition, which precedes a noun phrase

- He is **different from** your average shop owner.

Different than is a preposition which precedes a noun clause

- London is**different than** we had imagined.

Differ from/Differ with

- To **differ from** is "to be dissimilar." Men differ from women physically.
- To **differ with** is "to disagree with." I differ with you on this issue. (I disagree with you)

elicit/illicit

- *Elicit* is a verb that means to draw out. *Illicit* is an adjective meaning unlawful. "No matter how hard I tried to elicit a few scandalous stories from her, she kept all knowledge of illicit goings-on discreetly to herself. "

emigrant/immigrant

- *Emigrant* is a noun that means one who leaves one's native country to settle in another: "The emigrants spent four weeks aboard ship before landing in Los Angeles." *Immigrant*is a noun that means one who enters and settles in a new country: "Most of the immigrants easily found jobs." One emigrates *from* a place; one immigrates *to* another.

Enough

Enough is an adverb, which precedes a noun and follows an adjective:

- He knows **enough** English to study in England.
- She is fast**enough** to win the race.

Every so often/Ever so often

Every so often is an adverb meaning "occasionally"

- They come **every so often**. I wish they could come more frequently.
  Ever so often is an adverb meaning "frequently"
- They come **ever so often**. I wish they would stay home.

Emigrate/Immigrate

- To **emigrate** means, "to leave one country to live in another."
  My grandfather emigrated from Europe to the USA in 1864.
- To **immigrate** means, "to move to a new country."
  Many immigrants living in Greece work on farms and in construction.
- It's probably **easiest** to remember that to emigrate means to leave a country while immigrate means to enter to live.

Economic/Economical/Economics/Economy

- Mrs. Young is said to be an **economical** housekeeper.
- He is going to study **economics** in the university.
- Tourism plays an important part in the **economy** of Greece.
- The **economic** indicators say we are headed towards a depression.

Eligible/Legible

- She is **eligible** for promotion due to her hard work and dedication.
- Mr. Kontogeorgakis' handwriting is almost not **legible**.

elicit, illicit

- *Elicit* means to bring out or draw forth: His comments ***elicited*** groans from the audience. ***Illicit*** means unlawful: His ***illicit*** affair broke up their marriage.

eminent, imminent

- *Eminent* means famous or prominent as in: His *Eminence,* The Pope. *Imminent* means soon to take place: The Christmas concert is *imminent.*

enormity, enormousness

- *Enormousness* refers to something of extraordinarily large size. *Enormity,* used to describe something monstrously evil should never be confused with *enormousness.*

Eminent/Imminent

- Dr. Chevereney is an **eminent** surgeon in our city.
- Most people were in a hurry to go home as a typhoon was **imminent.**

Equal/Identical/Similar

- The tow applicants are of **equal** ability.
- Your book is **similar** to the one that I lost last week.
- They are surprised to find that their shirts are **identical.**

Error/Mistake

- I took his book by **mistake.**
- An **error** of judgment can be disastrous.
  There are so many **errors** in this letter I don't understand it.

Exciting/Excited/Excitement

- The boys became **excited** when they watched such an **exciting** basketball match.
- When they heard that he had passed the examination, he jumped up and down out of **excitement.**

exacerbate/exasperate

- *"Exacerbate"* means "to make more violent, brutal or severe." *"Exasperate"* means "to excite the anger of," or "to cause irritation or annoyance to." In general, people are exasperated; situations are exacerbated. Make sure you're using the right one.

- Jim was **exasperated** by Blair's sloppiness.
- Closing the factory will **exacerbate** unemployment problems.

Everyday/Every Day

- What do you do **every** day?
- John seems to be very busy with **everyday** work.
- She writes ten letters **every day**.

Fare/Fee

- A student has to pay the **fare** when he takes a bus.
- The **fare** is more by taxi than by minibus.
- When will the students pay the school **fee**?

Farther/Further

- **Farther** means "towards a more distant point in space." (actual distance)
  The beach is a few miles farther away.
- **Further** means "towards a more distant point in time, degree, or quantity." (figurative distance)
  Let us consider this problem a bit further. (time)
  We should do further research on this matter. (quantity)
  Be careful not to excite the children any further. (degree)

farther, further

- *Farther* means more remote; more distant: He threw the ball *farther* than anyone else. *Further* means at or to a more advanced point in time; to forward , as a work: He was *further* along with the count than expected.

fewer, less

- *Fewer* pertains to a smaller number: *fewer* oranges,

fewer girls, *fewer*cars. *Less* means a smaller amount or quantity: *less* money, *less* coal, *less* weight.

flotsam, jetsam

Flotsam means wreckage found afloat. *Jetsam* means objects thrown overboard and then washed ashore.

Flout and **flaunt**. One *flouts* a rule or law by flagrantly ignoring it. One *flaunts* something by showing it off.

- *Standard*: If you've got it, flaunt it.
- *Standard*: He continually flouted the speed limit.
- *Non-standard*: If you've got it, flout it.
- *Non-standard*: He continually flaunted the speed limit.

fiancé/fiancée

- A *"fiancé"* is a male person who's engaged to be married. If the person is female, it's *"fiancée"*. In English, both these words tend to be used without the acute accents fairly often, just because accents are hard to type on an English keyboard. Technically, though, the words are borrowed from French, and the accent is correct.
- Before they were married, Carolyn was Jim's **fiancée**, and Jim was Carolyn's **fiancé**.

flaunt/flout

"Flaunt" means "to display or obtrude oneself to public notice" or "to display ostentatiously or impudently." It generally has to do with showiness and attention-getting. *"Flout"* means "to treat with contemptuous disregard" or "to indulge in scornful behaviour." In the U.S., it's not uncommon to see "flaunt" used in place of "flout," and not all dictionaries say this is non-standard, but if you use "flaunt" in this way, many readers will think it's wrong.

- Harry was known for **flouting** Professor Snape's rules.
- Amidala tried not to **flaunt** her expensive clothes.
- Hermione sometimes **flaunts** her knowledge.

Formally/Formerly

- **Formally** means "in a formal way."
  He was formally charged with the crime.
- **Formerly** means "previously," or "at an earlier time."
  She was formerly a dancer in a club.

fallow/follow

"Fallow" has several uses, mostly, relating to farming. If a farmer decides not to plant in a particular field one season, he's letting that field lie fallow. It's much more likely that you want to use *"follow"*, which means, generally, to come after something, or to obey something.

- Farmer McDonald decided to let twenty acres lie **fallow** this year.
- Don't forget to **follow** the directions.

forceful, forcible

- *Forceful* means powerful; vigourous; effective: His *forceful*personality dominated the interview. *Forcible* means exercising force or by force or violence: He made a *forcible* entry into the hose by kicking down the door.

former, latter

- *Former* and *latter* are used to designate one of two persons or things: When given a choice between chocolate and ice cream, I prefer the *former* to the *latter*. If more than two things or people are involved: He had the choice of coffee, tea, juice or milk. He preferred the *first* and *last* to the others.

fortuitous, fortunate

- *Fortuitous* means an event which happens by accident that may or may not be favourable. *Fortunate* means lucky or receiving good from an uncertain or unexpected source.

founder, flounder

- *Founder* is a nautical term referring to the collapsing

or sinking of a boat. ***Flounder*** means to move clumsily or to struggle to gain footing: The horse ***floundered*** in the deep snow.

fulsome

- ***Fulsome*** means excessive and insincere. NEVER use it to mean plentiful. The critic gave ***fulsome*** praise to the sculpture, which angered the artist.

First/Former

First as an adjective refers to three or more items:

- The **first** five skiers fell.
- Former as an adjective refers to two or fewer items
- The **former** Secretary of State for the U.S., Colin Powel, was the first black to hold that position.

From/Since/For

- **From** is a preposition followed by a noun or noun phrase.
  As a time marker, it requires **to** or another preposition.
  From now on I will lead the way.
  From Monday **to** Friday, I work like a slave.
- **Since** is a subordinate conjunction followed by a clause.
  It expresses "the time something began" or "the beginning of time"
  Since Wednesday, I have walked 6 miles a day.
- **For** is a preposition followed by a noun or noun phrase.
  It expresses "the length of time (**duration**) something has lasted."
  For two weeks I have walked to work every day.

farther/further

- ***Farther*** is an adjective and adverb that means to or at a more distant point: "We drove 50 miles today;

tomorrow, we will travel 100 miles farther." ***Further*** is an adjective and adverb that means to or at a greater extent or degree: "We won't be able to suggest a solution until we are further along in our evaluation of the problem." It can also mean in addition or moreover: "They stated further that they would not change the policy."

few/less

- *Few* is an adjective that means small in number. It is used with countable objects: "This department has few employees." **Less** is an adjective that means small in amount or degree. It is used with objects of indivisible mass: "Which jar holds less water?"

figuratively/literally

- **Figuratively** is an adverb that means metaphorically or symbolically: "Happening upon the shadowy figure, they figuratively jumped out of their shoes." **Literally** is an adverb that means actually: "I'm not exaggerating when I say I literally fell off my chair." It also means according to the exact meaning of the words: "I translated the Latin passage literally."

flammable/inflammable

- These two words are actually synonyms, both meaning easily set on fire. The highly flammable (inflammable) fuel was stored safely in a specially built tank. Use nonflammable to mean *not* flammable.

flaunt/flout

- To **flaunt** means to show off shamelessly: "Eager to flaunt her knowledge of a wide range of topics, Helene dreamed of appearing on a TV trivia show." To **flout** means to show scorn or contempt for: "Lewis disliked boarding school and took every opportunity to flout the house rules."

foreword/forward

- ***Foreword*** is a noun that means an introductory note or preface: "In my foreword I explained my reasons for writing the book." **Forward** is an adjective or adverb that means toward the front: "I sat in the forward section of the bus." "Please step forward when your name is called." *Forward* is also a verb that means to send on: "Forward the letter to the customer's new address."

founder/flounder

- In its primary sense **founder** means to sink below the surface of the water: "The ship foundered after colliding with an iceberg." By extension, *founder* means to fail utterly. **Flounder** means to move about clumsily, or to act with confusion. A good synonym for*flounder* is blunder: "After floundering through the first half of the course, Amy finally passed with the help of a tutor."

hanged/hung

- **Hanged** is the past tense and past participle of hang when the meaning is to execute by suspending by the neck: "They hanged the prisoner for treason." "The convicted killer was hanged at dawn." **Hung** is the past tense and participle of hang when the meaning is to suspend from above with no support from below: "I hung the painting on the wall." "The painting was hung at a crooked angle."

Healthful/Healthy

- **Healthful** means "good for ones health."
  Vegetables and fruits are healthful foods.
- **Healthy** means "in a good condition of health."
  Due to their outdoor lifestyle, all of his children are healthy.

Hang/Hanged/Hung

- Last night the criminal was **hanged** to death.

- John **hung** a picture on the wall a few minutes ago.

Handed/Hand

- He took her by the **hand** to cross the street.
- John was **handed** an award for being on time all semester long.

Hard/Hardly

- **Hardly** had he finished his work when the bell rang.
- He could **hardly** see in darkness.
- He tried **hard** to improve himself.

Hire/Let/Rent

- This house is not to **let**.
- The young couple **rented** a flat in the building.
- They **hired** a truck to take the furniture to their new flat.
- Hear, hear!/Here, here!

historic/historical

- In general usage, **historic** refers to what is important in history, while **historical** applies more broadly to whatever existed in the past whether it was important or not: "a historic summit meeting between the prime ministers;" "**historical** buildings torn down in the redevelopment."

Hope/Expect/Wish

- I don't **expect** to see him at the airport next Monday. What do you expect him to do?
- I **wish** I could help you to solve the problem. She **hopes** she will be admitted to the university.

hoard/horde

- ***"Horde"*** is a noun, meaning "a teeming crowd or throng."
- Genghis Khan led the Mongolian **hordes**.
- Anakin was amazed by the **horde** of people on Coruscant.

- The noun *"hoard"* means "a supply or fund stored up and often hidden away." Hoard can also be used as a verb, meaning "to lay up a hoard of."
- Harry needed to access his **hoard** of Galleons.
- Squirrels **hoard** acorns for the winter.
- Hermione **hoarded** her thoughts.

Illusion/Allusion

- An **illusion** is "a false idea" or "unreal image." The magician's illusion convinced the crowd that he was flying.
- An **allusion** is "an indirect reference." The professor made an allusion to modern art. Imply/Infer
- To **imply** is "to suggest without saying directly." A speaker or writer can imply. Susan implied that she was not happy with her studies.
- To **infer** is to "to make a conclusion based on evidence not stated." Only a listener or reader can infer. I inferred from the report that our taxes would be raised again.

It's and its.

It's is a contraction that replaces *it is* or *it has* (see apostrophe). *Its* is the possessive pronoun corresponding to *it,* in the same way that *his* corresponds to *he.* In standard written English, possessive **nouns** take an apostrophe, but possessive **pronouns** do not.

- *Standard*: It's time to eat!
- *Standard*: My cell phone has poor reception because its antenna is broken.
- *Standard*: It's been nice getting to meet you.
- *Non-standard*: Its good to be the king.
- *Non-standard*: The bicycle tire had lost all it's pressure.

Its is the singular possessive pronoun for things.

The car had its tires stolen last night.
It's is the contraction for "it is."
It's a nice day today. (It is a nice day today.)

Imaginary/Imagination/Imaginative

- This story was about an **imaginary** situation.
- Why does John have so much **imagination**?
- He's got an **imaginative** mind.

Interesting/Interested/Interest

- These story books do not seem to **interest** the students.
- He is very **interested** in taking photographs.
- You can never find this book **interesting** if you don't read it.

i.e./e.g.

- The abbreviation *e.g.* means for example (from Latin *exempli gratia)*: "Her talents were legion and varied (e.g., deep sea diving, speed reading, bridge, and tango dancing)." The abbreviation *i.e.* means that is or in other words (from Latin *id est):* "The joy of my existence (i.e., my stamp collection) imbues my life with meaning."

Insist/Persist

- John **insisted** on going for a walk despite the heavy rain outside.
- The boy **persisted** in his plan though it was not very practical.

Intense/Intensive

- Most of the onlookers felt hot because of the **intense** heat.
- Last year I took an **intensive** course in Japanese.

in spite of, despite

- ***In spite of*** means in opposition to all efforts of; notwithstanding: We held the picnic ***in spite of*** the rain. ***Despite*** means the same, but is written or spoken as: ***Despite*** the rain, we held the picnic. ***Despite*** also means extreme malice; contemptuous hate; and act of spite or contempt: His voice full of***despite***, he said, "You will pay for that!"

imply, infer

- ***Imply*** means to indicate more than the words plainly say; to hint: The politician's smile ***implied*** he could be trusted to keep his promises. ***Infer*** means to draw a conclusion; as by reasoning; to deduce; to indicate as a conclusion: The reporter ***inferred*** from his manner that the politician was sincere.

impracticable, impractical

- ***Impracticable*** means unfeasible; unmanageable; not useful for an intended purpose. ***Impractical*** means not taking a common sense view; not workable: He was ***impractical***, always wasting his allowance on candy.

intense, intensive

- ***Intense*** means stretched out or tight; existing or occurring in a high or or extreme degree: She blushed, unable to endure the ***intense*** passion in his gaze. ***Intensive*** means increasing in intensity or degree, more labourious. expensive or concentrated methods of cultivation: As in ***Intensive*** Care Unit of a hospital.

invaluable, priceless

- ***Invaluable*** means having a value so great that its worth cannot be evaluated. ***Priceless*** means having a value beyond all price; or in slang, very amusing or absurd.

its, it's

- ***Its*** (no apostrophe) is the possessive case of ***it***: ***Its*** tail was too long. ***It's*** is the contraction of ***it is***: ***It's*** too soon to tell.

Journey/Voyage/Tour/Trip

- We shall take a **trip** to Vienna on Sunday.
- Mr. Chan had a tour in Europe during the summer **vacation**.
- How long does a **journey** from Chicago to New York take?
- One of the **tourists** caught a cold on the voyage.

kind of, sort of, type of, variety of

- Never use ***a*** or ***an*** after these expressions: ***Variety of an apple*** is confusing because ***an*** is used for one particular member of a class. ***Variety of apple*** is preferable because apple by itself correctly refers to the general idea of apple.

Lay

Lay (*lay, laid, laid, laying*) and **lie** (*lie, lay, lain, lying*) are often confused. *Lay* is a transitive verb, meaning that it takes an object. "To lay something" means to place something. *Lie,* on the other hand, is intransitive and means to recline (and also to tell untruths, but in this case the verb is regular and causes no confusion). The distinction between these related verbs is further confused by the fact that past tesne of *lie* is *lay*. A quick test is to see if the word in question could be replaced with *recline*; if it can you should use *lie*.

- *Standard*: I lay my husband's work clothes out for him every morning. Yesterday I decided to see if he paid attention to what I was doing, so I laid out one white sock and one black. He didn't notice!
- *Standard*: You should not lie down right after eating a large meal. Yesterday I lay on my bed for half an hour after dinner, and suffered indigestion as a result. My wife saw me lying there and made me get up, she told me that if I had waited for a couple of hours I could have lain down in perfect comfort.

- *Non-standard*: Is this bed comfortable when you lay on it?
- *Non-standard*: Yesterday I laid down in my office during the lunch hour.
- *Non-standard*: There was no reason for him to have laid down in the middle of the path, it unnerved me to see him laying there saying nothing. (Should be "have lain down" and "him lying there")

Loathe

Often incorrectly used for 'loth' or 'loath' in phrases such as "She was loathe to accept." 'Loathe' is only properly used as a verb.

Leave/Let

- To **leave** means, "to go away from."
  He leaves work at five o'clock every day.
- To **let** means, "to permit."
  Jane let me borrow her bike.

lead/led

Let's start with the most common verb form of ***"lead"***: It's pronounced *leed,* with a long e, and it means, more or less, "to guide," "to direct," or "to be first." So far so good. Its past tense is ***"led,"*** pronounced with a short e. So, "lead"=present, "led"=past. Sounds easy, right?

The reason this gets confusing is that "lead" can also be a noun. With a long e it means "the person in front" or "leash" or "the first card played" or "the distance a base runner is from the base," as well as some others. But it can also be pronounced with a short e, in which case it's the metal that's in a pencil. (Or was, before lead poisoning, but anyway.) So because "lead" can properly be pronounced with a short e, it's easy to think that that's how the past tense of the verb is spelled—but it's not.

- Harry **leads** his year in detentions
- Jack has **led** SG-1 into some interesting situations.
- The **lead** in my pencil needs sharpening.

- Why isn't your dog on a **lead**?
- You can **lead** a horse to water, but you can't make him drink.
- Jim **led** Blair to the temple.

leech/leach

"Leech" is a noun, meaning an aquatic bloodsucking worm. As a verb, it means to apply leeches to someone, as a method of bloodletting. Ninety-five per cent of the time, this is the only meaning 'leech' should have. (The other five per cent: if you write Age of Sail fic, "leech" can mean "the vertical edge of a square sail;" if you write LotR or medieval fic, "leech" is an archaic word for "physician," and can also can mean "to heal.") *"Leach"* is a verb. It means "to percolate a liquid through some material"; its subject may be the liquid or the person causing the action; its object may be the material the liquid goes through, or the substance it dissolves and carries away. "**Leach**" may also be used figuratively, if you want to talk about some intangible quality (e.g., courage) being taken away.

As a rule of thumb, if it's a verb, you probably want "leach"; if it's a noun, you probably want "leech."

- **Leeches** lived in the mud by the lakeshore and would attack any student who went wading.
- Théoden to Gríma: "Your **leechcraft** ere long would have had me crawling on all fours like a beast."
- Snape **leached** the phoenix ashes of their magical components.
- Rain has **leached** nutrients from the topsoil.
- The dementors closed in on the house, **leaching** warmth and courage from everyone inside.

Loose/Lose

- The adjective **loose** means "not tight."
- This shirt is too loose. I need a smaller size.
- To **lose** is a verb meaning "to leave (forget) behind by accident"
- I often lose my house keys.

lie/lay

Everyone's favourite. Basically, *"lie"* is ***intransitive,*** meaning it doesn't have an object. *"**Lay**"*is ***transitive,*** which means it does have an object. (Yes, lay does have some intransitive usages, too, but they're not the ones that get confused with lie.) So, you lay something on a table. You lay down your cards. You lay the baby in the crib. But when you go to bed, you lie down. You lie in wait. You lay a book on the desk, and then the book lies on the desk.

This is made more complicated by the various forms of these verbs.

- **Lie**: Past tense, lay; past participle, lain
- **Present**: *I lie down.*
- **Past**: *I lay down.*
- **Past participle**: *I have lain down.*
- **Lay**: past tense, laid; past participle, laid
- **Present**: *I lay the book on the table.*
- **Past**: *I laid the book on the table.*
- **Past participle**: *I have laid the book on the table.*

Then there's the other meaning of "lie": "to make an untrue statement." Its forms are different from those of the other "lie":

- Past tense, lied; past participle, lied
- **Present**: *She lies habitually—she never tells the truth.*
- **Past**: *She lied to her teacher.*
- *Past participle: She has lied to everyone.*

Both forms of "lie," however, have the same present participle: "lying."

I am lying on my bed.

I am lying about my age.

- Harry **lies** in his bed, waiting.
- Harry **lay** in his bed, waiting. (past tense of "lie")
- Ron **lays** the scroll in front of Hermione.
- Ron **laid** the scroll in front of Hermione.
- Harry's Gringotts vault **lies** deep below ground.
- The route **lies** to the west.
- Ginny **lays** the table for dinner.
- Draco **lied** to his father.

"Sit" and ***"set"*** work the same way: "Sit" and "lie" are used similarly, as are "set" and "lay."

I'm **sitting** in the chair.

Please **set** the papers on my desk.

There are three different meanings of these words.

Lay means **to place or set,** and it always has an object. The past tense and past participle are laid and the present participle is laying.

- *I now **lay** down my books on the desk.* (present tense)
- *I **laid** down my books on the desk.* (past tense)
- *I **have laid** my books on the desk.* (past participle)
- *I **am laying** down my books on the desk* (present participle)

Lie means **to recline**, and unlike lay it does not have an object. The past tense is lay, the past participle is lain and the present participle is lying.

- *I am going to **lie** down for an hour.* (present tense)
- *Last night I **lay** down for an hour.* (past tense)
- *I **have lain** here for over an hour.* (past participle)
- *I **am lying** down for an hour.* (present participle)

Lie also means **to tell an untruth**, it also does not have an object. The past tense and past participle are lied and the present participle is lying.

- *I can tell you **lie.*** (present tense)
- *I know that you **lied** to me.* (past tense)
- *You **have lied** to me in the past.* (past participle)
- *You **are lying** right to my face.* (present participle)

Less/Fewer: The rule is that if you can separate items into a countable number then use fewer. If the items cannot be separated use less.

- *Ted didn't get the job because he has **less** skill in writing than the other applicant.*
- *That store has **fewer** DVDs than Best Buy.*

Like/As: As or as if should be used as a conjunction to introduce a clause, and such as should be used to mean **exactly or similar to**. Like should be used as a preposition for comparisons.

- *Ben was waiting in the library after class for Mike,*

just ***as*** *he said he would be.* (introduces a clause)

- *Ken played the piano* ***as if*** *he had been playing it his whole life.* (introduces a clause)
- *She looks* ***like*** *an athlete.* (preposition comparing the subject, she, to the object of the preposition, athlete)
- *Earthquakes* ***such as*** *the one that occurred yesterday are common.* (the earthquake is similar to the ones that are common, don't use like)

Lie is an intransitive verb meaning "to recline"
He **lies** down for a nap after his lunch.
Lay is a transitive verb which means "to put or place"
He **lay** the book on the desk and left the room.

Late/Lately/Later/Latter/Latest/Last

- I haven't seen Mary **lately**.
- Both John and Jack are hardworking students, but the **latter** was more active at school.
- Mary is always fascinated by the **latest** fashion.
- Read the **last** line of the third paragraph carefully.
- Jane is always **late** for school.

laid/lain/lay

- **Laid** is the past tense and the past participle of the verb lay and not the past tense of lie.**Lay** is the past tense of the verb lie and **lain** is the past participle: "He laid his books down and lay down on the couch, where he has lain for an hour."

lend/loan

Although some people feel *loan* should only be used as a noun, **lend** and **loan** are both acceptable as verbs in standard English: "Can you lend (loan) me a dollar?" However, only *lend* should be used in figurative senses: "Will you lend me a hand?"

lightening/lightning

Lightening is a verb that means to illuminate; **lightning** is a noun referring to the electrical charges the cause flashes of light during storms: "The lightning struck, lightening the sky."

Loud/Loudly/Aloud

- Would you mind not talking so **loud**?
- You have to speak **aloud**; otherwise your classmates can't hear what you say.
- It's impolite to speak in a loud voice.
- A woman shouted **loudly** that her handbag was stolen.

loath/loathe

"Loath," usually pronounced with a soft th, means unwilling or reluctant. (It's sometimes spelled "loth" in Britain.)*"Loathe,"* pronounced with a hard th, means to dislike greatly or to detest.

- arry and Ron **loathe** Draco Malfoy
- Blair was **loath** to tell Jim that his fly was undone.

Me, myself and I.

In a traditional prescriptive grammar, *I* is used only as a subject, *me* is used only as an object, and *myself* is used only as a reflexive object, that is to say when the subject is I and the object would otherwise be *me*.

- *Standard*: Jim and I took the train.
- *Standard*: He lent the books to Jim and me.
- *Non-standard*: Me and Jim went into town.
- *Non-standard*: It was clear to Jim and I that the shop was shut.

Myself is often used in way that makes usage writers bristle, particularly when someone is trying to be "extra correct". Like the other reflexive pronouns, in prescriptive usage, *myself* should be used only when both the subject and object of the verb are the speaker, or as an intensifier.

- *Standard* (intensifying): I myself have seen instances of that type.
- *Standard* (reflexive): I did it myself. I'll take it there myself. I want to enjoy myself.
- *Non-standard*: As for myself, I prefer the red. (Just use *me* here)

- *Non-standard*: He is an American like myself. (Just use *me* or *I am*)
- *Non-standard*: He gave the paper to Jim and myself. (Just use *me*)
- *Non-standard*: My wife and myself are not happy with all the development going on in town. (Just use *I*)

loose/lose

"Loose" is usually used as an adjective, meaning "not tight." It can also be a verb, but only if it means "to release" or "to make less tight." *"Lose"* is a verb that means "to not win," or "to misplace," or "to get rid of."

- If Neville were to **lose** weight, his pants would be **loose**.
- Did you **lose** your way?
- "Obi-Wan, how in the world did you **lose** your tunic?"

Most/Almost

- The adjective **most** is the superlative of many or much; meaning " largest number/amount."
- Most coffee comes from Brazil.
- **Almost** is an adverb meaning "not quite," or "very nearly" or "nearly all"
- Almost all the students are here.
- He is almost ready to leave.
- He almost won the race.

Maybe/May Be

- **Maybe** he is unable to solve the problem himself.
- David **may be** doing his work now.

Memorize/Memory/Memorial/Memorable/Remember

- I shall never forget taking part in such a **memorable** occasion.
- I remembered seeing him read a newspaper a few **minutes** ago.

- I do not take history because there are too many facts to **memorize**.
- My uncle has bad **memory** for dates.
- A **memorial** school is built for the chairman of the association.

Movable/Portable

- The large cupboard in the kitchen is not **movable**.
- You may bring along your **portable** cassette recorder when you go for the picnic.

Neglect/Negligent/Negligible

- Good parents never **neglect** their children.
- It was said that John was rather **negligent** in his work.
- He was dismissed because he was **negligent** of his duties.
- The manager did not report the burglary to the police because the amount of money stolen was **negligible**.

minuet/minute

A ***"minuet"*** is "a slow graceful dance in 3/4 time characterized by forward balancing, bowing, and toe pointing." If you're looking for the unit of time, or for notes taken during a meeting, you want ***"minute"***. "Minute" can also be an adjective meaning "very small."

Obi-Wan had to learn to dance the **minuet** for a diplomatic mission.

Just a **minute**!

militate, mitigate

- *Militate* means to oppose; to fight or act for or against; to manifest weight or influence; usually followed by **against**: His anger *militated against* a reconciliation. *Mitigate* means to lessen; to diminish in severity; to become milder: The heating pad on my back *mitigated* my suffering.

myself

- *Myself,* like **yourself, himself, herself, itself, themselves** is an intensive and reflexive pronoun. It should never be used in a sentence without its corresponding noun or pronoun: I hurt ***myself***. They sent for Susan and I. (NOT ***myself***)

mysterious, mystic

- ***Mysterious*** means not revealed or explained; unintelligible; beyond human comprehension: The ***mysterious*** light appeared in the sky and disappeared without explanation. ***Mystic*** means hidden from human knowledge or comprehension; involving some secret meaning, often religious: The appearance of the angel was a ***mystical*** experience.

moot/mute

In its most common American usage, ***"moot"*** can mean "open to question" or "deprived of practical significance: made abstract or purely academic." Law schools often have moot courts. In British English, naturally, "moot" has a rather different ***meaning***: "tending to be discussed or argued about and having no definite answer." As an adjective,***"mute"*** means "unable to speak" or "silent."

- Jim said, "It's a **moot** point whether the suspect was home that night."
- The question is **moot**.
- Merry and Pippin attended the **Entmoot**.

nonplussed

Meaning perplexed or bewildered, **nonplussed** is very often thought to mean just the opposite—calm, unruffled, cool-as-a-cucumber. A common mistake is to think the word means not "plussed," but no such word exists.

Nonplussed originates from the Latin *non*(no) and *plus* (more, further), and means a state in which no more can be done—one is so perplexed that further action is impossible. "The lexicographer grew increasingly agitated and nonplussed by the frequency with which she noted the misuse of*nonplussed.*"

Noise/Sound

- Don't make any **noise**; otherwise you'll be punished.
- Some strange **sounds** were made by the wild bird.

Of and **have**. In spoken English, *of* and the contracted form of *have, 've,* sound the same. However, in standard written English, they aren't interchangeable.

- *Standard*: Susan would have stopped to eat, but she was running late.
- *Standard*: You could've warned me!
- *Non-standard*: I should of known that the store would be closed. (Should be "I should've known")

navel/naval

- A ***"Naval"*** refers to the navy or to warships. Sounds simple, but mixing them up can lead to some very strange images.
- Ewan McGregor's **navel** is no stranger to the big screen.
- Horatio Hornblower learned a great deal about **naval** warfare.

Over/More than

Very simply, more than (also less than) refers to a number or an amount, whereas over (and under) refers to spatial locations.

- *Saturday's picnic is expected to attract a crowd of* ***more than*** *100 people.*
- *Put your hands* ***over*** *your head.*

Passed/Past

Passed is a transitive verb and past participle of the verb pass:

- She barely **passed** the exam.
- **Past** is a preposition or adjective meaning "by"
- We will keep school open **past** June.
- She walked **past** without saying hello.

- *"Passed"* is the past tense of "pass."
- Harry **passed** Potions with an O.
- Jim **passed** the basketball to Blair.
- Obi-Wan's speeder **passed** Qui-Gon's.
- Also, if someone dies, he or she has **passed** away.
- *"Past"* is not a verb, but it can be an adjective, adverb, preposition or noun.
- Obi-Wan was Anakin's master in the **past**.
- We drove **past** his house.
- Harry has been working hard for the **past** few months.

pacific, specific

This is a mispronunciation. *Pacific* means making peace; conciliatory. *Specific* means explicit or definite.

precede, proceed

- *Precede* means to go ahead of: The introduction will *precede* the reading. *Proceed* means to go ahead with an action: *Proceed* with the reading.

presently, at present

- *Presently* means soon or will happen shortly: We are waiting for our test results, which will be posted *presently*. *At present* means now, happening currently: At *present*, he is in the office.

pedal/peddle/petal

A *"pedal"* is the thing your foot uses on a bicycle. When you ride a bike, you "pedal." *"Peddle"* means to sell. A" petal is the colourful leafy thing on a flower.

Blair **pedaled** his bicycle.

peek/peak/pique

- We're talking verbs here: *"Peek"* means "to look furtively" or "to glance." *"Peak"* means "to reach a maximum" or "to come to a peak." (It can also mean "to grow thin or sickly," as in "You look peaked."

But most people would use a different word.) *"Pique"* means about the same thing as "provoke." So curiosity is piqued.

- The inscriptions **piqued** Daniel's curiosity.
- Harry **peeked** around the corner.
- The temperature **peaked** at 95F.

"Pique" can also be a noun, meaning "a transient feeling of wounded vanity." I'll assume you can figure out "peek" and "peak."

- Pansy stormed out of the room in a fit of **pique**.

per se/per say

- *"Per se"* is a Latin phrase meaning "as such" or "intrinsically." **"Per say"** is totally incorrect. In general, you shouldn't use a foreign word or phrase unless you're very sure of its usage. If you're not sure, there are usually ways to get the point across in English.

It was a good enough film **per se**, but as an adaptation of the book it was based on, it left a lot to be desired. (Thanks, Fox!)

Partisanship **per se** does not preclude political action.

perfect/prefect

This one's mostly for HP writers. A *"prefect"* is a kind of official—in particular, it's a student monitor in a private school. Notice that the "r" comes before the "e" in this case. *"Perfect"*, of course, means "without flaw."

- Ron was stunned to find he'd been chosen as **prefect**.
- Percy always thought he was the **perfect prefect**.

phase/faze

- *"Faze"* means "to disturb the composure of."
- Daniel wasn't **fazed** by Jack's sarcastic remarks.
- *"Phase"* means "to adjust so as to be in a synchronized condition," or "to conduct or carry out by planned phases," or "to introduce in stages."
- The Nimbus 2000 brooms are being **phased** out.

Plane/Plain

- The noun **plane** usually means "airplane."
  His plane arrives in New York at 9:00am.
- The adjective **plain** means "simple," "not fancy."
  Her dress was very plain.

Principal/Principle

- The **adjective** principal means "chief" or "very important."
- The **noun** principal means "chief official."
- The **principal** reason for his failure was lack of support.
- I am the **principal** of this school.
- The noun **principle** means "fundamental truth."
- He is studying the **principles** of accounting.

passed/past

- **Passed** is the past tense and past participle of *pass*. ***Past*** **refers** to time gone by; it is also a preposition meaning beyond. "In the past decade, I passed over countless opportunities; I was determined not to let them get past me again."

penultimate

- Meaning "next to last," *penultimate* is often mistakenly used to mean "the very last," or the ultimate: "The perfectionist was crestfallen when he was awarded the penultimate prize; the grand prize went to another."

precede/proceed

- The verb *precede* means to come before. *Proceed* means to move forward. "He preceded me into the room; once I caught up with him I proceeded to tell him off."

principal/principle

Principal is a noun that means a person who holds a high position or plays an important role: "The school principal has 20 years of teaching experience." *Principal* is also an adjective that means chief or leading: "The necessity of moving to another city was the principal reason I turned down the job offer." *Principle* is a noun that means a rule or standard: "They refused to compromise their principles."

Pretense/Pretext

Pretense means a false appearance or action intended to deceive, and pretext is **a false or fabricated reason developed to hide the truth**.

- *The CEO later realised that the applicant's claim that he had a bachelor's degree was only a* ***pretense.*** (The claim of the degree was false and it was intended to deceive the person hiring him.)
- *The woman called in sick, but it was only a* ***pretext*** *to hide the fact that she going on a vacation.*

Personal/Personnel

- It is only my **personal** opinion. What's yours?
- The **personnel** manager of the firm interviewed all the candidates for the job.

Presently/Recently

- A new metro will be built in Thessaloniki *presently*.
- John has made much improvement **recently**.

pore/pour

- ***"Pore"*** means "to read studiously or attentively."
- Harry **pored** over the Divinations text.
- Jim **pored** over the report.

prescribe/proscribe

- ***"Prescribe"*** means "to lay down a rule" or "to designate or order the use of as a remedy." ***"Proscribe"*** means "to condemn or forbid as harmful or unlawful." Completely different meanings, but it's easy to get them confused.

- The doctor **prescribed** antibiotics for Blair's strep throat.
- The doctor **proscribed** drinking as long as Blair was taking the antibiotics.
- Dumbledore **proscribed** entering the Forbidden Forest.

prostate/prostrate

- The ***"prostate"*** is the gland that is mentioned so often in slash and in which men occasionally get cancer.
- All men over 40 should have a **prostate** exam.
- ***"Prostrate"*** can be an adjective that means "lying on the ground," or a verb that means "to throw on the ground," or "to put in a humble and submissive posture or state."
- Lucius **prostrated** himself before Voldemort.
- Luke was **prostrate** from the cold on Hoth.

Quiet/Quite

- **Quiet**is an adjective meaning "not noisy."
  It was a very quite party."
- **Quite** is an adverb meaning "completely" or "to a degree."
- He is **quite** upset today.
- He is **quite** short.

rain/rein/reign

- ***"Rain"*** is the water that falls from the sky, and that's pretty much all it refers to. It can also be used figuratively, as in "raining cats and dogs" or "it's raining men."
- ***"Rein"*** is the piece of leather that keeps a horse under control. It's used figuratively rather often—you keep someone on a tight rein, or give them free rein.
- ***"Reign"*** has to do with monarchy—as a noun, it's the period of time during which a monarch rules; as a verb, it's the act of ruling.

- Harry hated playing Quidditch in the **rain** because his glasses fogged up.
- Hermione kept a tight **rein** on her thoughts.
- Professor Dumbledore tended to give Harry free **rein**.
- Professor Snape never allowed chaos to **reign** in his classroom.
- Silence **reigned** for several minutes.

rare, scarce

- *Rare* means coming or occurring far apart in time; seldom seen; unusual; uncommon: The *rare* works of Van Gogh are worth millions. *Scarce* means small in quantity in proportion to the demand; not plentiful or abundant; deficient; **rare**, uncommon: The supply of fresh vegetables is *scarce* during the winter.

ravish/ravage

To *"ravage"* is to "wreak havoc on" or to "commit destructive actions." *"Ravish"* means "to seize and take away by violence," "to overcome with beauty," or "to rape." If it's being done to a person, it's probably "ravishing. "*Bartleby.com* has a good *note* on this. (Incidentally, *"ravishing"* can also mean "unusually attractive, pleasing, or striking"—like **ravishing** beauty.)

- The Death Eaters **ravaged** the house.
- The Death Eaters **ravished** Hermione.
- A hurricane **ravaged** the coast.

Redundant does not mean useless or unable to perform its function. It means that there is an excess of something, or that something is "surplus to requirements" and no longer needed.

- *Non-standard*: Over-use of antibiotics risks making them redundant. (This should read: over-use of antibiotics risks making them worthless)
- *Standard*: A new pill that will instantly cure any illness has made antibiotics redundant. (Antibiotics could still be used to cure illnesses, but they are no longer needed because a better pill has been invented)

- *Standard*: The week before Christmas, the company made 75 workers redundant.

Reluctant/Reticent

If you are reluctant, you are unwilling or against something. If you are reticent, you are unwilling to speak.

- *He was **reluctant** (unwilling) to take a position at IUP at first.*
- *Prisoners are sometimes become **reticent*** (unwilling to speak) *when asked by reporters about their crime.*

reason is because

- The words ***reason is (was, etc)*** should always be followed by a statement of the reason: The ***reason*** for his error ***was*** lack of knowledge. The words ***reason*** and ***because*** convey the same meaning. To use them together is redundant: ***Because*** he lacked the knowledge he made an error.

regardless, *irregardless

- ***Irregardless*** is a nonstandard word, probably patterned after irrespective. ***Regardless***, which means without regard or to despite is the correct form: ***Regardless*** of the weather, the picnic will proceed.

respectable, respectful

- ***Respectable*** means worthy of respect; having a good reputation: He has a ***respectable*** command of computer languages. ***Respectful*** means showing respect for something or someone else: He treated the cliff he was climbing with ***respectful*** caution.

respectively, respectfully

- ***Respectively*** means individually, in their respective (listed or given) order: He mentioned taxes, education, and health care ***respectively***, as the most serious issues. ***Respectfully*** means showing respect, courtesy, regard for something or someone else: He answered the judges questions ***respectfully.*** *Note*: ***respectfully*** is always used to define an action and must refer to the verb preceding it.

Respectfully/Respectively

- **Respectfully** means "with respect."
- The audience rose **respectfully** when the President entered.
- **Respectively** means "in the order given."
- The Suttons lived in Chicago, Los Angeles and New York **respectively**.

Raise/Rise

- **Raise** is a transitive verb meaning to move to a higher place.
- Tom **raised** his hand to answer a question.
- **Rise** is an intransitive verb meaning to go up or ascend.
- The sun**rises** in the morning.

Respectable/Respectful/Respective/Respectively

- The candidates went to their **respective** classrooms when the bell rang.
- He belongs to the **respectable** upper classes.
- The crowd stood at a **respectful** distance from the governor.
- Our principal is a **respectable** man.
- The students went back to their classrooms **respectively** after the assembly.

Raise/Rise/Arouse/Arise

- Many problems **arise** after the government announced the new taxation policy.
- You may **raise** your hands if you have questions.
- The minibus drivers usually **raise** the fare when a typhoon comes.
- The food price has **risen** a lot recently.
- Two young men wearing sunglasses **arouse** the policemen's suspicion.

Refuse/Reject/Decline

- He refused to help us organize the annual carnival.
- He was disappointed to hear that this application was rejected again.
- He was so busy that he declined his friend's invitation to dinner.
- The committee had considered carefully before rejecting his proposal.
- Mr. Wright refused to discuss his plan with his colleagues.

roll/role

"Role" is a noun that can mean "a socially expected behaviour pattern usually determined by an individual's status in a particular society," or "a part played by an actor or singer," or "a function or part performed especially in a particular operation or process." For any other meanings, or a verb, use *"roll."*

- Harry must figure out his **role** in the wizarding world.
- What **role** did Alec Guinness play?
- It depends on the **roll** of the dice.
- Jack was on a **roll**.
- Hermione gave the teacher the **roll** of paper.

rightfully, rightly

- *Rightful* or *rightfully* means having a right or just claim, as to some possession or position: He was the *rightful* owner of the vehicle. *Rightly* means properly or correctly, without the legal claim: She *rightly* refused to sign the petition.

Say/Tell

- Say is a transitive verb meaning to express in words
- I **said** that she should stay home tonight.
- Tell is an intransitive verb also meaning to express in words
- **Itold** him to stay home but he didn't listen.

- (Never, **never, NEVER** told **to** him)

same

Same is not a pronoun and should NOT be used as one: I have your request for the instructions and I will fax **them**. (NOT will fax **same**)

Sit/Set

- Sit is an intransitive verb meaning to rest on something.
- **Sit** on the bench and not on the grass.
- Set is a transitive verb meaning to place something.
- She **set** the soup and spoons on the table.

sheer/shear

As a verb, ***"shear"*** means to cut the hair or wool off, or "to subject to a shear force," or "to become divided under the action of a shear." As a noun, it's the scissor-like implement used for shearing, or "internal force tangential to the section on which it acts."

"Sheer" is usually an adjective that means transparent or diaphanous—it can also mean unqualified, like **sheer** ignorance. "Sheer" can also be a verb or noun having to do with changing direction.

- "There's no way I'm wearing leggings made of such a **sheer** fabric!" complained Obi-Wan.
- Jim wondered where Blair had put the kitchen **shears**.
- It's time to **shear** the sheep so we can sell the wool.

should of/should have

3would of/would have

could of/could have

In all these cases, it's "have." "Of" is wrong.

- Ron **should have** finished his Transfigurations homework.
- Jim **would have** kissed Blair, but he missed his chance.

- In speech, you can contract it to *'ve*. "Of" is still wrong.
- "I **could've** gone to Hogsmeade," Harry said.

stationary/stationery

Stationary is an adjective that means fixed or unmoving: "They maneuvered around the stationary barrier in the road." **Stationery** is a noun that means writing materials: "We printed the letters on company stationery."

Sight and site.

A site is a place, a sight is something seen. The internet may be dazzling to some, but it is not a web-sight!

- *Standard*: You're a sight for sore eyes.
- *Standard*: I literally found lots of sights on the internet—I was looking at a tourist site for Rome.
- *Non-standard*: I found lots of sights on the internet.

Speak/Speech

- Speak is a verb meaning "to say out loud"
- "**Speak** louder. I can't hear you!"
- Speech is a noun meaning "what is said aloud"
- Politicians give the same boring **speech** over and over again when running for political office.

So/So that

- **So** is a conjunction joining a clause of result to a main clause.
  It rained a lot last year, so there were lots of wildflowers to enjoy.
  (result)
- **So that** joins a clause of purpose to a main clause.
  We wore raincoats so that we would not get our clothes wet.
  (purpose)

Stationary/Stationery

- **Stationary** means "in a fixed position."

The car was stationary parked in the driveway.

- **Stationery**refers to writing supplies.
  That stationery store sells writing paper, envelopes and office supplies.

stanch/staunch

"Stanch" means "to check or stop the flowing of" or "to stop or check in its course." ***"Staunch"*** means "steadfast in loyalty or principle" or "watertight." "Stanch" is a verb; "staunch" is an adjective. In the U.S., the two words are sometimes used interchangeably, but it's generally best to stick with their strict definitions.

- Harry was glad to have a **staunch** friend like Ron.
- Horatio thought the Indefatigable was the **staunchest** ship in the British Navy.
- Blair tried to **stanch** the flow of blood from Jim's wound.
- Obi-Wan managed to **stanch** his tears after Anakin threw his teddy bear out the window.
- The police are working hard to **stanch** the crime wave.

Scene/Scenery

- They were fascinated by the scenery of the countryside.
- That soldier never forgets the scene of a great battle.
- The drama consists of five scenes.

Sometime/Sometimes/Some time

- He will leave for Scotland sometime next year.
- Sometimes I watch television till midnight.
- We haven't seen Amy for some time.

Successive/Succession/Success/Successful

- They were busy with their work in five successive days.
- They did not give up in spite of a succession of defeats.

- It is said that John will be in succession to his father's property.
- Congratulations! Your plan is really a treat success.

supine/prone

"Supine" means lying on one's back. *"Prone"* means lying on one's front.

- Snape lay **prone** before Voldemort.
- Blair lay **supine**, staring up at the ceiling.

That/Which

Which should be used to introduce essential clauses, and that should be used to introduce nonessential clauses. An essential clause is needed in order for the sentence to convey its message; however, a nonessential clause is simply extra information added to the sentence for description or other purposes. The distinction between essential and nonessential information is also described in the comma section.

- *The meal, which was delicious, was served promptly at 7 p.m.*
- *The food that was served at the dinner was delicious.*

Than/Then

Than is a conjunction used in comparisons:

- She is taller **than** her sister.
- Then as an adjective or adverbial conjunction relates to time
- First we will work; **then** we will go out for lunch.

There, their and they're.

While they all sound the same, in standard written English they all have separate, definite meanings, and are not interchangeable. *There* refers to the location of something. *Their* means "belonging to them". *They're* is a contraction of "They are".

- *Standard*: Since they're all coming to the restaurant for their dinner, we'll meet them there.
- **Their** is the third-person plural possessive pronoun.

They sold their car last week.

- **There** is an adverb of place or an expletive that tells of existence.
  "Your package is there on the counter."
  "There are fifty states in United States."
- **There're** is the contraction of "they are".
  "They're ready to see you now."

tenet/tenant

"Tenants" are people who rent property. ***"Tenets"*** are principles or doctrines.

- I have to follow the **tenets** of my religion.

To/Too/Two

- **To** is (1) part of the infinitive form or (2) a preposition.
  "I like to walk in the snow."
  "I walked to the park on Saturday."
- **Too** is an adverb indicating an excess.
  "It is too cold to go swimming."
- **Two** is a number (2).
  "I have two cats; one named kitty and one called whiskers."

Than/Then

- ***"Than"*** is used in comparisons.
- Hermione is older **than** Harry.
- Jim is taller **than** Blair.
- Harry would rather eat dirt **than** study Potions.
- Otherwise, you want ***"then"***, which usually involves some sort of sequences, but not necessarily.
- They ate dinner, **then** they had pudding.
- If you want to learn to drive, **then** you must take lessons.
- Your mind is made up, **then**?
- Killing Voldemort will require all Harry's determination and **then** some.

- Blair lost the election, but **then** he didn't expect to win.
- Since **then**, Obi-Wan has been practicing.
- Teal'c misses his family now and **then**.
- Than is a conjunction used in comparisons
- She is taller **than** her sister.
- Then as an adjective or adverbial conjunction relates to time
- First we will work; **then** we will go out for lunch.

their/they're/there

- *"Their"* is the possessive form of "they." See below for more on this.
- *"They're"* is a contraction of "they are."
- Everything else is *"there."*
- Jim and Blair bought **their** tickets for the Jaguars game.
- Jack yelled, "**They're** coming to take me away!"
- The landspeeder is over **there**.

Thorough/Through

- The police carried out **thorough** investigation into the murder case.
- That window is too narrow to get **through**.
- I wondered how he got **through** his examination.

Tired/Tiresome

- He felt **tired** after Working for a long time.
- The **tiresome** students made the teacher very angry.

that/which/who

"That," "which" and *"who"* are all ***relative pronouns,*** but there are some differences in how they're used.

First, though, let's talk about restrictive vs. non-restrictive clauses. A restrictive clause is information that's necessary to figure out what's being talked about. For instance, let's say I'm standing on a sidewalk in front of two blue houses. I could say, "I live in the blue house that has the red door." In this case, "that has the red door" is necessary because, without it, you wouldn't know which blue house I'm referring to. This is a restrictive clause.

Now, let's say we're standing on a sidewalk, and there's only one blue house in sight. I could say, "I live in the blue house," and you'd know exactly which house I meant. I could also say, "I live in the blue house, which has a red door." In this case, the fact that the door is red is *not* necessary to identify which house we're talking about; it's just extra information. This is an unrestrictive clause.

You may notice that I used "that" for the restrictive clause and "which" for the unrestrictive clause. That's the traditional way of doing it. These days, however, "which" is sometimes used for restrictive clauses. Michael Quinion has a terrific ***article*** about the whole thing, including cases where it's still necessary to use "that." If you're not sure what's correct, you'll never go wrong using "that" with restrictive clauses and "which" with unrestrictive.

(Incidentally, if it's an unrestrictive clause, you have to use "which." "That" is incorrect.)

In these examples, you'll also notice that there is a comma before "which" in the unrestrictive clause, but not before "that" in the restrictive clause. This is always how it's done: Never use a comma before a restrictive clause, regardless of whether you're using "that" or "which." Always use a comma before an unrestrictive clause.

So that's "that" and "which." Now, what about "who"? Basically, "who" is used in place of "that" or "which" when it's referring to a person. You can get away with using "that" or "which" if the person or persons are not specified (*The students that finish first will get a prize* and *The students who finish first will get a prize* are both correct), but "who" is always safe.

The House **that** has the most points at the end of the year wins the House Cup.

Gryffindor House, **which** has fewer points than Slytherin, needs to win the next Quidditch match. Blair Sandburg, **who** is a doctoral student in anthropology, is teaching that class. The Weasley **who** gets out of bed first starts breakfast.

The rules governing these two words are a bit flexible, but "which" is too often used where "that" should be. "That" is preferable when you are limiting or restricting a noun:

A law that does not have public support cannot be enforced. ("A law that" helps to limit the meaning to just one kind of law.)

The air dry loss moisture factor appears to control the amount of airborne respirable dust that is liberated from the product. ("Airborne respirable dust that" restricts the dust just to that liberated from the product.)

The following line from a nursery rhyme is instructive here, because all of the "thats" are correct: This is the rat that ate the cat that lived in the house that Jack built.

In contrast, "which" introduces a phrase that provides descriptive yet incidental information, and "which" often requires commas on one or both ends of the phrase it introduces: Approximately 71 per cent of the earth's surface is covered by a worldwide body of sea water, which is interconnected. The trawl consists of five net bags in a row which are collected on board one at a time as they become filled with oil.

In short, you use "that" to complete a noun and "which" simply to describe a noun.

threw/through

"Threw" is the past tense of "throw." *"Through"* isn't a verb, although it can be a lot of other things. Make sure you're using the right one.

- Oliver Wood **threw** the quaffle to Katie Bell.
- The path goes **through** the Forbidden Forest.

throe/throw

A *"throe"* is a pang or spasm, or a hard, painful struggle. A *"throw"* is the act of tossing something, or it can be a light cover or wrap.

- The injured dog was in its death **throes**.
- France was in the **throes** of revolution.
- Qui-Gon bet Watto on the **throw** of the die.

trooper/trouper

A "*trooper*" is a soldier or a policeman. A "*trouper*" is a member of an acting troupe, or "a person who deals with and persists through difficulty or hardship without complaint." If you want to say someone is a real trouper, it's the word with the "u." The four-year-old was a **trouper** for not complaining while he was in the hospital.

venal/venial

Venal is an adjective that means corruptible; *venial* is an adjective that means a slight flaw or offense: "In the Catholic church, a venial sin is one that is minor and pardonable, whereas a mortal sin is a serious transgression involving more venal or depraved behaviour."

Valuable/Invaluable/Priceless/Worthless

- I would like to thank Sergeant Alexander for his **invaluable** service to us.
- This is really a very **valuable** gift.
- She was given a **priceless** diamond ring for her wedding anniversary.
- Nobody will take care of a **worthless** old car.

tortuous, torturous

- *Tortuous* means full of twists, turns or bends: *tortuous* road. *Torturous* means full of, involving, or causing torture: *Tortuous* devices, such as the rack, were use during the Spanish Inquisition.

unique

- *Unique* means without a like or equal; unmatched; unequaled; single in its kind; uncommon or rare. It cannot logically be used in a comparative or superlative for. Something may be more or less rare but NOT more or less *unique*.

vial/vile

A "*vial*" is "a small closed or closable vessel especially

for liquids." ***"Vile"*** means despicable, repulsive, abhorrent, or "disgustingly or utterly bad."

- Snape put the potion in the **vial**.
- Snape is known for his **vile** temper.
- What **vile** weather we're having!

vicious/viscous

"Vicious" means depraved, impure, spiteful, damaged or malicious. ***"Viscous"*** means "having a glutinous consistency." Make sure you're choosing the right one and spelling it correctly.

Harry, Ron and Hermione thought Fluffy looked **vicious**.

Wake/Awake/Awaken/Waken

- Mary got up late this morning because her mother forgot to wake her up.
- It is difficult to make him awake to the problem.
- The accident awakens him to the danger of careless driving.
- Is the patient awake or asleep?
- He woke up at half past six yesterday.

waist/waste

The ***"waist"*** is the part of a body where you'd wear a belt. All the other meanings are ***"waste"***.

- Jim wrapped the belt around his **waist**.
- If you don't eat, you'll **waste** away to nothing.
- Television has been referred to as a vast **wasteland**.
- Don't **waste** food; there are children starving in China.
- A mind is a terrible thing to **waste**.
- A **waist** is a terrible thing to mind.

Weather/Whether

"Weather", in general, is what's going on outside—rain, snow, wind, sun, etc. It can also be a verb meaning "to subject to the elements" or "to bear up against and come safely through." ***"Whether"***, on the other hand, is either a pronoun or a ***conjunction*** having to do with choosing one of two alternatives.

Blair **weathered** the storm of the dissertation fiasco.

What's the **weather** like today?

I can't decide **whether** to watch the first or second Harry Potter movie.

Weather is a noun meaning "atmospheric conditions."

"The weather was not nice enough to go out."

Whether is a conjunction meaning "if."

"I don't know whether he will stay at home or not."

Won't and **wont** (rhymes with *font*). Won't is a contraction for "will not", and wont is a rarely-used archaism: as a noun it means *habit*; as a verb it is an auxiliary with the same function as *used*.

- *Standard*: He won't let me drive his car.
- *Standard*: He spent the morning reading, as was his wont (or "as he was wont to do").
- *Non-standard*: I wont need to go to the supermarket after all.

Who's/Whose

- **Who's** is the contraction for who is.
  "I don't know who's coming tonight."
- **Whose** is (1) a question word or (2) a possessive relative pronoun.
  "Whose pen is this?"
  "I met the man whose child scored the winning goal."
  Who's is the contraction of *who is*. *Whose* is the possessive form of *who*. "Who's going to figure out whose job it is to clean the stables?"

who/whom

"Who" is the subject form; ***"whom"*** is the object form. If you're trying to figure out which to use, try replacing it with "he" or "him." If "he" is correct, then use "who." If "him" is correct, use "whom."

- Ask not for **whom** the bell tolls. (The bell tolls for him.)

- **Who** was at the door? (He was at the door.)
- **Whom** did you speak to? (You did speak to him.)

  The prize is for the student **who** has the highest score. (He has the highest score.)

You're, your, yore and **ewer**. While they sound the same in many dialects, in standard written English they all have separate meanings. *You're* is a contraction for "you are", and *your* is a possessive pronoun meaning "belonging to you". When in doubt, just see whether you can logically expand it to "you are". The third homonym, *yore,* is an archaism meaning in the distant past, and is almost always used in the phrase "in days of yore". The fourth is the name of a once common piece of household equipment made obsolete by indoor plumbing: the large jug holding washing water.

- *Standard*: When driving, always wear your seatbelt.
- *Standard*: If you're going out, please be home by ten o'clock.
- *Non-standard*: You're mother called this morning.
- *Non-standard*: Your the first person to notice my new haircut today!

wrack/rack

This one gets really complicated; use it at your own risk. The ***"wrack,"*** as a noun, can mean "wreckage," "ruin," "destruction" or "marine vegetation (like kelp)." As a verb it means "to utterly ruin." American dictionaries say the phrase "wrack and ruin" is proper usage. ***"Rack"*** has a lot of meanings, but the ones that tend to get confused with "wrack" generally have to do with pain. It can mean "to torture on a rack," or "to stretch or strain violently," or "to cause anguish." A "rack" is a torture instrument on which a person is stretched—it can also be "a cause of anguish and pain" or "the action of straining or wrenching."

In British English, "wrack" definitely has the "marine vegetation" and "shipwreck" meanings, but after that, things get a little confusing. Its usage tends to vary by geography; in some areas, "wrack and ruin" would be correct, but other areas would use "rack and ruin."

Chapter 5

Words and Phrases

A whole	:	Used when a man of substance is belittled e.g See how mobile police trash the guy, a whole managing director for dat matter
Abeg	:	Please.
Abi?	:	Is it not?
Abi na wetin!	:	What is it?
ABU	:	Amadu Bello University.
Acada	:	1. Intellectual 2. University student 3. Book worm.
Acata	:	1. USA or UK 2.Someone who lives in those places.
Acting big man	:	Deputy exercising power in the absence of the boss.
Adire	:	Dyed cloth.
Adonkia	:	contraction for I don't care attitude
Afang	:	Efik soup made from Afang leaves, beef, dried fish, crayfish, palm oil, and periwinkle.
Afraid catch me	:	I was scared.
Afta	:	After
Afta much	:	Inebriated after much alcohol.
Agaracha	:	Woman of easy virtue.
Agbada	:	Large traditional garment usually worn by men over a shirt.
Agbepo	:	Night soil man. (See - Onioburu).
Agbero	:	Labourer who carries heavy goods for a fee.

Agip : Any Government In Power. Derisory term for person who changes alliances as goverments come and go.

Agument : Argument.

Ah-ah : For goodness sake.

Aircon : Abbreviation for air conditioner.

Ajasco : Dancing with fanciful footwork. Also called Ajasco Toronto.

Ajebota : One used to butter; rich spoilt kid.Literally means -one used to eating wood i.e. uses a wooden chewing stick as toothbrush.

Akamu : Pap made from corn.

Akara : Bean cake made from fried ground black-eyed beans.

Akara school : Nursery school.

Akata : 1. Recent arrival from abroad (especially UK or USA) into Nigeria 2. Nigerian nickname for an African American

Alaba : Abbreviation for Alaba International Market, Lagos. Famed for the sale of electrical goods.

Alau : Allow.

Alau him : Give him a break.

All na : It is all a.e.g All na wayo.

All night : Night vigil.

All Weda : Shoes worn all the time, come rain come sunshine.

Amebo : 1. Gossip 2. Name of a character in a Nigerian soap opera (The village headmaster), with a penchant for gossiping.

Amerika : America.

Amugbo : One habitually smoking Indian Hemp. (Marijuana)

And Co : Wearing the same clothes or fabric with someone else especially married couple.

Andrew : One wishing to emigrate out of Nigeria. Term originates from government sponsored advert in which the main character - Andrew threatens to 'check out' of the country due to various hardships.

Angola : Prison. Also Angola.

Animal and Sontin : Elephant and Castle (in Southeast London).

Anoda : Another.

Ansa : Answer.

Any attempt! : Don't even think about it!

Anyhow : 1. Shoddy 2. Inappropriate

Akpere : 1. Basket 2. Bad goalkeeper in soccer match.

Apoti : Yoruba word for small stool

Appear : 1. Arrive unexpected usually to something good such as a meal. Host will then say 'you waka well o'. 2. Arrive uninvited.

Apketeshi : 1.Illicit gin. 2.Native gin. Also called Kai Kai, Ogogoro, Push me-push you, Sapele water and Burukutu.

Apkroko : Gossip.

Apku : Cassava flour.

Apollo : Conjunctivitis. (an epidemic swept Nigeria around the time of the Apollo 11 moon landing hence the name)

Arrange yua sef : 1. Make your own arrangements 2. Everyman to himself.

Arrangee : 1.Soiree. 2. Exclusive 3.Preplanned set up.

Area boys : Unemployed street-wise youth loitering in the neighbourhood. Also called 'Alaye boys' in Lagos.

Area girls : Female Anopheles mosquitoes.

Ariya : Good time.

Aro : 1.Abbreviation for large psychiatric

	hospital in western Nigeria. 2. Lunatic.
Aromental :	1. Lunatic 2. Eccentric personality.
As :	How it e.g. 'Tell am as e take happun'.
As for :	That's the way it is.
Ashewo :	Prostitute. See Agharacha.
Askology :	Sarcastic reply to irritant question. Also- Askor.
Aso oke :	Tradition Yoruba fabric worn on special occasions. Means Upper class cloth.
At-all :	Not at all. Also- At-all ah-tall.
Atachee :	1. Hanger on 2. Social climber forcing themselves on the in-crowd
Attachment :	Small stool placed along the aisle of luxurious buses for passengers who can't afford proper seats.
Aunty :	Any older female. Used when first name terms not appropriate.
Awa :	Our.
Awoko :	Burning the midnight oil.
Awoof :	Freebie. Without charge.
Away :	Foreign especially Europe and America.
Away Baffs :	Imported clothes from Europe and America; especially designer labels.
Baba Jiga :	Derisory name for a person suffering from Jiga infestation. Also Baba sore.
Babawilly :	Internet pen name of the author of this dictionary.
Babar :	Verb. Hair cut
Babariga :	Large traditional robe worn by man.
Babo! :	WOW! Also Ibabo!
Babi :	1.Baby 2. Pretty girl.
Babi pancake :	Girl fond of make-up.
Back :	Carry a baby tied to the back with lappa
Backyard :	Bottom. See Yarnsh.
Bad bad :	1. Severely e.g Di man wey moto jam wound bad bad. 2. Absolutely e.g She fain bad bad.

Bad-belle	: 1 Malice. 2 Player hater.
Baffs	: Trendy clothes. See Away Baffs Bakassi: 1. Name of Igbo vigilante group. 2. Bottom
Bale	: Eat greedily.
Baler	: One who eats greedily.
Bam	: In good condition.
Banga	: Palm tree fruit.
Banga soup	: Soup made from Palm tree fruit.
Barawo	: Thief
Basia	: Large aluminium metal basin.
Bata	: Shoe.
Battalion	: Large family.
Baze	: Woo a girl. See Spin.
Beat am die	: Beat to the point of death.
Been to	: Well travelled.
Beg beg	: One always begging.
Begin go	: On your bike mate.
Belle	: 1. Stomach 2. Abdomen 3. Mind 4. Heart
Belle full	: Satiety.
Belle-sweet	: Happiness.
Belle-turn me	: 1. Diarrhoea 2. Abdominal colic. 3. Nausea.
Bend-bend	: Illegal.
Bend down boutique	: Second hand clothes. Usually spread on a mat at the roadside.
Bending corner	: Sharp corner of a road
Betta	: 1. Good times e.g. 'Betta don come'. 2. Improvement e.g. things don betta.
Betta dey for Okra soup	: 1. There's something good in store. 2. Good times are here.
Betta follow	: Good fortune
Bi	: Be.
Bi as e get	: See Get as e bi.
Biam Bia	: Beard.Also- Byah-byah.
Bico	: Please.

Bicos	:	Because
Bicos why?	:	The reason is
Bifor	:	Before.
Bifor-bifor	:	Long time ago.
Bifor nko?	:	What did you expect?
Big grammar	:	Long and difficult English words.
Big eye	:	1 Ambitious 2. Greedy
Big man	:	1. Rich and well connected man 2.Man in position of authority.
Bingo	:	1. Dog 2. Cooked dog meat. See Four-o-four. 3. Common dog name in Nigeria.
Black soap	:	Traditional soap made from Palm oil. Also called Ose Dudu in Yoruba.
Bleach	:	Use of skin lightening creams. Also Bleaching.
Block	:	1. Defecate 2. Meet up with someone.
Blokkus	:	Scrotum.
Blow	:	1 Punch 2 Speak with arrogance e.g. sofri-sofri blow Oyinbo.
Blow oyinbo	:	Use of long English words especially with a foreign accent.
Blom-blow	:	1. Balloons 2. Condoms
Bo	:	For Pete's sake e.g. Comot bo!
Bobbi	:	Breasts.
Bobo	:	Trendy guy.
Bobo	:	Misinform.
Bodi	:	Body.
Bodi dey inside cloth	:	I am surviving.
Bodi do me	:	Premonition.
Bodi no bi firewood	:	The body has its limitations.
Boi	:	Boy.
Boju-boju	:	Yoruba word for 'cover your eyes. 1.Hide and seek 2. Pay eye service e.g. Dis Boju-boju friend go stab you for back o! 3. Deception
Bole kaja	:	Yoruba for come down and let's fight and used for over crowded commuter bus in Lagos.

Bold face : To bluff one's way through a situation.
Boli : Roast plantain.
Bom-boy : Baby boy.
Boma boi : Thug. Derived from Burma boy. Term probably originates from Nigerians who served under the British in Burma during WW2.
Bone : 1. Frown 2. Disagree e.g. e don bone for am!
Bones : Sun glasses.
Bonga Fish : A kind of blackened dried fish used to prepare local soups
Booze man : Drunkard.
Borkotor : Cooked cow's foot.
Borku : Very plenty. Full ground remain and Plenti plenti.
Born throway : Not in touch with one's cultural heritage.
Borrow-borrow : One always borrowing from friends.
Borrow-borrow make me fine : One well dressed up in borrowed clothes. Also Borrowed Baffs.
Bosaut : 1. Burst out 2. Come out 3. Explode.
Bottom Box : Treasured attire worn only on important occasions. e.g Dat yua dress na real bottom box o!
Bottom-pot : Dregs at the bottom of the pot.
Bottom Power : Undue favouritism toward's a female lover e.g Na bottom power she use get dat job o!
Bou-bou : Large voluminous dress worn by women.
Bow : 1. Surprised e.g. Man bow! 2. Applaud or be impressed e.g. everybodi bow when I land wit away baffs.
Boy's quarters : Small bungalow behind main house where hired domestic staff or extended family reside.

Boyi-boy	:	Houseboy.
Branch	:	Detour during pre arranged trip.
Bread	:	Naira (money)
Break Kola	:	Ritual breaking of the Kola nut at the beginning of a ceremony.
Brekoyan	:	Yoruba slang for Brassiere.
Broda	:	Brother.
Broda-broda	:	Nepotism.
Broke	:	1. Break e.g Na you broke di plate.2. Speak with big English words e.g Abeg sofri broke the grammar now.
Brokun	:	1. Broken English 2. Pidgin English.
Brokun plate	:	Breakable plates especially China.
Brush	:	Hit someone hard.
Buba	:	Traditional blouse.
Bubble	:	1 Dance 2 Party.
Bukka	:	Roadside restaurant.Also- MamaPut and Food is ready.
Bulala	:	Horse whip. See koboko.
Bulgary proof	:	Iron bars built into windows for security
Bullet	:	Grammatical error especially in spoken English. Also Ibon.
Burukutu	:	Illicit homemade gin.
Bush man	:	Unsophisticated man. (derisive usage)
Bush meat	:	Game.
Bust	:	1 Write off 2 Ignore.
Butta my bread	:	Answered prayer. E.g God don butta my bread.
Butter	:	Another name for Ajebota. Also Omobota
Buredi	:	Bread.
Call	:	To be beckoned by unseen forces. Juju is usually implied e.g. dem dey call you?
Cantab	:	Run full circle and over take fellow athlete in long distance race.
Carbon copy	:	Dead ringer for someone else e.g See im face. Na real carbon copy of im papa.

Carbu-carbu : Unregistered taxi cab operating illegally. Not painted in official taxi colours.

Carry am for head : 1.Take up too much responsibility for something. 2. To become obsessed with something e.g See how e carry politics for head.

Carry dey do : Behave badly.

Carry go : Used playfully to mean -Get away or Get out of here.

Carry woman : verb 1. Womaniser e.g. you too carry woman.

Catch : 1. Enough salt in food. e.g. salt no catch dis soup at all. 2. Intoxication e.g. Ogogoro don catch am. 3. Excited e.g. Bodi dey catch am.

Cease light : Power failure.

Chai! : Good grief

Characteristics of Tombo : Sang to the tune of Michael Jackson's You wanna be starting something.

Chance : 1 Take advantage of. 2 Intimidate 3 Cheat e.g. abeg no chance me jo!

Changer : Hifi

Charge : Loose one's temper.

Chassis : Brand new car

Chei! : Goodness.

Chickito : Young pretty girl.

Chin : 1. Frowning 2. Angry. Also - Chinning.

Chin-chin : Fried bits of pastry served as appetiser.

Chineke! : Oh my God!

Chipay : Cheap.

Chipeleke : 1. Cheap 2. Cheap article.

Chop : 1. Food 2. Income 3. Bribe 4. Embezzle money e.g Dat Oga chop belle-full bifor e retire.

Chop bottle : Eat glass. Part of pre fight preamble during which various threats and

		questions are asked to measure of toughness of the opponent e.g. you dey chop bottle?
Chop bullet	:	Get shot.
Chop life	:	Enjoy life.
Chop money	:	Monthly or weekly house keeping allowance.
Chop mouth	:	Kissing.
Chop-remain	:	Leftovers of meal.
Christmas goat	:	Used for one was sweats excessively e.g. which one you dey sweat laik Christmas goat. i.e. the goat sweats for its life as Christmas draws near.
Chuk	:	1. Prick 2. Stab e.g Why you chuk me naif?
Chuk body put	:	1. Squeeze into tight corner. 2. Getting involved with other peoples buisness.
Chuku-chuku	:	Thorny.
Ciga	:	Cigarette
Clear	:	1. Leave e.g Make you clear commot. 2. Malicious sliding tackle during football game e.g See as them dey clear leg, abi na fight? 3. Finish large meal e.g Di guy clear the Eba finis o!
Close eye	:	Grin and bear it e.g close eye drink dat medicine ojare.
Close marking	:	Following spouse to every social event for fear of husband or wife snatchers.
Cock-shoe	:	Court shoe. Any low cut ladies' shoe not bearing laces.
Coke and Fanta	:	Derisory term used to describe the mottled complexion one who uses skin bleaching products.
Colo	:	Loose ones mind e.g. Dat guy don dey Colo.
Come chop	:	Small party.
Comot	:	1 Come out 2 Get away! E.g. comot for here jo! 3 Excuse me e.g. comot road

make I pass.

Comot for road : 1. Make way 2. Get away!

Compin : Company.

Compound : Fenced off house, bungalow or groups of huts.

Condemn : Spoilt beyond repair e.g. see how she juss condemn the moto.

Condition make crayfish bend : Saying used when one is forced to do the unthinkable due to prevailing financial circumstances.

Confido : 1 Confidence 2 Self confidence.

Confra : University Campus Fraternity.

Congo-meat : Cooked snail

Coolee : 1 Relaxed 2 Cool 3 Chill.

Coolu-down : Simmer down.

Coolu temper : 1. Control your temper! 2. Title of song by Nigerian saxophonist Lagbaja.

Corner-corner : Illegal.

Corofo : Army recruit.

Coror : 1. Dark corner 2. Crevice.

Corporate begging : High class begging e.g. A rich man or business with cash flow problems begging for loans.

Correct : Very good. e.g Di bobo na correct guy.

Correct Correct : Extremely good.

Cortex : Nail varnish.

Cortina : Type of school sandals.

Count : Afford e.g You fit count Twenty thousand as you stand so?

Country paper : 1 Passport 2 Right of abode in foreign country.

Court! : Rallying cry for everyone in a public building to rise and leave. Usually done to embarrass speaker or performer on university campuses.

Cover beer : Aluminium beer bottle cover.

Cost : Expensive. Also Too cost.

Crape	:	Defraud completely e.g. e crape all my money or E don crape my head pata-pata. 2 Finish (food) completely.
Crash helmet	:	Prominent forehead. Also Opun.
Craw-craw	:	Skin ailment especially rashes.
Craze	:	Crazy.
Cross leg	:	Idleness. e.g see as e cross leg dey wait awoof.
Cruise	:	Use excessively.
Cry blood	:	Threat. E.g. you go cry blood today today.
Cry-cry	:	Cry baby.
Cry dey call you	:	Threat to a child before a smacking. See Trouble dey call you.
Cross no gutter	:	Tight and long skirt i.e. it would be difficult to skip across gutter.
CU	:	1. Christian Union 2. Born again Christian.
Cubes	:	Sugar cubes
Cult guy	:	One belonging to secret societies, nocturnal fraternities or clubs especially in higher institutions.
Cuni	:	Contraction of cunning. Also Cunny or Cuni-cuni.
Cuni man die cuni man bury am	:	It takes one to know one.
Cut	:	Share of the loot. Usually involves a bribe.
Cut and sew	:	Bespoke tailor.
Dabaru	:	Spoil.
Dada	:	Dread locks. Also called Bob Marley.
Damn	:	To rudely cut short someone who is speaking. Also Idanminashon.
Dance blues	:	Slow dance with couple in each other's arms. Also Hold tight.
Danfo	:	VW Combi bus.
Dash	:	1. Gift 2. Bribe.
Dat	:	That.

Dat na question? : Rebuff to a silly question.

Dat one na grammar : That is not practical.

Dem : 1. Them. 2. They.

Dem-dem : A group of people with an affiliation such as students or soldiers.

Dem no born you reach : Threat or dare meaning "Don't even think about it".

Dem no send me message : I will not get involved.

Dem send you? : Have you been sent to torment me?

Denge : Strike a fine pose.

Dey : 1. Is e.g. wetin dey happun 2. Location e.g. where you dey 3. Stance in the matter e.g. which one you dey sef. 4. In existence 5. Spectacular e.g. dat car dey well-well.

Dey go : Keep on going.

Dey laik Dele : (Dele is a Yoruba name) 1. I am barely surviving e.g Man juss Dey laik Dele. 2. Being idle e.g You juss dey there laik Dele. Also - Standing like Standard Bank, Looking like Lucozade and Dey like you no dey.

Dey there now : 1 Keep on in self deceit 2 It is there at present.

Deshine : Public humiliation.

Die for : In love with.

Di : The.

Di thing wey mai eye no fit talk am : Words fail me.

Dia : 1.Their 2. Dear or expensive eg Dat moto too dia.

Different eye : Individual variations on interpreting what is seen.

Different different : Assorted e.g Na different different kain fish dey inside dat soup.

Dig am out	:	Fight e.g We two go dig am out.
Diopka	:	Elderly wise one.
Direct entry	:	(Obsolete as A-Levels no more in place in Nigeria) Gaining admission into University after A-Level examination. JAMB examination not done in this case. See JAMB.
Dis	:	This.
Dishi	:	Embarrass. See Deshine.
Do	:	Participate e.g. I no do again. 2. Afflicting one's health e.g. Wetin dey do am?
Do anyhow	:	Unruly.
Do betta	:	Show us the colour of your money.
Do quick	:	Hurry up!.
Do river	:	Well done. Joke using the word 'river' as opposed to 'well'.
Do well	:	Well done e.g you do well.
Dodo	:	Fried plantain
Dodge	:	1. Avoiding someone 2. Escape e.g. man juss dodge comot.
Doing laik dis	:	Acting this way e.g. Why are you doing laik dis now?
Don	:	1. Has e.g. e don come. 2. Has it? E.g. e don come? 3. Have e.g. I don tell am (present tense) 4. Have e.g. I don been tell am (Past tense).
Don run	:	Has ran away.
Donatus	:	(Derisory) One in habit of giving their services to others for free. Derived from-donate.
Done	:	Cooked e.g. yua own done?
Dormot	:	1 Door mat 2 Area in front of main door to house.
Dorti-dorti	:	Garbage.
Dorti slap	:	dirty slap Hard slap across the face.
Doz bin	:	Garbage can.
Drain duck	:	Cleaners employed by Lagos state

		government to clean un block public gutters.
Draiv	:	1. Drive 2.Chase away.
Draiva	:	Driver.
Draw	:	Slimy e.g Di Okra soup draw well well.
Draw bodi take	:	1. Withdraw 2. Make hasty exit. 3. Avoiding getting drawn into a dicey situation.
Draw my throat	:	1 Stimulate my appetite 2 Entice me.
Draw rain	:	Make an empty boast. Also Rake and Shakara.
Draw soup	:	Slimy soup usually containing Okra.
Dress	:	1. Any kind of clothing. 2. Move your butt.
Drink garri	:	1.In trouble e.g. you go drink garri today.2. Meal of garri and water.
Drop	:	1. A taxi journey e.g Oga, na fifty Naira per drop. 2. To alight from a bus. 3. Pay up 4. Monetary bribe.
Dros	:	Voluminous underwear.
Dry	:	1 Slim person.
Dub	:	1. Make extra copy of music tape 2. Copy neighbour's work during examination.
Dudu	:	Dark skinned person.
Dundi	:	Fool.
E	:	1. He 2. She.
E Dey hard	:	It is a rarity e.g E dey hard make Saturday night meet am for house.
E don do	:	It is enough.
Eagles	:	See Super Eagles.
Eba	:	Meal made with garri and hot water. Usually eaten with soup with bare fingers of right hand. See Garri.
Econs	:	(Abbreviation of economy) Stingy.
Edikang Ikong	:	Traditional Efik soup made with beef, stock fish, snails, crayfish, periwinkle, peppers, pumpkin leaves and onions.

	Usually served with pounded yam or Fufu. Folklore has it that when an Efik maiden prepares this dish for a man she steals his heart away.
Effa	: Ever.
Efritin	: Everything.
Egbe	: Fool.
Ego	: Money.
Egunje	: 1. Bribe or 2. Kick back..
Eh?	: 1. What? 2. What!
Eh-eh	: 1. No 2. Not at all.
Eh-yah	: 1. Sorry 2. What a pity 3. How touching
Ehen?	: So what?
Ehen	: Is that so.
Ejika ni shop	: Tailor walking on the street with his portable sewing machine on his shoulder. Ejika ni is Yoruba for "shoulder is".
Enjoi	: Enjoy.
Eko	: Lagos
Eniwe	: Anyway.
Enta	: Enter.
Enta road	: 1. Get out of control. 2. Drive car into the streets.
Enta market	: 1 Go crazy.
Enta trouble	: Get into trouble.
Esusu	: Thrift society where members contribute a monthly sum into a pot and then take turns in collecting the total sum. Also- Moni of by turn - by turn.
Essenco	: Abbreviation for term 'essential commodities' i.e. Milk, Sugar, and Salt.
Everyday everyday	: Daily
Everywhere tinted	: Wearing really dark sun glasses.
Ewa	: Beans.
Ewa Agoyin	: 1. A kind of beans 2. Street hawkers who sell cooked beans.
Expo	: 1. Leaked examination question paper.

		2. Contraction of exposed
Eye glass	:	Spectacles.
Eye go come down	:	Come back to reality.
Fabu	:	1. Unlikely tale. 2. Tall Tale
Fa fa fa foul!	:	1. That is totally objectionable.
Face to face	:	Rooms rented to families which all open onto a long corridor. Also Room and parlour.
Face yua front	:	Face forward.
Fada	:	Father.
Fain	:	See Fine.
Fain-fain	:	Completely.
Fain for face	:	Pretty face.
Faif	:	Five.
Fait	:	Fight.
Falcons	:	Nigerian national female football team.
Fap	:	Steal. Also Tap or Tapping.
Fashie	:	1. Ignore 2. Forget.
Fawul	:	Fowl.
Faya	:	Fire.
Feferity	:	1. Showing off 2. Pretending to be classy.
Felele	:	1. Light plastic football. 2. Neighbourhood in Ibadan
Fence	:	Exclude.
Festac	:	(Acronym for Festival of Arts and culture) Name of large estate in Lagos originally built to house participants of the arts festival and later sold to members of the public.
Fiam	:	At lightening speed.
Fillage	:	Village.
Fine fine	:	Extremely well.
Firee cinema	:	1. Public fight especially one in which clothes are torn off. 2. Free public spectacle 3.
Find me something	:	Give me a bribe.
Find my mouth	:	To extract a comment.

Find my trouble	Get on one's nerves.
Fine	1. Beautiful person or object 2. Alright.
Fine boy connection	Handsome lad.
Fi si	See Jara.
Fit	Possess ability to carry out task.
Fly	1. Jump across a fence e.g the tief fly di fence fiam. 2. Jump across open drainage gutter.
Fly your polo	Wear shirt with collar turned up. Also- Fly your shirt.
FOC	Free of charge.
Follow fight	Fight with.
Follow-follow	One easily lead.
Follow laugh	Laugh with.
Follow play	1. Play with. 2. Joke with e.g. I bi yua age wey you wan dey follow mi play?
Fone	Derived from Phonetics. To speak in a foreign accent e.g. why you dey blow fone?
Food is ready	1. Buka 2 Wording of sign placed in front of Buka 3. Food is being served.
Fool pass garri	Extremely foolish
Footron	Derived from Citroen. One who has no car and goes everywhere on foot.
For	1. From. E.g. Comot for road. 2. At e.g. Na for Tombo bar I see di booze man.
Forbid	Have an aversion to certain foods e.g. I dey forbid goat meat on Sundays. Usually related to Juju.
For life	No chance in a million
For where?	Impossible
Form fool	Fool around.
Foto	Photograph.
Four-o-four	1. Peugeot 404 2. Cooked dog meat i.e. the dogcatcher needs to be fast to make the kill
Four one nine	1. Advance fee fraud 2. Cheating 3. Deception.

Four to six	:	Children's birthday party. Usually lasts from 4pm to 6pm.
Fren	:	Friend.
Fren-fren	:	Favouritism.
Front	:	Presence e.g Who born am to talk dat nonsense for mai front
Frovlem	:	Problem.
Fufu	:	Dough like meal made from hot water and either cassava or plaintain flour. Usually served with soup
Fun won ton	:	Meaning - Give dem finish. 1. To make a memorable entrance. 2. Dress very well.
Full ground remain	:	Excess e.g. See how food full ground remain for the party. Shoo!
Gaining calories	:	Couple in tight embrace. Also-Gaining electrons.
Gallop	:	Pot holes in road.
Garium Sulphate	:	Garri. [pseudo chemical composition of Gari]
Garri	:	Dried cassava flour.
Garuwa	:	Aluminium container for fetching water. Garuwa is used as a metaphor for private business e.g. everybodi carry im Garuwa meaning mind your own business.
Gather	:	1. Own a lot of an item 2. Hoarde.3. To be muscular e.g. See how the man gather. You no bow? 4. Beat up. e.g. See as e gather di man.
Gauge	:	Bellyful.
Gbagam	:	Loud clapper of bells.
Gbagbati	:	Excessive display.
Gbagbe!	:	Dismissive. Means Forget that one!.
Gbaladun	:	Enjoyment.
Gba summer	:	Enjoy.
Gba winter	:	1. Suffer 2. Loneliness
Gbanjo	:	Cheap market sale.

Gbedu : 1. Rhythmic Afro beat sound 2. Loud sound system.

Gbegiri soup : Yoruba soup made from ground beans, red capsicum, onions, tomatoes and palm oil. Served with Amala, Pounded Yam or Eko.

Gbomogbomo : Child snatcher usually for fetish.

Gbosa : Loud explosion.

Gboyen : Fine girl.

Gen : Electricity generator. Also Standby Gen and Plant.

Gen-gen : 1. Exciting 2. On the edge.

Gerrout : Get out of here.

Geisha : Brand of sardines in tomato sauce.

Get : 1. To have or own e.g. I get shirt like dat. 2. To understand e.g. I don get wetin you dey yarn.

Get as e bi : There's something odd about it.

Get belle : Get pregnant.

Get bodi : Overweight.

Get gist : Important information to tell e.g. I get gist for you.

Get head : 1. Sensible 2. Genuine e.g that deal no get head at all

Get mouth : 1 Talkative 2 Acid tongue. 3 Gift of the garb.

Get road : 1. Right of way while driving e.g. Na mi get road but e come shunt me. 2. Delusions of grandeur e.g. See poor man dey waka as if na im get road.

Get sense : Intelligence e.g. So you think say na you get sense pass?

Gettaway you : Get out.

Ghana must go : Large woven red or blue plastic carrier bag which was used by Ghanaians when they fled Nigeria during a mass deportation exercise.

Giam : Give it to him or her.

Giddying	:	Kissing.
Gidi	:	Lagos. Also Las Gidi.
Gif	:	Give.
Gi mi	:	Give it to me.
Giraffe	:	Examination malpractice were the neck is stretched to spy neighbour's work.
Girls follow me	:	Hair cut with horizontal parting on back of head.
Gism	:	GSM phone.
Gist	:	1. conversation 2. Idle chat
Give chance	:	1. Excuse me! 2. Get lost!
Give dem finish	:	Big entrance.
Give raps	:	See Spin.
Go	:	1. Will 2. Indicating intent. (In present tense) e.g. I go beat you O!
Go come	:	See you when you get back.
Go come no dey	:	No dilly dally.
Go here go there	:	1. Indecisive. 2. Neither here nor there.
Gonosheen	:	Gonorrhoea.
Go slow	:	Traffic jam
God forbid	:	God will not allow that to happen.
God forbid bad thing	:	God will not allow that to happen. Also God forbid.
Gorimapka	:	Derived from name of soap character with clean- head. Clean shaven head. See Moro-moro.
Got gist	:	Hear through the grapevine. Also Gotten gist and Them say.
Grab	:	Muscular.
Grabeez	:	Big muscles.
Gra-gra	:	1. Commotion 2. Hustle 3. Overactive 4. Aggressive
Gree-gree	:	See Gra-gra.
Gree	:	Agree.
Gree yua own	:	1. Takes a fancy to you e.g. di bobo gree yua own o! 2. Agree with you.
Ground no level	:	I don't have enough money.
Gulder	:	Brand of Nigerian beer.

Guud	:	Good.
Guguru	:	Pop corn.
Guy	:	Man about town.
Guy name	:	Trendy nickname.
Guy way	:	Acting cool.
Gwaince	:	To eat.
Haba!	:	Good grief!
Hala	:	1. Raise ones voice 2. Scream.
Half field	:	When the ball remains in the weaker team's half of the field during soccer match.
Handsup	:	Put your hands above your head.
Hanlele	:	Start marching.
Harmattan	:	1. Dry and dusty winds blowing Southwards from the Sahara occurring during the dry season. 2. Financial hardship.
Haus	:	House.
Haysobay!	:	1. Wake up call to action 2. Rallying cry. Used to psyche up people who then respond by shouting Hey! Might have originated from the shouts of workers and their foremen during railway construction in Nigeria. The foreman would have shouted Chaps (or Hey) obey.
Head	:	On your account. Eg Why you wan dey chop credit for mai head?.
Head no correct	:	1. Mad 2. Eccentric e.g Why you dress laik yua head no correct. See Craze. Hear : 1. Understand a language 2. Obey instruction. 3. Comprehend what is being said.
Hear di smell	:	Smell the aroma.
Hear word	:	Obey instruction. e.g. you no dey hear word
Heart cut	:	Frightened e.g. My heart juss cut.
Heavy men	:	Tough guy.

Helele : Exceptional.
Highway manager : Public cleaner of major roads in Lagos.
Hiss : sound emitted while sucking ones teeth. Duration is proportional to emotional state ay the time
Hold belle : Prevent hunger e.g Abeg take dis chin-chin hold belle till the yam cook.
Hold this one for hand : 1.Take 2.Take this monetary gift.
Hold-up : Traffic jam.
Home delivery : Girl sent off to meet husband for first time following arranged marriage.
Home training : Well brought up. E.g. e no get home training meaning she wasn't brought up well.
Home trouble : A personal disaster blamed on a family member using Juju to cause problems.
Hor! : See Shoo!
Hot drink : Alcoholic beverages.
House : 1. Room 2. Anywhere inside a house.
How bodi? : How are you?
How dey go dey go? : 1. How are things with you? 2. How are things going?
How e bi? : How is it?
How far? : See How bodi?
How for do? : How are we going to do it?
How I go come do? : What am I supposed to do?
How manage? : How did it happen?
How now? : How bodi?
How pepper ? : How are you financially?
Hungri : 1. Hunger 2. Strong desire for something e.g. New moto dey hungri me. 3. Poor e.g. Look im Byah byah laik hungri man own.
Hungry man : Poor man.
Hyper-jack : Read too much.
I beg : Abeg.
I dey fear you o! : I am afraid of you. Also- You dey fear

		me o.
I don die	:	I'm finished!
I never see!	:	Oh, I never!
I no get yua time	:	I have no time for you
I think?	:	Is it not so?
Iacon	:	Air conditioner.
Iapot	:	Air port.
Ibeji	:	Twins.
Ikebe	:	Bottom.
Ikpekere	:	Fried unripe plantain chips.
Igbo	:	1. Language spoken by the Igbo people of Eastern Nigeria 2. Indian hemp.
Iyama!	:	1. That's gross! 2. Filthy! 3. Yuck!
Innocenti	:	1. Guiltless. 2. Chastity.
Inside inside	:	Deep in the interior.
Isiewu	:	Igbo soup made from goat's head (including the mashed brain), vegetables, palm oil and potash. Served as a starter.
Isu	:	1. Yam. 2. Prominent Calf Muscles
ITK	:	I too know. One who thinks they know everything.
Ivinin	:	Evening.
Iwe Ilu	:	Right of abode in a country.
Ja	:	Run away.
Jab	:	1. Profession 2.Place of work.
Jack	:	Read seriously especially for examination.
Jaga-jaga	:	Haphazard
Jaki	:	1. Very hard worker 2. Worker being taken advantage of.
Jaku-jaku	:	Carelessly put together.
Jagbajantis	:	Nonsense
Jaguda	:	Crook.
Jam	:	1. Collision, especially cars. 2. Meet up
Jam bodi	:	Rough bodily contact.
Jamb	:	Joint Admission and Matriculation Board. Body in charge of University

entrance in Nigeria who organise a yearly entrance examination.

Jambite : Freshman in Nigerian university.

Jambito : Jambite.

Jambress : Female freshman in Nigerian universities.

Jandon : London.

Jankara : 1. Market in Lagos 2. Fake products.

Janglova : 1.Merry-go-round. 2. Playground swing

Jara : Extra helping. Also Fi si.

Jare : Ojare.

Jazz : Nonsense. e.g Ol' boy why you dey talk Jazz laik dat?

Jedi Jedi : Piles.

Jeje : 1.Gentle. 2. Polite. 3. Up standing individual.

Jejeli : Adverb of Jeje meaning Gently.

Jibiti : Fraudster.

Jiga : Parasitic worm infestation on legs or foot such as Guinea worm.

Jim-jim : Over zealous.

Jin jin jin : Party.

Jinta : Crook.

JJC : Johnny juss come. Slang to denote a Nigerian who has just returned from abroad especially after a long absence.

Jo : Please; Yoruba word.

Jogba : 1.Trickery 2. Gambling. Urhobo word.

Join : Board a bus.

Joke na joke : This is no longer funny! Also - If na joke stop am!

Jollof : Paella like dish of rice made with tomatoes, peppers and spices. A Nigerian party dish.

Joint : 1. Watering hole where food and drinks are sold.

Judge : Say ones side of the story in a dispute.

Jugunu : Rough neck.

Juju	:	Black magic.
Jump up pee	:	Koko ise trousa
June 12	:	1. Date election result was annulled in Nigeria. 2. Fraud 3. Election malpractice.
Jungle city	:	Ajejunle. A rough part of Lagos.
Juss	:	Just.
Juss dey patch am	:	Just surviving
K-leg	:	1. Knock-knees 2. Unexpected Complications in a situation 3. Unexpected problems e.g. K-leg don enta di matter.
Kabu-kabu	:	carbu-carbu.
Kack	:	Dress well.
Kai-kai	:	Home made gin.
Kain	:	Kind of.
Keke Marwa	:	Yoruba for 'Bicycle of Marwa'. Name given to 3 wheeled vehicle used as Taxi in Lagos. They appeared during the tenure of Gorvenor Marwa.
Kakaraka	:	Strong and stiff. E.g. the stork fish bodi strong Kakaraka laik say dem never cook am.
Kalakuta	:	House of the late Fela Anikulapo Kuti, which was burnt down by soldiers.
Kalo-kalo	:	1. One armed bandit. 2. Amusement arcade game machines.
Kampala	:	1. Kind of African print fabric thought to have originated in the city of the same name the capital of Uganda. Also called Ankara. 2. Jail house.
Kampke	:	1.Complete 2. Completely at ease.
Kanda	:	1. Peelings 2. Hide 3. Skin.
Kari	:	Carry.
Kashi	:	Gambling especially with cards.
Kata-kata	:	Commotion.
Kaun	:	Potash.
Keep Lagos clean	:	Large bell bottomed trousers that drags

		on the floor.
Khaki bois	:	The army.
Khaki no bi leather	:	Phrase meaning 1. Things are getting very tough. 2. Threat to someone telling him that - More trouble than bargained for is on the way.
Kia-kia bus	:	Quick-quick buses; Yoruba word. Danfo buses known for always being in a hurry.
Kick moto	:	Turn car engine on.
Ki lo de	:	What is wrong? Yoruba phrase.
Ki lon' haps	:	Whazuuppp??
Kill and divide	:	Make a killing and divide the spoils. Usually refers to corruption among public officers.
Know book	:	1. Literate 2. Intelligent.
Kobo	:	Nigerian coin. 100 kobo= 1 Naira.
Kobo-leg	:	Bow leg.
Ko ko e se	:	Trouser that barely reaches ankle. Also Jump up pee.
Kol	:	Call.
Kondishon	:	Condition.
Korodoome	:	Large vessel for storing water.
Koro-koro	:	1. Very clear vision e.g. na for mai two eye korokoro I see am hapun 2. Clear daylight e.g na daytime Korokoro.
Kudi	:	Money.
Kuk	:	1. Cook. 2. To be given protective charms by witch doctor e.g Babalawo don kuk am well well.
Kuku	:	Word placed in sentence for emphasis e.g. I no Kuku sabi am, meaning I really don't know him. Also Kukuma.
Kulikuli	:	Small fried balls of peanut paste.
Kunu	:	Refreshing Nigerian drink made from Sorghum or Millet. Drunk in Northern Nigeria.
Kwik	:	Quick

Labu	:	Bell bottomed trousers.
Lahila Hilalau!	:	Oh gosh!
Lai	:	Lie.
Lai lai	:	Not in a million years. Also Lai lai to lai lai.
Lait	:	1. Light 2. Electricity e.g. NEPA don commot lait again.
Lakuli!	:	Oh my word!
Lama	:	Cow.
Land	:	Arrive e.g. e don land
Land you slap	:	Threat meaning I will slap you face e.g I go land you slap o! Also Wipe and Tear you slap.
Lanko	:	Guinness stout drink. Also called Odeku.
Lap	:	Carry someone on your laps during ride in a car or bus.
Las Gidi	:	Lagos.
Lasu	:	Lagos State University.
Last year tori	:	Old news.
Launch	:	Use newly brought item for first time.
Learn work	:	Do apprentice.
Lef	:	Leave.
Leg no dey comot	:	Someone who seems to always be present e.g. dat bobo leg no dey comot church.
Leg no dey house	:	One who goes out too much. Also Waka about and Waka waka
Leg no dey stay one place	:	1. Restless 2. Constantly moving about.
Legedis Benz	:	Derived from Mercedes Benz. Denotes one without a car who 'legs it' everywhere.
Legle	:	Sit spread eagled
Leg-xus	:	(Derived from Lexus). Someone who walks everywhere because they don't own a car. also see Footron.
Leke leke	:	Type of bird. Cattle Egret

Lepa Shandy	:	Slim (skinny) girl
Let my people go	:	Result that is barely above the pass mark in examination.
Level	:	Eat and finish a substantial amount of food.
Like play like play	:	Before you knew it. Also - No do no do.
Light	:	Electricity power supply.
Listen well well	:	Pay good attention.
Load	:	Eat too much E.g. E juss load poundi finis come dey ask for eba.
LOC	:	Local organising committee. Usually formed to run a major sporting event.
Local champion	:	A provincial super star.
Lokito	:	Uninformed and not travelled.
Lookery	:	Looking at things one's eyes are not supposed to see.
Long leg	:	Well connected. e.g. na long leg e use enta dat school
Long throat	:	Greed. Also Lagga throat.
Love in Tokyo	:	Excessive public show of affection by couple.
Machine	:	Motor cycle.
Mach	:	Trample upon. Also Mash.
Madam Kofo	:	1. Character in Nigerian soap opera Second Chance famed for wearing large head scarves. 2. Lady with large head-scarf.
Made in England	:	Eat food and lick plate clean till Logo at the bottom of plate is visible.
Made in China	:	See Made in England.
Magani	:	Native aphrodisiac.
Maggi	:	Maggi cubes. Brand of seasoning cubes for cooking containing herbs and spices.
Mago-mago	:	Ilegal deal.
Magun	:	Spell put on woman said to kill her partner if involved in adulterous relationship.

Mai	:	My. e.g Commot mai front
Make	:	1. Made e.g. Wetin make am sick. 2. Should I? E.g. Wetin make I do? 3. Let me e.g. Make I warn you o! 4. Parade one's self e.g. E juss dey make up and down.
Make eye	:	Wink.
Make mouth	:	Boast.
Make yeye	:	1. Make fun 2. Crack jokes 3. Misbehave.
Mek	:	Make.
Make I hear word	:	Shut up.
Make I see road	:	Get out of my face.
Malu	:	Cow. Also Lama.
Mama, dash	:	Hand me down clothes from a lady.
Mama-put	:	Road side food seller so called because customers frequently beg for extra helpings by saying 'Mama abeg

put more now'
Mammar:Hit.

Mammy wagon	:	Wooden construction on the chassis of a lorry for carry passengers.
Mammy water	:	Mermaid.
Man	:	1 Myself.
Man picken	:	1. Me.
Man no die, man no rotten	:	1. I am barely surviving.
Manage	:	Make do with second best.
Many leg	:	Complications e.g. Dat business don get Many leg.
Markit	:	1. Merchandise
Mash	:	Trample upon.
Mate	:	1. Age group. 2. Same social class. e.g. which day we become mate?
Matric	:	Matriculation into university.
Matric gown	:	Matriculation gown.
Mayguard	:	Night watch man.
Meanwilli	:	Mean while.

Mede-mede : 1. Salads 2. Foreign cuisine.

Medicine : 1. Juju 2. Tablets. Also called Melesin and medi.

Megida : Big man. Also Oga.

Mentalo : See Aromental.

Me shio nu : Shut up; Igbo word.

Mescaform : Mess up e.g Ol'boy, why you kon dey mescaform now?

Mesej : Message.

Mess : Fart. See Pollute.

Micro stuff : Small print information.

Miliki : Enjoyment.

Minerals : Soft drinks

Mind tell me : Intuition.

Mister man : Hey you!

Mm-mm:

Mobile : Abbreviation for Mobile Police force which is a rapid response anti-riot arm of the police. Also called Kill and go (derogatory).

Mobile tailor : Tailor who slings sewing machine on shoulder and roams the streets in search of clients. Also Obioma.

Moda : Mother.

Moin moin : Steamed cake of ground black eyed beans containing pepper, bits of fish or corned beef. Also spelt Moyin moyin.

Monkey coat : Fanciful waistcoat.

Money for hand : No credit.

Money make iron float : 1. The iron float refers to large ships and the phrase means it cost money to do anything outstanding. 2. Money can do a lot.

Money miss road : Nouveau riche throwing money around.

Money yab man : Condition where desires can't be accomplished due to financial constraints.

Moni	:	Money.
Monkey dey work babon dey chop	:	The workers don't partake of the harvest despite their hard work.
Molue	:	Rickety bright yellow bus used for transportation in Lagos.
Moro-moro	:	Clean-shaven head. Also Gorimapka.
Morning food	:	Breakfast.
Morocco	:	Indian hemp.
Mono mono	:	Lightening.
More-more	:	In addition.
Moto	:	Car.
Mouth organ	:	Cob of roasted or boiled corn.
Move	:	Brisk trade.
Move stuff	:	Show off one's academic prowess. Also Vibrate
Mugun	:	Fool.
Mumu	:	See Mugun.
Murd	:	1. Die e.g. Di Baba don murd o! 2. Murder e.g. Wo, if you touch mi I go murd you o!
Muritala	:	Slang for twenty Naira note which bears the photograph of the late Nigerian Head of state; General Muritala Mohammed. Also called Muri.
My own don betta	:	My good fortune has arrived.
Na	:	It is.
Na dat time	:	That is the time.
Nada	:	Nothing
Na fight?	:	1. Rebuff to someone being unduly aggressive. 2. Is it by force?
Na go bi dat?	:	Are you going ?
Na im	:	It is.
Naif	:	Knife
Nait	:	Night
Na one	:	Exclusive or distinctive item. Eg That Bobo Opon na one.
Na kwensh	:	See Na die.

Na sò : 1. That is true. 2. That is how e.g. Na so e come dabaru everything.

Na so? : 1. Is that how it is now? 2. Is that true?

Na so I see am o! : That's the way it is.

Na una sabi : That's your business not mine.

Na wa : It is wonderful. Also Na wah.

Na wetin? : 1. What is it this time? 2. So what?

Na you bico : You the man please!

Na you o! : You are the man! Also Na you we dey look o!

Na you we dey look o : We look up to you.

Na yua eye bi dis? : Long time no see.

Naija : 1. Pertaining to Nigeria 2. Nigerian citizen e.g. Naija no go change.

Nak : 1. Tell 2. Hit e.g. Why you nak me for bodi laik dat now? 3. Eat 4. What someone is wearing e.g. See the shoe wey e nak.

Natin : Nothing.

Natin spoil : 1. No sweat 2. Hey, no worries.

Native doctor : 1. Juju practitioner 2. Herbalist.

NEPA : National Electric Power Authority. Also Never Expect Power Always.

Next tomorrow : Day after tomorrow.

NFA : National Football Association. Also No future ambition.

NFAite : Student lacking in ambition.

Ngwo ngwo : Soup made from goat intestines, heart, liver, vegetables, onions and pepper. Served as a starter.

No bi? : Is it not?

No be me and you : Just count me out of that

No bi person : Persona non-grata E.g Dat one no bi person.

No bi classmate : Not in the same category.

No bi small : A lot. E.g. E get money no bi small.

No bi today : It didn't start today. e.g No bi today that man begin tief.

No dey : 1. Not at home. 2. Not available.
No dey stay one place : 1. Can't stay still. 2. Adventurous.
No dey take eye see : Can't see without touching e.g Dat guy no dey take eye see woman.
No do no do : Before I could say Jack Robinson.
No face : No time.
No how no how : One way or the other. Also - No do no do.
No go : 1. Will not.
No know : 1. Not aware.
No know im sef : 1. Ignorant or clueless person 2. One with exaggerated ideas about their true station in life.
No let : Do not allow e.g. No let am come here again.
No money for pocket : Financially broke.
No size in London : Very large size E.g. Im leg na no size in London.
No wan hear : Refusing instruction or advice.
Not to : It is not.
Notice me : One desperately carving attention.
Now : Placed at end of question for emphasis E.g Wetin dey do you now?
NTA : 1. Nigerian Television Authority 2. Gossip.
Number six : Intelligence.
Nyanfu-nyanfu : Plenty. See Borku and Plenti plenti.
Nyanga : Showing off. Also Nyanga Tolotolo.
Nyarsh : Bottom. Also Backyard.
NYSC : National Youth Service Corps. One-year compulsory national service undergone by all Nigerian graduates. After an initial 4 week military style training camp the graduates are posted throughout Nigeria to fill various posts. Also Now Your Suffering Commences.
O! : Placed at the end of sentences for emphasis and effect E.g. I go broke

		bottle for yua head O!
Oba	:	Traditional ruler. Also Olu, Ovie and Sultan.
Obey the wind	:	Skinny, Very underweight individual.
Obioma	:	See Mobile tailor.
Obito	:	1. All night wake.
Objectiv	:	Multiple choice examination.
Obobo canda	:	Light skinned person.(Derogatory).
Obodo	:	Homestead.
Obokun	:	1. Cat fish 2. Mercedes Benz limousine
Obrokotor	:	Obese person.
October rush	:	Frantic chasing of female freshmen (Jambitoes) in Nigerian universities by senior male students.
Oda	:	Other.
Odeku	:	Large bottle of Guinness stout.
Odu	:	Shady business.
Odudoof	:	(Derisory) Overweight individual.
Ofofo	:	Yoruba word for Gossip.
Oga	:	Person in charge. Also Oga pata pata.
Ogbele o!	:	Goodness gracious! See Ye pa!
Ogboju	:	Bluff your way through.
Ogbologbo	:	Old hand
Ogbono	:	Soup made from ground Ogbono seeds, crayfish, beef, dried fish, okra, spinach and pepper.
Ogi	:	Pap made from corn. Also Akamu.
Ogogoro	:	See Apketeshi.
Ojare	:	Said at the end of sentences for emphasis. E.g Comot for road Ojare!
Oje marina	:	Big lie.
Ojoro	:	Cheating.
Ojuju	:	Masquerade.
Okada	:	1. Name of Nigerian Airline. 2. Motor cycle taxi.
Okirikpotor	:	1. Eczema. 2. Dermatitis.
Okpetu	:	1. Trouble 2.It has happened!
Okporoko	:	Stork fish.

Okrika wake up	:	Second hand clothes. Also Gorgio Amadi.
Ol'boy	:	Yo my man.
Ole	:	Theif. Also Teif.
Olodo	:	Dunce.
Olofofo	:	Gossip (Yoruba word). Also Tatafo and Amebo
Olopa	:	Police officer.
Omi ni polish	:	Patent leather shoes.
Omo	:	1. Child 2. My friend 3. Popular detergent powder.
Omo ale trousa	:	Literally means Prisoner's trousers i.e. Trousers that barely reach the ankles.
Omolanke	:	Labourer for hire who carries goods in a large custom made wooden wheelbarrow.
Omoge	:	Fine girl. Also Chinani, Chickito, Gboyen, Si si and Babi.
Omota	:	Ruffian or rude boy.
One day one day	:	One of these days. Used as a warning for those involved in dodgy acts e.g One day one day monkey go go market e no go come back meaning everyday foe the thief one day for the owner.
One kain	:	Odd E.g Dat guy dress one kain.
One thousand and four	:	Popular block of flats in Lagos Island.
Onioburu	:	Night soil man. Also Agbepo.
Opaks	:	Worthless.
Opari	:	It is finished.
Opeke	:	Good looking girl.
Open eye	:	1. Wise up. 2. Become sexually active.
Open mouth	:	1. Talk e.g Abeg no open mouth laik dat.2. Astonishment e.g Ol' boy, the way dem spray money nyanfu nyanfu for dat party, Omo na so I open mouth.
Open ya sense	:	Use your intelligence.
Operation	:	Armed robbery.

Operation sweep : (Defunct) Special police anti-crime task force.

Opkor : Juju.

Opon : Yoruba word for prominent forehead. Also Crash helmet.

Oppressor! : Owner of big car.

Orenj : Orange.

Osa straight : Molue. Literally means Straight into the lagoon. Called so because of accidents involving Molue Buses plunging into the lagoon in Lagos.

Otopiapia : Rat poison.

Over-graduate : Postgraduate student. (As opposed to undergraduate).

Overs : Overseas.

Over stone : Disallowed goal when stones are used for goal posts and the ball goes directly above the stone.

Ovie : King.

Owambe : Yoruba word meaning it is there, denoting a lavish party with live music.

Owo : Urhobo soup made from palm oil, dried meat and fish, crayfish, potash, pepper, cassava starch and Egidije. Also called Oil soup.

Oyinbo : 1. Caucasian 2. English 3. Big English words.

Oyoyo : 1. Good times 2. Jollification..

Paale : Old man.

Paddy : Good friend.

Pafuka : 1. Give up the ghost 2. Collapse

Pain : Physical deformity e.g Una sabi dat guy now, di one wey leg dey pain.

Pali : See Paddy.

Pammi : Palm wine taped from tree top.

Pammy : See Pammi

Pan cake : Make-up.

Panda : Cheap gold plated jewellery.

Pangba : Astonishing e.g. Dat man Byah byah na Pangba.
Pangolo : Tin can.
Panla : Dried stork fish. Also Opkoroko.
Para : Abbreviation of Parasite. 1.
Papa : 1. Dad 2. Granddad 3. Old man.
Papa battalion : Man with many children.
Papa dash : Hand me downs from a man.
Papa dozen : See Papa battalion.
Papa-lolo : Dandy old man.
Parapo : Kinsman.
Parsha : Partiality.
Pass : 1. More than or bigger than e.g. E big pass am. 2. Beyond me e.g. Dat one pass me o! 3. Obsolete e.g. Dat style don reign pass. 4. Relating to a bygone era e.g. Dat time don pass.
Pata : Underwear.
Pata pata : Completely.
Patch am : Managing.
Pay smol smol : Pay for goods in instalments.
Pepper : 1.Trouble e.g. You go see pepper.
Pepper don reach : I am alright financially
Pepper eye : 1. Jealousy 2. Sour grapes.
Perm : 1. Commit to memory 2. Woo a girl.
Persin : Person.
Petty trader : Road side vendor of assorted cheap articles.
Phichemba : Physics, Chemistry and Biology.
Pick pin : Punishment where one stoops on one leg to touch the ground with one finger and maintains the position. (Popular in boarding houses).
Pick race : Sprint off.
Picken : Child.
Picken wey say im mama no go see, im sef no go sleep : Admonition to disobedient child - "You

		think you are giving me trouble but it's you who will suffer most."
Pipo	:	People.
Piss for bodi	:	1.Incontinence of urine 2. Paralysed by fear
Pkomo	:	See Ponmo.
Pkaje	:	Share of fraud money.
Pkokiripko	:	Rackety.
Pkopo garri	:	Dried Tapioca usually eaten with salt and ground nuts.
Pompoo	:	Navel.
Plant	:	Electricity generating plant. Also Gen or Standby Gen.
Play	:	1. Trick e.g. No play mi wayo jo.
Plenti plenti	:	Abundant.
Pollute	:	Fart. Also Mess.
Pololo	:	Prostitute.
Ponmo	:	Boiled animal hide. Also Pkomo, Show-boy and Rain coat.
Popular jingo	:	Man about town.
Popular side	:	1. Cheap seats 2. Standing only tickets in stadium.
Populo	:	1. Cheap seats. 2. Cheap or very common article.
Port	:	Port Harcourt. Town in Rivers state, Nigeria. Also called the Garden city.
Poto-poto	:	Mud.
Poundi	:	Pounded yam.
Pozza	:	Poser.
Pregnapoline	:	Pregnant lady.
Presido	:	President.
Press	:	1. Demonic oppression especially in bed at night 2. Ironing of clothes. 3. To be dominated during soccer game.
Price	:	1. Haggle over price with market trader. 2. Inquire as to the cost of items for sale.
Proper proper	:	Very well.
Provisions	:	Tinned beverages.

Puff puff	:	Fried balls of flour.
Pull your ears	:	Get ready to run off.
Pump	:	Public or outdoor tap.
Pure water	:	1. Bottled water sold by street vendors in Nigeria 2. A very common commodity. e.g Dat car dey everywhere laik pure water
Push me push you	:	See Apketeshi.
Put	:	Appoint to position.
Put am for ground	:	Floor with a punch.
Put eye	:	Look at something with longing.
Put fire	:	1. Stir up strife 2. Depress the accelerator pedal. (speed up) 3. Incite/ goad two quarrelling parties into a fight.
Put mi for trouble	:	Get me into trouble.
Put leg for road	:	Start going.
Quaya	:	Choir.
Quayet	:	Quiet.
Quanta	:	1.Collide 2. Fight 3. Clash
Quarter pass four	:	Squint.
Quench	:	1. Switch off e.g. quench dat light. 2. Die e.g. Di man don quench. Also Yamutu.
Queer-queer	:	Useless.
Quick	:	Used to comment on 1. Punctuality e.g. Since im promotion e no dey quick return from work 2. Rarity e.g Rain no dey quick fall this time of year
Ra-re	:	Trendy guy.
Rain beat you	:	Drenched in the rain.
Rain coat	:	See Ponmo
Raise hand	:	Salute e.g. I raise hand for you o!
Rake	:	Empty boasting.
Ranka dede	:	Hausa greeting.
R.R.S	:	Rapid Response Squad. (An arm of the police Force).
Reach	:	1. Arrive e.g. Which day you reach? 2.

Afford e.g. Na dat one my hand (pocket) reach.

Reach ground : Completely.

Reach mai place : Pay me a visit. e.g. you come town no even reach mai place.

Ready made : Off the peg (rack) and ready to wear.

Reign : In vogue e.g Na dat trousa dey reign now o.

Reign pass : Out of fashion.

Remain small : 1. Nearly 2. Almost.

Remember me : Remind me.

Remember the day yua mama born you : Threat e.g. I go beat you sotey you go remember the day yua mama born you. Means the beating will cause you to relive your birth.

Remi : (Derived from Remnant). Left overs. Also Chop remain.

Return match : Returning faulty electrical goods to point of purchase especially at Alaba International market.

Rhyme : Go well together e.g Dat yua trousa no rhyme di shirt.

Richard Lander : One who uncannily times his visits to your house to coincide with meal times.

Rimuv : Remove.

Rockeez : Party.

Rofo rofo : Rough.

Room and parlour : One room apartment rented out to families with shared toilet facilities. The room is usually divided with a curtain into the sleeping area (room) and the sitting area (Parlour). Mats are placed under the bed to be fished out at night for the kids to sleep.

Rush : 1. Struggling for a place on a bus e.g. Na when I dey rush for Molue na im pick pocket teif mai money. 2. Flow. e.g.

The pump dey rush well well.

Sabi : Know.

Sabi book : See Know book.

Sacrifice : Bribe to Police at road junctions.

Sagalo : Overhead kick in Football game.

Saka : Know too much (sarcastic) e.g Na you saka.

Sake of say : The reason is.

Sake of what? : Why should that be?

Salenza : Exhaust pipe if vehicle. Derived from Silencer.

Salot : 1. Salute 2. Greetings

Samba : 1. Bottom. 2. A generous rear end.

Samma : Hit e.g I go samma you slap o!

Sam-sam : 1. Never 2. Not in a million years. Also Lai-lai.

San sand : 1. Sand 2. Dirt.

Santana : also Apku. Named after the car which normally comes in white and handles smoothly like Apku.

Sapele water : Native gin.

Saraa : Sacrifice. (Yoruba word.)

Satellite : 1. Abbreviation for Satellite Town , Lagos. 2. Large head scarf worn by women dressed in traditional attire.

Sawa : Sour.

Say : Is it not that e.g Say na you be di Oga?

Say wetin : 1.Why? 2. What?

Scata : Scatter. Also Scata-scata.

School Father : Male mentor to junior student in Nigerian boarding school.

School Mother : Female mentor to a junior student in Nigerian boarding school.

Scope : 1. To look at an object or person longingly 2. Tell a lie

Sebi? : Isn't it?

Sekon : Second.

See Blood! : Look at trouble!

See im place see mai place	:	We are close neighbours.
See Oba	:	See trouble; threat. E.g. If mai hand touch you you go See Oba.
See Pepper	:	See- See trouble.
See trouble!	:	What a fine mess!
Sef	:	1. In particular e.g. You sef. 2. Placed at end of question when irritated or impatient e.g. Wetin sef?
Senior	:	1. Elder 2. Someone in a higher class in secondary school.
Serve Juju	:	Worship idols.
Set	:	Hi-fi system. See Gbedu and System.
Set blow	:	Adopt a fighting stance.
Shack	:	1. Drink alcohol. 2. Be intoxicated or mesmerised by anything e.g. The house wey e build juss dey shack am.
Shackeez	:	1. Act of drinking. 2. Alcoholic drinks. Also Shak.
Shaded up	:	Wearing dark sun glasses.
Shakabula	:	Dane gun.
Shakara	:	1. Showing off. 2. Boasting about the impossible. See Raking or Draw rain.
Shake bodi	:	1. Spend some money 2. Pay the bill.
Shaki	:	Sheep or cattle cooked intestine.
Shako	:	Yoruba word meaning Show off.
Shalanga	:	Pit latrine.
Sharrup!	:	Shut up.
Sharp mouth	:	1. Acid tongue 2. Gift of the garb.
Shenj	:	Change.
Shenlele-coolele	:	Chant usually sang by kids at each other before a fight in Warri.
Shey?	:	Yoruba word meaning- Is it not?
Shicoco	:	See Omoge.
Shift	:	Verb. Move out in convoy of cars.
Shimi	:	Slip worn under dress.
Shinani	:	See Omoge.
Shine	:	1. Look well 2. Look glamorous.

Shine eye : 1. Keep your eyes open 2. Be on your guard

Shine shine : Glittering.

Shockazoba : Shock absorbers of vehicle.

Shoe maker : Shoe repairer.

Shomo : 1.You know 2. You understand? Also You sabi say.

Shoo! : 1. Wow!

Short knicker : Shorts.

Show : 1.Make life difficult for you e.g I go show you o!

Show boy : See Ponmo. Also Pkomo and Rain coat.

Show face : 1. Turn up. 2. Show up briefly at a function to avoid being accused of snubbing the host.

Show ma fefe : Pretending to be fragile and sophisticated.

Show them : Give them something to think about. Also Show dem Pepper and Show dem finis.

Sidon : Sit down.

Sidon look na dog name : Phrase used to tell someone off for being too passive.

Sidon there now : Sit there day dreaming (sarcastic).

Sight : See e.g. I juss sight di guy dey come.

Sima : Simmer down.

Sime sime : 1. Weak 2. Too gentle e.g Ol' boy, why you dey make Sime sime.

Si si : Young trendy girl.

Sista : Sister.

Six to six : ref. Apku. Phrase coined up because some claim a meal of Apku can keep hunger away for 12 hours.

Skenchi : Greedy.

Slacki : Slow thinking person.

Slap : Walking e.g As man no get car na so so slap man dey slap go everywhere.

Slipas : Slippers.
Small chop : Pre meal appetisers such as Chin Chin, Peanuts, Puff Puff and Kuli Kuli.
Smallie : Small statured individual.
Small-small : 1. Gently. Also Sofri sofri. 2. Little by little.
Small time : 1. Next thing you know. 2. Before you know it.
Smol : Small.
Soak away : Septic tank.
Soakeez : Act of drinking garri.
Soda : Wield together.
Soja : Soldier. Also Soja man.
Sokoto : Traditional trouser.
Sontin : Something.
Sontin dey do you : There is something wrong with you.
Sontin dey there : There's something special going on.
So so : 1. Something always being done e.g. Na so so drink e dey drink.
Sotey : For such a long time.
Soyoyo : Trendy.
Sound you : Slap you in the face.
Soup wey sweet na money kill am : Good things cost money.
Spark : Lose temper.
Spin : Woo a girl. Also Toast , Approach, Tune, Give raps and Baze.
Spoots : Designer or very nice clothes.
Spoil : Talk badly of someone behind their back. e.g I hear as you dey spoil me for dat party.
Spoil mai garri : Also Put san sand for mai garri, Spoil mai show or Spoil show for man.
Spree spree : Speak with a foreign accent especially English one.
Sput : 1. Dressed to kill e.g Di guy Sput o! 2. Designer chlothes.Also Sputeez.
Square : 1. Pay up. e.g Ol' boy square me dat

moni wey you borrow now 2. Receive one's salary.

Squat-o-metre	:	Name given to a squatter's mattress on some campuses.
Stand dey look	:	1. Not using one's initiative. 2. Being unduly passive.
Standard	:	1. Very good 2. Perfect
Star	:	Brand of Nigerian beer.
Stay yua own	:	Keep to yourself.
Stock Fish	:	Chemically dried fish
Stone ground	:	1. Fall heavily
Stomok	:	Stomach.
Stranger	:	Visitor.
Stroke	:	Tease.
Strong head	:	1. Stubborn 2. Persistent.
Stud	:	Rough tackle during football game e.g No stud me o! 2. Hamper one's progress.
Suegbe	:	1. Dunce 2.Slow person.
Suffer head	:	1. One prone to recurrent hardships.2. Poor man.
Suffer man	:	Poor man.
Suppose fit	:	Should be able to.
Suppose to	:	Should.
Suya	:	Barbecued Beef or chicken served with special Nigeria spices.
Swear	:	1. Cursed e.g dem swear for you? Meaning- are you cursed?
Sweet mouth	:	1. Sweet tooth 2. Silver tongued
System	:	Hi-Fi System
Taba	:	Tobacco.
Taim	:	Time.
Tanda	:	1. Stand 2. Loitering.
Taffia	:	Gossip.
Take	:	1.How did you do it? e.g. How you take build house on yua salary?
Take breeze	:	Sit out in the fresh air.
Take light	:	Power cut.

Take me shine : 1. Show me up 2. Look good at my expense

Take style : 1. In a round about sort of way e.g the tailor take style get the dress o! 2. Use of guile e.g the bobo wan take style thief mai money

Talk anoda thing : (Dismissive).Say something better.

Tap leather : Play football.

Tap soccer : See Tap leather.

Tapping : Stealing.

Tapping electrons : Caressing a Lady.

Tatafo : Gossip.

Taya : 1. Tired 2. Do something to exhaustion or full satisfaction. E.g. I don chop taya.

TDB : Till Daybreak

Te slow : 1. Doing things slowly. 2. Slow Down, what's the hurry!

Tear shot : Kick a hot shot during football ball.

Tey : 1. Take too long a time. E.g. You don too tey for dat toilet, abeg commot one time jo.

That one : 1. That person 2. That situation.

Them say : I heard it on the grape vine.

Them send you : Were you sent to torment me?

Thermacool : 1. Relax 2. Chill or Stay cool. 3. Brand name of refrigerator.

The thing bi say : The fact of the matter is.

The thing wey-happun for fowl-haus dey happun-for chicken haus : What's good enough for the goose is good enough for the gander.

Throway face : 1. Ignore. 2. Snub. 3. Avoid eye contact.

Throway salute : Big shout out to.

Tie am : Cast a spell on someone.

Tie neck : Street criminals known for grabbing neck chains forcefully from car occupants' necks.

Tie yua Sokoto : 1. Tighten your belt 2. Brace yourself.

Tief : Thief.

Tight hand : Stingy.

Timber and calibre : Men of repute e.g. Those are men of Timber and calibre.

Time wey I small : When I was young.

Tineja : Teenager.

Ting : Thing.

Tinigboko : Extremely thin individual.

Tiro : Khol used as eye liner.

Tip : Dribble opponent during football game.

Titi : Young girl

Titrate : Urinate especially at road side or in a bush.

Toast : Woo a lady. Also Spin, Approach, Base and Tune.

Today na today : This problem must be fully resolved today

Tokunbo : (Yoruba word) 1. Second hand goods. 2. Child born overseas

Tolotolo : 1.Turkey. 2. Show of e.g E dey make Nyanga Tolo tolo.

Tombo : Palm wine.

Tommorow : Procastination.

To nonsense : To excess E.g E Grab muscles to nonsense.

Too dey : 1. Always doing something. E.g. You too dey snore.

Too get : 1. Have in abundance.

Tori : 1. Interesting or humourous story.

Tori get k-leg : The situation has become complicated.

Tori get many leg : Tori get K-leg.

Toro : 1. Old Nigeria 3 pence coin with circular hole in it's middle. 2. Problem e.g. Dat one na yua Toro. .

Toronto : Fake goods.

Tortoise car : Volkswagen 'Bettle'. Also Volks.

Tory don wowo : The story or situation has turned ugly.
Totori : 1. Tickle 2. Excite
Traficate : Indicate while driving. (using the turn signal in your vehicle)
Travul : Travel.
Tri : Three.
Triangular student : (University campus slang). Student with little time for anything other than studies. Goes from the hostels to the canteen then to lectures and back to the hostels thus completing the triangle.
Trying : Doing very well.
Tu : Two.
Tu tu : Two each.
Tuffia : God forbid!
Tuke tuke : Buses used for transport.
Tune : See Toast.
Tuwo Shinkafa : Hausa meal made from mashed boiled rice and served with soup.
Ukodo : Meal of yams, spices, fish and pepper soup boiled in the same pot.
U.I. : University of Ibadan
Una : You people.
Una go marry una sef : Two people forced on each other by a Molue conductor who runs out of change and suddenly darts off leaving the two with a single bank note to share.
Una two : The two of you.
Uniben : University of Benin.
Unilag : University of Lagos.
Uniport : University of Port Harcourt.
Up stair : One storey building.
Uselu : 1. Area in Benin city where the Psychiatric hospital is located. 2. Mad man 3. Eccentric.
Vamoosh : 1. Make hasty retreat.
Veks : Vex.

Venue : Location of party.
Vess : 1. Vex. 2. Provoke to anger.
Vex-comot : Storm off in anger.
Viagragra : 1.Viagra.2. Aphrodisiac.
Vibrate : 1. Exert one's self. 2. Show off one's grasps of a subject.
Village persin : Someone who hails fron one's tribe or village
Wad : Rich e.g Dat business man wad well-well.
Wadded : Rich e.g Di guy dey wadded no bi small.
Wado : Urhobo greeting e.g Internet surfers Wado.
Wahala : Trouble.
Waffi : Warri. Town in Delta State, Nigeria.
Wak : Eat.
Waka : 1. Walk.2. Frequent visits to a Juju practitioner e.g. Dat man sabi waka o!
Waka about : 1. One who is always on the road.
Waka-jugbe : One constantly loitering about.
Waka waka : See Waka about.
Waka pass : To act as extra in Nigerian movie. i.e. - to have a walk on role.
Walahi : I swear. Also Walai.
Wan : One.
Wan wan : One each.
Wash hand now : Come and join me in this meal.
Waszup guy : 1. Young up start. 2. One trying hard to be trendy.
Watch night : 1. Night vigil 2. Security guard.
Wata : Water.
Wata and garri-make eba : Rude reply to a question beginning with 'What'.
Wata pass garri : Things have reached breaking point.
Waya : 1. Wonderful 2. Tough like steel wire. 3. Pangs of hunger.

Wayo : Trickery.

Weak for bodi : In a state of shock e.g Dat news make us weak for bodi.

Wear : 1. Board a bus e.g I go wear bus reach Tinubu.

Wear same trousa : 1. We would fight e.g If you chop dat money we go wear di same trousa today.

Wee wee : Marijuana.

Weather man : Poor man.

Wetin : 1. What is? E.g Wetin bi yua name?

Wetin call : Private parts.

Wetin concern-government : What is my business?

Wetin concern Ag-bero with over load : 1. That's not my business. 2. I don't care.

Wetin dey do you? : What's wrong with you?

Wetin time talk : What is the time?

Wetin yua eye find-go dia : 1. You should not be looking there. 2. Mind your own business.

Wetin yua time talk : What is the time?

Wey : Who e.g The Obioma wey sew mai trousa dey pass.

What's doing you? : What is wrong with you? Also Wetin dey do you?

What's your own? : What's your problem? also - Wetin be yua own now? And Na wetin?

Which day? : When? E.g Which day you begin go gym?

Which one : 1. Hello e.g Ol' boy which ones now. 2. What is e.g Which one be dis?

Which one you dey? : 1. What's wrong with you? 2. Whose side are you on anyway?

Which level? : Hello.

Whinch : Witch.

Whinchi : 1. Bedevil.

Who born?	: Derisive. Used when someone claims to be able to do the unattainable. 1. You can not do it e.g. Who born monkey?
Who born monkey?	: See Who born.
Who know man	: 1. Nepotism. 2. Being well connected especially in government.
Who no know-go know	: Threat meaning - Whoever is claiming not to know will know without a shadow of doubt. Also Who no sabi go sabi.
Whosai!	: 1. Never! 2. Impossible. Also For where!
Wipe	: Slap across the face e.g If you talk am again I go wipe you now now. Also - Land you slap, Land you dorti slap, Sound you and Tear you slap.
Wit	: With.
Woman Lappa	: Man easily controlled by his woman.
Won	: One. see also - Wan.
Wor wor	: Ugly.
Wuru-wuru	: Underhanded methods. See Mago mago.
Xerox	: 1. Plagiarism. 2. Examination malpractice of copying someone's work. Derived from Rank Xerox. Also - Dub.
Ya	: Your.
Yab	: 1. Make fun of. 2. Abuse
Yabbis	: 1. Act of poking fun. 2. Joke at another's expense.
Yafu yafu	: Plenty. See Nyanfu-nyanfu, Borku and Plenti plenti.
Yakata	: 1. Heavily e.g. I juss fall Yakata.
Yam	: Large calf muscles.
Yama-yama	: Nonsense!.
Yamiri	: Cannibal.
Yamutu	: 1. Die 2. Break down.
Yanga	: 1. Pride. 2. Flamboyance. Also Nyanga.
Yarn	: 1. Story 2. Tale 3. Speaking.
Yarnsh	: Bottom. Also Backyard, Ikebe and

Samba.

Yawa don gas : 1.Things have exploded.2. Trouble!

Yawa go gas : (Threat) Things will explode or get out of hand.

Yawn : Loneliness. See Gba Winter.

Yellow fever : 1. Traffic warden with bright orange khaki shirts. 2. Lady who bleaches skin lighter. (derogatory).

Yesterday talk : Obsolete news. See Last year tori.

Ye ye : 1. Useless. 2. Worthless.

Ye pa! : 1. Yikes!

Yonda : Far away. (Yonder)

You are on without Nepa : 1. You're the man. 2. You are too much.

You chop I chop : Mutual corruption.

You dey fear me o : I am afraid of you.

You go see : (Threat) You will see. Also You go see blood.

You hear? : Do you understand?

You sabi now : You know how it is.

You're on o! : You are the man!

Your hand reach : 1. Afford e.g Na dat one my hand reach meaning That's what I can afford.

Your money don come : You have hit the jackpot.

Yua : Your.

Zero one zero : (University slang) No breakfast , have lunch and no dinner due to financial hardships.

Zero zero one : Eat only dinner.

Zombie : Derogatory name for Soldiers originally used by Fela Anikulapko-Kuti.